Manchester United: Sir Ale>
1986-2013
Re-Live The Rollercoa
By Andrew Hys

Table of Contents

Chapter One: Appointment and Early Years

November 6 1986 is the day that Manchester United started on a journey that would last nearly 27 years. Alex Ferguson was appointed as Manchester United manager only hours after they had confirmed the sacking of Ron Atkinson after a poor start to the 1986/87 season. Ferguson arrived at Old Trafford having managed East Stirlingshire, St Mirren and Aberdeen in Scotland, while also taking charge of the Scottish national team at the 1986 World Cup following the untimely death of Jock Stein. United weren't the first English team to try to entice Ferguson south of the border, with Wolverhampton Wanderers, Tottenham Hotspur and Arsenal all trying but failing to get Ferguson. Despite taking United to a 4th place finish in the 1985/86 season, speculation was rife that Atkinson's position as the Manchester United manager was under threat and the man being linked with his job was Ferguson. Atkinson was determined to fight back and prove his critics wrong but United's poor start to the season only piled more pressure on Atkinson. They didn't taste success in the league until their sixth game of the season, that coming with a 5-1 win over Southampton. Results continued to be more negative than positive for United and Atkinson and the final nail in the coffin came as United suffered a 4-1 defeat to Southampton in a League Cup third round replay, having drawn the first game 0-0 at Old Trafford. On November 5 1986, Manchester United's board decided to dispense with the services of Ron Atkinson and less than 24 hours later, Alex

Ferguson was named as his successor. Ferguson was given a four-year contract at Old Trafford as he looked to move United up the First division table to safety. Alex Ferguson's first game as Manchester United manager ended in a 2-0 defeat to Oxford United, that was followed by a 0-0 draw against Norwich City and United fans had to wait until November 22 to see Alex Ferguson enjoy his first victory as Manchester United manager. That came with a 1-0 win over Queens Park Rangers at Old Trafford, right-back John Sivebaek scoring the only goal of the game.

December saw United drawing 3-3 in successive games against Tottenham Hotspur and Aston Villa, which was followed by a 2-0 victory over Leicester City. Boxing Day 1986 saw United travel to Anfield to face Liverpool. They went into this game yet to have won away from home while Liverpool were yet to have suffered a home defeat in the 1986/87 season. Norman Whiteside scored the only goal of the game as United won 1-0. That result lifted Ferguson and United up to 14th in the table, having been languishing in 20th place when the Scot took charge of the club. As they headed into 1987, United began their quest for FA Cup success with a third-round tie against neighbours Manchester City, United came out on top thanks to a goal from Whiteside. Though any hopes of a third FA Cup success in four years were ended at the fourth-round stage, with a 1-0 defeat to Coventry City at Old Trafford at the end of January. Defeat in FA Cup ended of any hopes of silverware for Ferguson and United, leaving them to concentrate on improving their position in the league table. March saw United and City playing for the 110th time in their histories. United winning the game 2-0 thanks to an own goal from Peter Reid in the 62nd minute before Bryan Robson sealed the three points on 85 minutes. The three points against City moved Ferguson's side up to 10th in the table, while City were left starring relegation in the face, 19th in the table. The following month saw United coming up against North-West rivals Liverpool. With United looking to do the double over the Merseysiders following their 1-0 victory at Anfield in December. Another 1-0 victory was secured by the reds of Manchester, with Peter Davenport scoring the only goal of the game. Davenport would finish the season as top goalscorer for United with 16 goals in all competitions. The curtain came down on the 1986/87 season with a 3-1 victory over Aston Villa at Old Trafford, thanks to three goals in ten second-half minutes from Clayton Blackmore, Mike Duxbury and Bryan Robson. The result meant that United finished the season 11th in the First Division table. Making it their lowest finish in the top flight since suffering relegation 13 years previous.

The 1987/88 season was Alex Ferguson's first full season in charge of United and he started to shape his team the way he wanted. He first forays into the transfer market saw United in bringing Brian McClair and Viv Anderson from Celtic and Arsenal respectively. While Frank Stapleton and Terry Gibson were deemed surplus to requirements by Ferguson. Manchester United's kicked off the 1987/88 season with a 2-2 draw against Southampton, Norman Whiteside scoring both goals for United. That was followed by a 0-0 draw with Arsenal. United then won their next three league games against Watford, Charlton Athletic and Chelsea, scoring eight goals in the process and conceding just two. The win against Chelsea, saw United going top of the league for the first time under Ferguson, though they wouldn't remain there for very long as the next three games saw them dropping seven points with draws against Coventry City and Newcastle United before suffering their first defeat of the season against Everton at Goodison Park. The game finished 2-1 with Whiteside scoring United's goal. The defeat to Everton left United sixth in the table.

Despite the good start to the season, Ferguson was still looking to add to his squad in both defensive and attacking areas. Rangers and England defender Terry Butcher was believed to be Ferguson's number one choice in defence but the centre-back signed a new contract at Ibrox, dashing any hopes United may have had of signing him. After that disappointment, Ferguson turned his attention to Norwich City centre-back Steve Bruce. United had an initial bid of £750,000 rejected by Norwich with Norwich valuing their player closer to £1million. United had a second bid of £850,000 rejected before Ferguson finally got his man for a fee in the region of £900,000. With Bruce now on board, Ferguson turned his attention to the other end of the pitch and made an offer for Luton Town striker Mick Hartford, but the player opted to remain at Kenilworth Road after the offer of a new four-year contract. The final game of 1987 saw United gain revenge on Everton for the earlier defeat with a 2-1 win at Old Trafford, McClair notching both goals for Ferguson's side, the second coming from the penalty spot. The win over Everton saw United going into 1988 fourth in the First Division table. January 1988 saw Ferguson taking his side to Portman Road to face Ipswich Town in the third round of the FA Cup. With Viv Anderson scoring the crucial second goal in the tie. 10 days later United suffered a blow to their silverware hopes as they were knocked out of the League Cup in the quarter-finals, losing out 2-0 to Oxford United. By the end of January United had reached the fifth round of the FA Cup thanks to a 2-0 with over Chelsea at Old Trafford with goals from Whiteside and McClair. Ferguson's quest to win the 1988 FA Cup was ended in February at the fifth-round stage, with United suffering a 2-1 defeat away to Arsenal, Brian McClair scoring United's goal. That goal was one of 31 for McClair in all competitions. Meaning he finished as United's top goalscorer in the 1987/88 season, his first season with the club. McClair had no real challengers for the top goalscoring award in the Unite squad, Bryan Robson the next best with 11 goals. McClair's league tally of 24 goals was only beaten by Liverpool's John Aldridge who netted 26.

Though United had been knocked out both cup competitions by the end of February, Ferguson saw his team second in the league table, behind the dominant force that was Liverpool. United stayed in second place until the end of the season but they were never really challengers to Liverpool as they would eventually win the league by nine points. United though did inflict some pain on their rivals with a 3-3 draw at Anfield on April 4 1988. Liverpool led the game 3-1 at half-time before second-half goals from Bryan Robson and Gordon Strachan pegged the Merseysiders back. Ferguson and United knew that if they were to overhaul Liverpool in the future as not only the top team in the North-West but in the Country, they had to start planning for the future, immediate and long-term. The move that United made on April 18 1988 was one for the long-term future of the first-term, that move was the signing of Torquay youngster Lee Sharpe. The 16 year-old was signed for a fee of £200,000, a record fee for an YTS player. Once the season had ended Ferguson finally got his man in attack, in the shape of Mark Hughes. Bringing the Welshman back to the club where he came through the youth ranks for a record fee of £1.8million. The signing of Hughes would be both for the immediate and long-term future of Manchester United's first-team. Another new addition to the United squad for the 1988/89 season would be Aberdeen and Scotland goalkeeper Jim Leighton for a fee of £500,000. One player that Ferguson and Manchester United missed out on though was Newcastle United midfielder Paul Gascoigne, Gascoigne was the up and coming talent in English football and had agreed to join United, even giving Ferguson his word that he would sign for him. Telling the manager to go and enjoy his summer holiday and not to worry that he would be a Manchester United player for the 1988/89 season. Sadly though for all parties concerned, the move never materialised as Gascoigne and his family were lured by all that Tottenham offered the midfielder for him to sign for them instead of United.

Despite finishing as runners-up the previous season, United were unable to enter the UEFA Cup in the 1988/89 season due to ban on English clubs playing in European Club Competitions since the Heysel Stadium disaster at the 1985 European Cup final defeat Liverpool and Juventus. At the end of the previous season Norman Whiteside and Paul McGrath had been put on the transfer list but there was a lack of interests in both players who were said to be at the heart of United's drinking culture that Ferguson targeted as soon as he walked through the doors at in 1986. McGrath would eventually come off the transfer-list while Scottish midfielder Strachan appeared set for a move to French side Lens but the deal fell through. Manchester United and Ferguson had to wait until the third game of the season for their first league victory of the season after a 0-0 draw with QPR on opening day and a 1-0 defeat to Liverpool. That victory came with a 1-0 win over Middlesbrough and was followed by 2-0 victories over Luton Town and West Ham United. The victory over West Ham on September 24 would be United's last until December 3 when they beat Charlton Athletic 3-0 at Old Trafford. The nine game winless streak saw United drop from fifth to eleventh in the league table. The victory over West Ham saw Ferguson giving debuts to two teenagers. 17 year-old Lee Sharpe and 19 year-old Mark Robins, both would be a big part of the Ferguson story further down the line. Sharpe and Robins were two of a group of young players that were dubbed "Fergie Fledglings". These young players were thrust into the limelight at Manchester United partly due to injuries and loss of form of first-team regulars. The group also included several players that were in the Manchester United youth team that reached the 1986 FA Youth final, these were Lee Martin, Tony Gill, David Wilson and Russell Beardsmore. These players all had a short-term impact on Manchester United's first-term with only Lee Martin and Lee Sharpe going on to make over 100 appearances for United. While Mark Robins was the only one that went on to enjoy success in the game with other clubs. Scoring 15 goals for Norwich City as they

10

finished third in the inaugural Premier League season. Robins has also gone on to enjoy a good career in management.

As well as going on a winless run in their league campaign, United's League Cup campaign ended at the third round stage in November as they lost 2-1 to Wimbledon at Plough Lane, having eased past Rotherham United 6-0 on aggregate in the second round. Boxing Day 1988 was a good one for United, with a 2-0 victory over Nottingham Forest, which was followed by a 3-1 victory over Liverpool at Anfield on New Year's Day. The victory over Liverpool was inspired by 19 year-old Russell Beardsmore, making only his second start in the first-team and scoring the decisive third goal. The win lifted United to sixth in the league and only one place behind Liverpool. A 2-0 win over Sheffield Wednesday on February 11 1989 courtesy of two goals from Brian McClair, lifted Ferguson's side to third in the league table though there was still some distance between them and the top two. United sat eight points behind Norwich in second and 11 points off leaders Arsenal, who had a game in hand. A 1-0 win over Bournemouth in the fifth round replay of the FA Cup meant United reached the quarter-finals of the competition for the first time since they lifted the trophy in 1985. In the quarter-finals they faced Nottingham Forest with United having the home advantage. United though couldn't make this advantage pay as they were beaten 1-0, ending any hopes of silverware for another season. Following the exit from FA Cup, United limped to the end of the season as they won just three out of their final 12 league games. That run of results meant that United dropped from sixth to eleventh in the league table and only a final day win over Newcastle lifted United up to 10th in the final league table. It was clear for everyone that if Ferguson and Manchester United were going to challenge for the major honours in the English game they needed to strengthen their squad further and were linked with several players including England and

Nottingham Forest midfielder Neil Webb, West Ham United midfielder Paul Ince and Southampton winger Danny Wallace.

Chapter Two: Saved by that goal

The 1989/90 season was the fourth of Alex Ferguson's reign at Old Trafford and will always be remembered as the season when it could have ended for the man who would go on to be awarded a knighthood and forever be known as Sir Alex Ferguson. After finishing tenth the previous season, pressure was beginning to mount and questions were being asked by those outside of the club as to whether Ferguson was the man to bring the glory days back to Old Trafford. Manchester United spent the summer reshaping their squad with the departures of Norman Whiteside to Everton for £750,000, Gordon Strachan to Leeds for £300,000 and Paul McGrath to Aston Villa for £400,000. These players were replaced with the summer signings of Mike Phelan from Norwich City for £750,000 and Neil Webb from Nottingham Forest for £1.5million. United kicked off the season on August 19 1989 with a home game against defending champions Arsenal and United ran riot, winning the 4-1 with goals from Bruce, Hughes, McClair and one of the new signings Neil Webb also got his name on the scoresheet. The win gave United fans renewed hope that they could challenge for major honours and even bring the league title back to Manchester. That optimism for the United fans soon evaporated as they lost three and drew one of their next four league games to leave Ferguson's men 16th in the table.

With pressure rumoured to be mounting on Ferguson, he made three further additions to his United squad before the end of September. In defence he added Gary Pallister, arriving for a fee of

£2.3million, at the time a record fee for a defender, from Middlesbrough. In midfield Ferguson finally completed the signing of West Ham United midfielder Paul Ince for a fee of £2.4million. The transfer was initially cancelled when Ince failed medical tests but was completed on September 14 1989 when Ince received the all-clear. The third new arrival was in attack as Ferguson signed Southampton winger Danny Wallace for £1.2million. Despite the new arrivals United continued to struggle in the bottom half of the table. Ferguson and United's position wasn't helped when they suffered a 5-1 mauling at the hands of Manchester City in the first Manchester Derby for three seasons. Despite the performances on the pitch, the Manchester United board offered Alex Ferguson a new contract that would take him to the end of the 1992/93 season and he accepted it. Any hopes Ferguson may have had that the League Cup would offer him some salvation were ended at the third round stage, as he saw his side defeated 3-0 by Tottenham Hotspur at Old Trafford. A 3-1 win over Luton Town would move United up to ninth in the table but that would be the last time United would earn three points until they defeated Millwall on February 10 1990. That run consisted of 13 games and saw United drop from ninth to 17th. During that terrible run of league form, United had the distraction of the FA Cup. While there was pressure in these games because it was Ferguson's last hope of bringing any silverware to Old Trafford in the 1989/90 season and failure to do so would probably mean this would have a very short book or one not even worth writing. Had United finished the 1989/90 season emptyhanded then the Manchester United and Alex Ferguson story would probably be one not worth telling. As it is this is just the start of that wonderful story.

The third round of the FA Cup pitted United away to first division rivals Nottingham Forest, managed by Brian Clough. If you believe the tabloids then defeat against Forest and Clough may have ended Ferguson's tenure at Old Trafford. Though senior board members such as Sir Bobby Charlton have always stated that sacking Ferguson was never discussed. And Ferguson himself stated in his autobiography that despite his teams dismal form in the first half of the season, he was always assured by the club's director that his job was safe. Going into the game against Forest, United were half-way through that run of thirteen games without a win in the league and the majority of experts were predicting another loss for United and that may have seen the end of Ferguson. The game was to be televised live on TV, expecting an adverse result for United. Ferguson and United though found a hero in 20 year-old Mark Robins. Robins had been given his debut in first-team the previous season. He was a young striker who knew where the goal was. Robins would make 23 appearances in the first-team in the 1989/90 season, scoring 10 goals. Several of his 10 goals were crucial ones none more so than his strike in the third round of the FA Cup against Nottingham Forest. Robins would often be asked about that goal and build-up to the goal for many years after the game. He said the FA Cup is a different sort of game and is a break from the league campaign especially in the third round. Which is the first round at which United compete in the competition. The players knew the pressure was on the manager going into the game. Forest were on a high compared to United and were looking to make home advantage pay. The TV cameras were there to see the game that could have been Alex Ferguson's last as United manager if you believe the media. Overall the game wasn't a memorable one and will only be remembered especially by United fans for the Robins goal. Robins would later reveal that Ferguson never thanked him for the goal but as a United fan he didn't want any thanks just pleased he was able to do the job the manager had asked of him.

The strike against Forest wouldn't be Robins last in United's cup run. Their reward for beating Forest was a fourth round tie against Hereford United again away from home. United came through 1-0 and were again drawn away from home in the fifth round, this time travelling to the North-East to face Newcastle United. Robins scored the opening goal in this one as United eventually won through by three goals to two. United were through to the FA Cup sixth round where they would face a trip to Sheffield and Bramhall Lane to face United of Sheffield. United's league form was still poor and instead of challenging for the title, Ferguson and his team were facing a battle to stay in the top flight. Manchester United went into the sixth round tie with Sheffield United on the back of a 4-1 win over Luton Town in the league, where Robins was on the scoresheet with the fourth goal. The tie with Sheffield United was settled by a goal from Brian McClair and set-up a semi-final clash with Oldham Athletic to be played at the neutral location of Maine Road. United went into the semi-final on the back of two wins, 2-0 and 3-0 against Southampton and Coventry respectively. United needed two games and extra-time in both games to see off Joe Royle's Oldham side. The first game played on April 8 1990 finished two goals apiece after 90 minutes, meaning the tie would go into extra-time. Oldham had opened the scoring through Earl Barrett before goals from Robson and Webb gave United a 2-1 lead after 72 minutes. Only for Oldham's Ian Marshall to level the game after 75 minutes. So into extra-time the game would go and United struck just two minutes into the extra 30 minutes through Danny Wallace. Once again Oldham levelled the tie up through Roger Palmer and the game finished 3-3 meaning they would have to meet again three days later. United won the replay 2-1 but needed extra-time to see off their North-West neighbours. McClair gave United the lead after 50 minutes, only for former United striker Andy Ritchie to equalise after 81 minutes. Just as the original tie three days earlier, extra-time was needed and with six minutes left on the clock, Robins once again popped up to score yet another crucial FA Cup goal. In the final Ferguson's side would face Crystal Palace who saw off Liverpool 4-3 in the semis. With their place at Wembley confirmed, United faced six games at the end of their league campaign. They won three, lost two and drew one. With a 1-0 over Charlton Athletic on the final day of the season thanks to a rare goal from Gary Pallister, United finished 13th in the final first division table for the 1989/90 season. The 13th place finish was the lowest final league position for United since their relegation 15 years earlier.

The final at Wembley took place on May 12 1990, United went into the game as favourites against a Crystal Palace side who were playing in the FA Cup final for the first time in their history. Palace took the lead after 18 minutes through Gary O'Reilly, but United pegged Palace back to 1-1 after 35 minutes through captain Bryan Robson and the score would remain at 1-1 until Mark Hughes struck the first of two goals for the Welsh forward in the 62nd minute. United's lead was short-lived as Palace striker Ian Wright made it 2-2 and it would stay that way until the full-time whistle. So once again United faced extra-time in their cup run. Two minutes into the extra 30 minutes, Ian Wright once again struck to give Palace the lead again. That wasn't the end of the scoring though as United drew level through Hughes second strike of the final. Just as in the semis United would have to return for a second game to decide who would win the 1990 FA cup. The replay would take place five days later on May 17 1990 and Ferguson made a big decision in his team selection. Goalkeeper Jim Leighton had played for Ferguson at Aberdeen and made the move to United at the start of the previous season, two years after Ferguson had left Aberdeen for United. Leighton's form throughout the 1989/90 season had been erratic at best and Ferguson decided the replay of the final was the time to make a change. A risky decision given that the man coming in for him, Les Sealey had only played two games for United having joined the club on loan from Luton Town in the December. In the end the risk payed off for Ferguson as United won the replay 1-0 thanks to a rare goal from full-back Lee Martin. The victory sealed United's first trophy under Ferguson and the first for United since winning the same competition in 1985. The success also meant United would enter the European Cup Winners Cup the following season following the end of the ban on English sides playing in European competition after the Heysel Stadium disaster.

Chapter Three: Success in Europe

With the first major success of his Manchester United reign under his belt, Alex Ferguson set about building on that success and had an extra prize to aim for. Winning the FA Cup the previous season meant that United entered the European Cup Winners Cup for the 1990/91 season. The summer was quiet one for United, with Ferguson just making two signings. The first one being the permanent signing of goalkeeper Les Sealey after his loan spell the previous season, after replacing Leighton with Sealey in the cup final replay, Sealey was now Ferguson's number one choice between the sticks. Leaving Leighton to fight it out with two young goalkeepers in Mark Bosnich and Gary Walsh as back-up to Sealey. The other new arrival ahead of the 1990/91 season was that of Republic of Ireland International Denis Irwin. The full-back arrived from Oldham Athletic for £625,000 after impressing Ferguson in the cup semi-final the previous season. The new arrival in defence was comfortable playing in either full-back position and would give United great service for many years to come.

Ferguson was starting to build a squad that had a blend of youth and experience and also had competition for places in many positions, he must have felt his team would mount a serious challenge on all fronts during in the coming season. Winning the FA Cup also meant that Ferguson and United would return to Wembley before the season kicked off to contest the FA Charity Shield against League champions Liverpool. The game finished 1-1 which saw the two teams sharing the Shield. A week after the

Charity Shield, United kicked off their season with a 2-0 win over Coventry City. The victory over Coventry was followed by two wins, one loss and one draw in their next four league games before a visit to Anfield on September 16 1990.United suffered the humiliation of a 4-0 defeat against Liverpool, the defeat by Liverpool was followed by United's return to European competition where they faced Pecsi Munkas of Hungary in the first round of the European Cup Winners Cup with the first leg being played at Old Trafford. Goals from Clayton Blackmore and Neil Webb gave United a 2-0 win. Before the second leg in Hungary, United beat Southampton 3-2 in the league and Halifax Town 3-1 in the second round first leg of the League Cup. The second leg of the Cup Winners Cup tie against Pecsi Munkas finished 1-0, meaning United won through to the next round 3-0 on aggregate. In the next round they would face Welsh Cup winners Wrexham.

Before the first-leg against Wrexham, United welcomed Arsenal to Old Trafford on Saturday 21 October 1990, United lost the game 1-0 but it will be remembered for ugly scenes when all 11 Manchester United players and 10 Arsenal players were involved in a brawl on the pitch. The incident occurred when Denis Irwin was involved in a fight for ball with Arsenal's Ander Limpar. Then Limpar's team-mate Nigel Winterburn made a challenge on Irwin that provoked a melee between both sets of players. Despite the brawl between the two sides, only Limpar and Winterburn were booked for their involvements. Both clubs were punished though, both clubs being fined £50,000 and Arsenal docked two points while United were docked one point by the Football Association. After the brawl against Arsenal came the first-leg against Wrexham in the second-round of the Cup Winners Cup. The first-leg took place at Old Trafford, United winning 3-0 with goals from McClair, Bruce (penalty) and Pallister. In the return game two weeks later, United completed a 5-0 aggregate win with a 2-0 victory in Wales. Robson and Bruce scoring the goals, the victory over Wrexham meant United were through to the quarter-finals where they would face French side Montpellier in the second half of the season. The end of October also saw United progressing in the League Cup with a 3-1 victory over Liverpool, which setup a fourth round tie against Arsenal just over a month after the brawl of Old Trafford. November 28 1990 saw United travel to Highbury for the League Cup tie with Arsenal. United won the tie 6-2 in a match lit up by a hat-trick from 19 year-old winger Lee Sharpe but the true star of night was Danny Wallace. Wallace asked to play as a centre-forward had a hand in all three of Sharpe's goals as he made four goals and scored one himself. The day before this tie Ferguson offered a five-year contract to rising star Ryan Giggs. The Welsh winger had been compared to George Best and was approaching his 17th birthday when he would be eligible to sign a professional contract with the club. Giggs duly accepted and signed the contract on his 17th birthday on November 29th 1990. It wouldn't be long before United fans would see Giggs making his first-team debut. Four days after the League Cup win over Arsenal, Ferguson took his side to Goodison Park to face an Everton team struggling in the bottom half of the table. Sharpe once again got his name on the scoresheet, scoring the only goal as United won the game 1-0.

Manchester United enjoyed a good start to 1991 with a 2-1 win over Tottenham Hotspur at White Hart Lane before beginning their defence of the FA Cup with a 2-1 win over Queens Park Rangers in the third round. The win over Tottenham will be remembered for the sending-off of Paul Gascoigne. Gascoigne became the first player to be sent-off in a First Division game televised live. January also saw United progressing to the semi-final of the League Cup coming through a quarter-final tie with Southampton after a replay. The first game ended 1-1, with United winning the replay 3-2 at Old Trafford, Mark Hughes scoring a hat-trick to set-up a two-legged semi-final with Leeds United. The first-leg of the League Cup semi-final against Leeds United took place on February 10 at

Old Trafford. The game was played in front of crowd of 34,050 and United won 2-1 with goals from Lee Sharpe and Brian McClair. Sharpe also scored the only goal in the return leg at Elland Road as United booked their place in the final as Ferguson looked to guide United to their first success in the competition. Two goals in the semi-finals meant that Sharpe had scored six goals as United navigated the road to Wembley. The final would be against Sheffield Wednesday, who were now managed by Ferguson's predecessor in the United managers chair Ron Atkinson. Any hopes United had of successfully defending the FA Cup were brought to an end in the fifth-round against Norwich City a week before booking their place in the League Cup final. The game against Norwich took place at Carrow road and Norwich won 2-1 with United's only goal coming in the 37th minute through Brian McClair. March saw the much anticipated debut of Ryan Giggs. It came on the March 2 1991 in a first division game against Everton at Old Trafford. Giggs appeared as a substitute in the game for an injured Denis Irwin, United lost 2-0 but the game will always be remembered by many as the first-time they saw Giggs in a United shirt. The Welshman would have to wait until the end of the season for first start though. March also saw United resuming their Cup Winners Cup campaign with a quarter-final against French side Montpellier. The first-leg took place at Old Trafford, finishing 1-1 and two weeks later United won the return leg in France 2-0 to book their place in the semi-finals against Poland's Legia Warsaw.

April 1991 was a big month for Manchester United and Alex Ferguson, they played the Cup Winners Cup semi-final against Legia Warsaw over two legs with the first game being played in Warsaw. Sandwiched between these two games was the League Cup final against Sheffield Wednesday at Wembley stadium. The first-leg in Warsaw took place on April 10 with United winning the game 3-1 to put one foot in the final. The goals in the game came from McClair, Hughes and Bruce. The trio would finish as United's top goalscorers in the 1990/91 season. McClair and Hughes finished level on 21 goals while centre-back Bruce bagged 19 in all competitions. Bruce's tally was helped by his penalty taking duties but he also proved a threat attacking balls in the penalty area from set-pieces. Going into the League Cup final United were favourites to lift the trophy, Wednesday were playing a division below United but their manager was no stranger to United's faithful. Ron Atkinson led his side to success in the final with the only goal of the game coming from Manchester United fan John Sheridan. Three days after the defeat to Wednesday, United faced Legia Warsaw in the second-leg at Old Trafford with a 3-1 advantage from the first-leg in Poland. A crowd of 44,269 saw United book their place in the final with a 1-1 draw, winning the tie 4-2 on aggregate. The result meant United fans could start looking forward to a trip to Rotterdam and a final against FC Barcelona.

The final in Rotterdam saw Mark Hughes coming up against his former side Barcelona and Hughes would prove to be the match winner as United won the game 2-1 to triumph in Europe for the first time since 1968. The first-half ended goalless but United would take the lead on 67 minutes through Mark Hughes or was it Steve Bruce's goal. Captain Bryan Robson floated in a free-kick that was met by Bruce who headed goalwards only for Hughes to touch the ball over the line or had the ball already crossed the line before Hughes touched it. Hughes later credited Bruce with the goal but the official records show that Hughes scored the goal. Seven minutes later Hughes made it two-nil and there was no dispute this time. Hughes through on goal took the ball around Barcelona keeper Carles Busquets and looked like he might have taken the ball too far before drilling the ball into the net from a tight angel. Barcelona defender Ronald Koeman pulled a goal back for his side on 79 minutes and Spanish side had a goal disallowed for offside and another effort cleared off the line as they pushed for an equaliser. United held out for the 2-1 win and Ferguson added a second major trophy in as many years after FA Cup success the previous season. The Cup Winners Cup triumph made it major trophies in successive seasons for the first time in 23 years for Manchester United. While United also reached the final of the League Cup and finished sixth in the league table. The season saw an improved league performance for United despite some inconsistent performances. United were heading in the right direction and were seeing the emergence of young players such as Ryan Giggs and Lee Sharpe. Giggs made his first United start in the Manchester Derby on May 4 1991, United won the game 1-0, Giggs credited with his first United goal despite the ball appearing to deflect into the net off City defender Colin Hendry. Sharpe and Mark Hughes picked up personal awards at the PFA Player of the Year awards. Hughes was voted PFA Player of the Year while Sharpe picked up the Young Player of the Year. With FA Cup success and a European trophy under his belt in successive seasons, Ferguson was now eyeing up a tilt at the league title in the 1991/92 season.

Chapter Four: First League Success

With successes in the FA Cup and European Cup Winner Cup under his belt, the target for Ferguson and Manchester United was now to end that long wait for a league title. There were several new additions to the United squad for the 1991/92 season as they looked to improve on their sixth place finish the previous season. One of those was winger Andrei Kanchelskis, who had joined the club towards the end of the 1990/91 season but United fans had to wait until the 1991/92 season for the speedster to make a real impact. While Kanchelskis added something to the United frontline, two major signings were made to bolster their backline. The first being Queens Park Rangers and England right-back Paul Parker for a fee in the region of £1.75million. The signing of Parker meant a switch from right-back to left-back for Denis Irwin. United's other major signing of the summer was that of Danish goalkeeper Peter Schmeichel from Brondby for a fee of £500,000. Schmeichel was a replacement for Les Sealey, who despite featuring heavily the previous season had left the club after only being offered a one year contract. Young Australian Mark Bosnich had also left the club, leaving Ferguson with Gary Walsh and forgotten man Jim Leighton before the arrival of Schmeichel. Leighton would eventually leave the club in February 1992, returning to Scotland and signing for Dundee. On paper the squad Ferguson was building at United would be a match for anyone in the first division. With established stars such as Robson, Bruce,

Pallister, McClair and Hughes, and young talent in Giggs and Sharpe coming to prominence at Old Trafford.

Now with his squad complete for an assault on the title United hadn't won since the days of Best, Law and Charlton. The last title success for United had come in 1967 and many believed they finally had a manager and team capable of bringing the league title back to Manchester. United would be in the top two positions all season as they thought tooth and nail with newly-promoted Leeds United for the First Division title. The first four games of the 1991/92 season saw United winning three and drawing one without conceding a goal. The fifth game of season saw United welcoming Leeds to Old Trafford, United went into the clash top of the table and remained there after a 1-1 draw. United would remain on top of the league until October 26 1991 when they suffered a 3-2 defeat to Sheffield Wednesday. The early season also saw United beginning the defence of their Cup Winners Cup title with a first-round tie against Greek side Athinaikos. United came through the tie 2-0 on aggregate with two extra-time goals in the second-leg at Old Trafford. The second-round in United's defence of the Cup Winners Cup saw them drawn against Spanish side Atletico Madrid with the first-leg being played in Spain on October 23. Any hopes United had progressing any further in the competition took a massive blow with a 3-0 defeat in Spain. The second-leg at Old Trafford took place two weeks later with the game finishing 1-1, meaning United were knocked out 4-1 on aggregate. Despite the exit from the competition, United still had a European trophy in their sight in the shape of the UEFA Super Cup. The competition saw United facing the winners of the European Cup the previous season Red Star Belgrade. The game was played at Old Trafford in front of the grounds smallest attendance of the season. A crowd of 22,110 witnessed a goal from Brian McClair that gave United and Ferguson another trophy for the cabinet.

Following the defeat to Sheffield Wednesday in the league United went on an eight game unbeaten run which included six wins and two draws before they suffered a shock 4-1 defeat at home to QPR on New Year's Day 1992. The unbeaten run saw United scoring a total of 21 goals including four against Coventry City and six against Oldham Athletic in a 6-3 win with former Oldham player Denis Irwin scoring two of the six goals. The defeat to QPR saw United dropping to second in the league table. Following the defeat to QPR, United recovered with another unbeaten run in the league, this time nine matches. That run though only included four wins as United struggled for goals in the second-half of the season. Meanwhile they had progressed to the semi-finals of the League Cup with victories over Portsmouth, Oldham and Leeds. While January saw them facing Leeds in the third round of the FA Cup. A goal from Mark Hughes gave United a 1-0 win and setup a fourth round tie against Southampton. United were drawn away from home for the fourth round tie and the game finished 0-0 meaning the two teams had to do it all again at Old Trafford, with Southampton winning the tie 4-2 on penalties after it finished 2-2 after extra-time. Despite the disappointing exit from the FA Cup, Ferguson still had his eyes fixed on the prizes of League Cup and First Division league title. United booked their place in a second successive League Cup final thanks to an extra-time goal from Ryan Giggs in the semi-final second-leg versus Middlesbrough at Old Trafford. The first game finished 0-0 and Giggs extra-time goal gave United a 2-1 win in the tie to a book a return to the League Cup final after finishing as runners-up in the 1990/91 season. The final would pit Ferguson against Brian Clough and his Nottingham Forest team. Forest would play a decisive role in United's trophy aims towards the end of the season. Forest inflicted the third and fourth defeats of United's league campaign. The second defeat to Forest was the start of three straight defeats, which also included a 1-0 defeat to West Ham United and a 2-0 defeat to Liverpool at Anfield in the penultimate game of the season. That defeat to Liverpool confirmed the end of any hopes Ferguson had that the 1991/92 season would bring an end to the long wait United fans had endured for a league title. Despite United's failure to beat Leeds to title, United had been a title contender for the first time in a number of seasons and they finished the season with two more trophies in the cabinet. United added the League Cup, winning the competition for the first time in their history to the UEFA Super Cup. The League Cup triumph came courtesy of a 1-0 win over Forest at Wembley Stadium. The match winner was United's top goalscorer Brian McClair with the goal coming in the 14th minute.

It was evident what United's problem had been in the second-half of 1991/92 season and that was scoring goals. This had cost Ferguson's side the league title and they had to watch their rivals from the across the Pennines celebrating a success that could have so easily been theres. With this in mind Ferguson looked to add to his striking options for the coming season. One name heavily link with a move to Old Trafford was that of 21 year-old striker Alan Shearer, and United hopes of prising the England International away from Southampton increased when manager Ian Branfoot announced that Shearer could leave the South-Coast for the right price. United eventually lost out on Shearer to Blackburn Rovers who were being bankrolled by steel baron Jack Walker. After losing out on Shearer it was reported that Ferguson expressed an interest in Tottenham's versatile player Paul Stewart. Stewart was equally adept at playing in the frontline or in midfield. He eventually signed for Liverpool though in a move that never worked out for either party. Eight days before the inaugural Premier League kicked off, Ferguson finally added a new striker to his ranks in the shape of Dion Dublin. Dublin had been a regular scorer as Cambridge United earnt successive promotions, rising from the fourth division to the second tier of English football. Dublin arrived at Old Trafford for a fee of £1million.

Dublin would be the only addition to the Manchester United first-team squad ahead of the big Premier League kick-off. United's supporters were hopeful that their side could go one better this season and become the first winners of the newly formed Premier League. United didn't have the greatest start to the new campaign though, with Ferguson's side not registering a win until the fourth game of the season. The opening day saw United travel to Bramhall Lane to face Sheffield United with the Yorkshire side winning the game 2-1 and Sheffield United striker Brian Deane taking the honour of scoring the first ever Premier League goal. The first home game in the Premier League era saw United welcoming Everton to Old Trafford and the visitors went home with the three points courtesy of a 3-0 win. The defeat was United's second worst home defeat since the arrival of Ferguson in 1986. After a poor start in which they picked up one point from the first three games and sat at the wrong end of the league table, Ferguson saw his side pick up five straight wins. Despite these victories United were still struggling for goals, scoring no more than two goals in each game but there was no problem at the other end of the pitch as Schmeichel and the defence kept five clean sheets. The run of victories saw United rise up the table to third place by mid-September. New signing Dion Dublin registered his first goal in the first of these wins, a 1-0 victory over Southampton but two games later the striker suffered a broken leg in a 1-0 victory over Crystal Palace, the injury ruled Dublin out for six months. The last of the five wins came on September 12 but United fans then had to wait until November 21 to see their side win again as Ferguson's side endured seven games without a win. This included five straight draws before two successive 1-0 defeats to Wimbledon and Aston Villa before a 3-0 win over Oldham ended the dismal run that had seen United drop from third in the table to tenth. As well as stuttering form in the league, September saw United exit the UEFA Cup at the first hurdle. Drawn against Russian side Torpedo Moscow, both legs finished goalless and Moscow defeated United

29

in a penalty shootout. The first-leg at Old Trafford saw the debut of 17 year-old defender Gary Neville. While United's defence of the League Cup ended at the third round stage with a 1-0 defeat to Aston Villa on October 28. United had defeated Brighton & Hove Albion over two legs in the second round with 17 year-old midfielder David Beckham making his debut in the first-leg. With United out of the UEFA Cup and League Cup, they just had the league and FA Cup to play for but Ferguson knew unless his team starting scoring goals and winning games any hopes of winning the league title would be over before the mid-way point of the season.

With the goalscoring problem in mind, Ferguson set about solving this issue in the transfer market. United were linked with several players including David Hirst of Sheffield Wednesday and Southampton's Matt Le Tissier. Ferguson had a £3million rejected for Hirst before Leeds United chairman Brian Fotherby rung his counterpart at United Martin Edwards, who at the time of the phone call was in a meeting with Ferguson to ask about the availability of Denis Irwin. Irwin was not for sale at any price. Ferguson instructed his chairman to enquire about whether Eric Cantona would be for sale and Fotherby said he would have to speak to manager Howard Wilkinson. Cantona had been a controversial character in French football and arrived at Leeds United after having a trial with Sheffield Wednesday, where manager Trevor Francis decided not to sign him. Cantona made 15 appearances for Leeds in the 1991/92 season and despite only scoring three goals he was identified by many as the difference between Leeds and United in the race for the title. He provided a number of assists to strike-partner and Leeds top scorer Lee Chapman. The transfer of Cantona from Leeds United to Manchester United was completed on November 26 1992 for a fee of £1.2million, a fee that would prove to a bargain for Ferguson and United.

The first game after Cantona's arrival was a visit to Highbury to face Arsenal but the game had come to soon for the Frenchman to make his debut and he watched from the stands as a Mark Hughes goal gave Ferguson's side a 1-0 win. Cantona made his debut as a half-time substitute in the Manchester Derby on December 6, United won the game by two goals to one with Hughes and Paul Ince grabbing the goals. Cantona scored his first goal for United in a 1-1 draw with Chelsea at Stamford Bridge that was followed by another draw. This time 3-3 with Sheffield Wednesday, where Cantona was once again on the scoresheet. 1992 was brought to an end with a 5-0 win over Coventry City that took United to the top of the table, this was followed by a 4-1 win over Tottenham and a 3-1 victory over QPR in the league. The arrival of Cantona had provided United with that extra dimension they were craving and would prove to the final piece in jigsaw that Ferguson had been working on since his arrival 1986. January 1993 also saw United dispose of Bury and Brighton & Hove Albion in the FA Cup to setup a fifth round clash with Sheffield United. Though defeat in the fifth round ended United's hopes of completing a league and cup double. It left Ferguson and his side with just the league to concentrate on. A 2-1 win over Liverpool on March 6 sent United to the top of the league, while Liverpool were struggling in the bottom half of the table and defeat left them just three points above the relegation zone. After the defeat of Liverpool, United went four games without a win, suffering a defeat to Oldham before three successive draws against Aston Villa, Manchester City and Arsenal. Next up for United was a visit to East-Anglia and Carrow Road and a top of table clash with Norwich. Norwich were surprise challengers for the first Premier League crown having been promoted to the top flight the previous season. There was a familiar name in Norwich ranks, that of Mark Robins, Robins had left United at the beginning of the season and would never have imagined he would end the season fighting it out with United for the title. Four games without a win had seen United drop to third but they beat Norwich 3-1 to move up to second with six games of the season left. All six of United's final games ended in victory for Ferguson side as they were finally crowned champions for the first time since 1967 following a defeat for closest challengers Aston Villa on May 2 1993. The following day was party time at Old Trafford as United celebrated their league title success with a 3-1 win over fourth placed Blackburn Rovers. Blackburn took the lead before goals from Giggs, Ince and Pallister put the icing on the cake of United's celebrations. After the game club captain Bryan Robson lifted the brand new Premier League trophy with Steve Bruce. Bruce had been the captain on the pitch for the majority of the season due to Robson's prolong absences with injury. The 26 year wait was finally over for Manchester United and its supporters and it was fitting that Sir Matt Busby was there to see the team lift the league title and now it was down to Ferguson to make sure the United fans didn't have to wait as long for the next one. The most important win for United in the title run-in came as United welcomed Sheffield Wednesday to Old Trafford on Saturday April 10 1993, after trailing to a 65th minute penalty converted by John Sheridan. United piled the pressure on and Steve Bruce scored two crucial late goals to confirm the three points. Ferguson and his assistant Brian Kidd both ran onto to the pitch to celebrate the second goal as if it was the goal that won the title.

Chapter Five: Double Success and Failure

With the first league title success secured, Alex Ferguson set about strengthening his squad for the 1993/94 season and the challenge of retaining the league title that United and their fans had waited 26 years for. Almost as soon as the 1992/93 season was over, it was reported that United were interested in bringing Nottingham Forest and Republic of Ireland midfielder Roy Keane to Old Trafford. United weren't the only team interested in signing Keane though, with Arsenal and Blackburn Rovers also reportedly keen to secure his signature. After losing out to Blackburn on the signing of Alan Shearer the previous summer. They also looked set to lose Keane to Blackburn until a paperwork mistake enabled Ferguson and United to step in and snatch Keane from under the noses of their rivals. Blackburn had agreed a £4million fee and agreed the contract with Keane but they didn't have the correct paperwork to complete the move. Ferguson found out and contacted Keane, the midfielder was signed for a British record transfer fee of £3.75million. Despite the record fee, Keane would have a fight on his hands to earn a regular starting position in Ferguson's line-up with the presence of Paul Ince and Bryan Robson.

Keane made his debut for Manchester United in the Charity Shield on August 7 1993, as United added another trophy to the cabinet with a penalty shoot-out win against Arsenal. The game finished 1-1 with Hughes scoring the opening for United before Ian Wright equalised for Arsenal. The defence of United's Premier

League title began a week later as they travelled to Carrow Road to face Norwich City. United won the game 2-0 and this was followed three days later with a three nil win over Sheffield United at Old Trafford. That game witnessed Keane's first goals in a United shirt. After six games of the new Premier League season, United had picked up five wins and a draw against Newcastle. The seventh league game of the season saw United suffering their first defeat with a 1-0 reverse away to Chelsea. Despite this defeat United remained on the top of the table and went on to win all nine of their next league fixtures. This included a 3-2 win over Manchester City, a game in which United were two nil down at half-time before Cantona struck twice to level the game and Keane scored an 87th minute winner. Winning the league title meant a return to the European Cup for the first time in 25 years. Now under the guise of the UEFA Champions League, they were drawn against Kispest Honved of Hungary in the first round. United travelled to Hungary for the first-leg on September 15 1993 and came away with a 3-2 win, Cantona and Keane were once again the scorers, this time Keane scoring two goals. The return leg at Old Trafford finished 2-1 in United's favour thanks to two goals from Steve Bruce. Their reward in the second round was a tie against Turkish side Galatasaray. The first-leg took place on October 20 at Old Trafford and finished in a 3-3 draw, meaning Galatasaray held the advantage of three away goals and United would need to go to Turkey and win in the return leg two weeks later. United couldn't breach the Galatasaray defence and the game finished 0-0, meaning United's return to the European Cup ended at the second round and Ferguson and his players were left to concentrate on the domestic competitions. By the time of their exit from Europe, United were dominating in the Premier League. They were sitting eleven points clear at the top of the league and had also reached the League Cup fourth round after seeing off Stoke City and Leicester City.

The last match of November saw United facing Everton in the fourth round of the League Cup, they travelled to Goodison Park and came away with a 2-0 victory with both goals coming from Welshmen in the shape of Hughes and Giggs. Blackburn Rovers were United's closest challengers in the title race and United welcomed Rovers to Old Trafford on Boxing Day. Blackburn looked like taking all three points but an 88th minute equaliser from Paul Ince secured the draw for United and preserved their fourteen point advantage at the top of the table. January saw United draw 3-3 at Anfield after leading 3-0 at half-time and also Ferguson took his side through to the next rounds of both the League Cup and FA Cup as the Red Devils stayed on course for a domestic treble. The League Cup fifth round saw United hosting Portsmouth and a 2-2 draw meant United had to travel to the South-Coast for a replay, which they won one nil to set up a two-legged semi-final against Sheffield Wednesday. While January also saw the third and fourth rounds of the FA Cup being played. The third round pitted United against Sheffield United. United travelled to Bramhall Lane and came away with a 1-0 win and their reward in the fourth round was a trip to Carrow Road in United's last fixture of January 1994. Goals from Keane and Cantona gave United a 2-0 win. After the defeat to Chelsea in the seventh game of the league season. Ferguson's side went on a 22 game unbeaten run until a 1-0 defeat to Chelsea at Old Trafford on March 5 1994. By the time of the second defeat to Chelsea, United had already booked their place in the League Cup final with a 5-1 aggregate win over Sheffield Wednesday and following the defeat to Chelsea, United faced Charlton Athletic in the FA Cup quarter-finals, after a 3-0 defeat of Wimbledon in the fifth round. United won the quarter-final against Charlton 3-1 but goalkeeper Peter Schmeichel saw red, ruling the Dane out of the League Cup final against Aston Villa. The dream of a domestic treble came to an end with defeat in the League Cup final to a team managed by Ron Atkinson for the second time in three seasons. The final result was 3-1 in a final which United were outplayed by Villa and United's goal scored by Mark Hughes was nothing more than a late consolation. The weekend after the League Cup final, United visited Ewood Park and a two nil defeat to second placed Blackburn saw United's lead at the top of the league cut down to goal difference. In the FA Cup semi-finals United faced Oldham Athletic at Wembley Stadium, a disappointing encounter saw Oldham taking the lead through Neil Pointon in the 106th minute of the game, only for Hughes to score a spectacular late equaliser and force a replay at Maine Road three days later. United booked their place in the final and a return to Wembley with a 4-1 win. Bryan Robson was on the scoresheet with a goal that would turn out to be his 97th and last goal for Manchester United.

Meanwhile in the league, United suffered another scare with a second defeat in three games, this time to Wimbledon but Ferguson's side remained on top of the table as Blackburn also faltered in the run-in. The month of April ended with United knowing they needed just one more victory in the league to complete successive title wins. The title was sealed on the first day of May with a 2-1 victory over Ipswich Town at Portman Road, the goals that sealed the win and the title for United were scored by Cantona and Giggs. Meaning United secured back-to-back Premier League titles with two league games to spare and could now concentrate on the upcoming FA Cup final against Chelsea as they looked to complete the double of league and FA Cup for the first time in the club's history. United eventually finished eight points clear of Blackburn at the top of the league and went into the FA Cup final on May 14 1994 looking to complete the double. Their opponents were Chelsea, who were playing their first FA Cup final in 24 years. After finishing 14th in the Premier League table, Chelsea were the underdogs coming into the final despite twice beating United one nil in the league campaign. Ahead of the final Ferguson made one of the most difficult decisions in his managerial career as he decided to leave long-serving captain Bryan Robson out of his matchday squad of 14. Robson would depart the club in the summer to take up the player-manager position with Middlesbrough. The match took place on a rainy afternoon and in the first-half, Chelsea were the better team with Gavin Peacock coming closest to opening the scoring. The second-half saw United take control with three goals in nine minutes, including two penalties from Cantona with the first goal coming on the hour mark. Brian McClair completed the scoring in the 90th minute following an unselfish pass from Ince. The final score was 4-0 and Ferguson had guided his side to the double of Premier League and FA Cup. Becoming only the fourth English team to complete the feat in the 20th century. Cantona's two goals in the showpiece final took his tally for the season to 25 in all competitions, making the Frenchman United's top scorer and he was voted as the PFA Player of the Year by his fellow professionals.

The close season between the 1993/94 and 1994/95 seasons saw a number departures from Old Trafford. Starting with that of captain Bryan Robson, who after 13 years at Old Trafford decided now was the time to take his first steps into the management with Middlesbrough. Robson would carry on playing while taking his first job in management as he was appointed player/manager with the North-East side. Joining Robson at Middlesbrough was Clayton Blackmore, Blackmore like Robson was given a free transfer by United having joined the club as a 14 year-old in 1982. After five years at the club midfielder Mike Phelan was also handed a free transfer by Ferguson and joined West Brom before returning to former side Norwich as assistant manager in December 1995. Les Sealey had returned to the club in January 1993 as understudy to Peter Schmeichel and only made a handful of appearances and was also handed a free transfer at the end of the 1993/94 season. The only new addition to the first-team was that of Blackburn Rovers defender David May for a fee of £1.4million. May had made over

100 appearances for Blackburn after starting his career with the club as a trainee and was seen by Ferguson as a long-term replacement for Steve Bruce. Just as in the previous season, Ferguson and United kicked off their season with a victory over Arsenal in the Charity Shield at Wembley Stadium. This time United were 2-0 winners with Paul Ince adding to another Wembley penalty from Cantona. The defence of the Premier League title kicked off six days later at Old Trafford and the visit of Queens Park Rangers, second-half goals from Hughes and McClair handed United an opening day win. This was followed by two away games. A 1-1 draw with newly-promoted Nottingham Forest and a 1-0 victory over Tottenham at White Hart Lane. The month of August finished with a 3-0 home win over Wimbledon. Meaning United started the season with three wins and a draw from their opening four league games and lay second in the league table with only Newcastle above them.

September saw the start of United's campaigns in the League Cup and Champions League. The League Cup second round drew United against Port Vale over two-legs with the first leg taking place at Vale Park. The game at Vale Park took place on September 21 1994 and will be remembered for the debut of a young Paul Scholes. This was the first of seventeen appearances Scholes would make for the first-team in his debut season, a season in which he scored five goals, two coming in this match against Port Vale. United won the return leg 2-0 to win through 4-1 on aggregate. Three days after the first leg against Port Vale, Scholes made his Premier League debut in a 3-2 defeat to Ipswich. Scholes once again found the back of the net but it was nothing more than a consolation for Ferguson's side. Meanwhile the Champions League had seen United drawn in a group with IFK Gothenburg of Sweden, FC Barcelona and Galatasaray. United kicked off their campaign with a 4-2 win against Gothenburg at Old Trafford and a 0-0 draw in Turkey against Galatasaray. United only played three league games in September but the month wasn't a good one as they suffered two defeats and finished the month fourth in the table. Another mixed month followed in October, starting with a 2-0 win over a struggling Everton side. Following this there was a 1-0 defeat to Sheffield Wednesday and a 1-0 win over West Ham. Four days after the win over West Ham, United resumed their Champions League campaign with a 2-2 draw with Barcelona at Old Trafford. The draw with Barcelona was followed by a trip to Ewood Park to face title rivals Blackburn Rovers. The game finished 4-2 in United's favour, with winger Andrei Kanchelskis scoring two goals and the result moved United ahead of Blackburn in the race for the league title. Though Ferguson's side still trailed Nottingham Forest in second by five points and leaders Newcastle by seven points. Before the end of the month United would get the opportunity to cut Newcastle's lead. Before the league fixture against Newcastle at Old Trafford, United and their fantastic away support travelled to Newcastle for the third round of the League Cup. Newcastle won the game 2-0 but Ferguson and United would have their revenge three days later as they welcomed Newcastle to Old Trafford for the league fixture. United won this game two nil with goals from Gary Pallister and young Northern Ireland winger Keith Gillespie. Gillespie had made his debut in 1992/93 season and made occasional appearances in the 1994/95 season but struggled to displace Kanchelskis and would be involved a transfer that shocked the country later in the season. The wins over Blackburn and Newcastle in the league were part of a nine game unbeaten run that came to end with a 2-1 defeat to Nottingham Forest on December 17.

Despite remaining unbeaten in the league throughout November, it wasn't all good news when goalkeeper Peter Schmeichel suffered a back injury in their 3-0 win over Crystal Palace on November 19, the injury ruled him out in the immediate future meaning he missed the next game against Arsenal but in the long-term Schmeichel would miss United's next ten games. His place in goal was taken by Gary Walsh with young Kevin Pilkington as the back-up to Walsh. Meanwhile in the Champions League, United faced two away games against Barcelona and Gothenburg. Two defeats, 4-0 against Barcelona and 3-1 against Gothenburg left United on the brink of going out of the competition in the group stages. To progress to the next round United would need to beat Galatasaray at Old Trafford and hope that Gothenburg beat Barcelona in final games of the group stages. United did their job, beating Galatasaray 4-0 at Old Trafford in a game which saw David Beckham making his Champions League debut and he scored United's second goal on the night. The opening goal had come courtesy of another academy graduate, Simon Davies. This would be Davies first and only goal for United's first-team as he went to make just 20 appearances before being sold to Luton Town in 1997. The result wasn't enough to see United through to the next round as they finished third in the group behind IFK Gothenburg and Barcelona. The exit from Europe left United with just the league title and FA Cup to aim for. If they could achieve success in both it would mean a second successive double for Ferguson and United. United went into 1995 second in the league table after missing several opportunities to go top of the table in December. The first missed opportunity came when they faced Nottingham Forest and lost 2-1 and the next opportunity came when facing Leicester City at Old Trafford on December 28. The game finished one goal apiece with United's goal scored by Andrei Kanchelskis and 1994 finished with another draw, this time 2-2 with Southampton. A game in which 19 year-old Nicky Butt struck his first senior goal. 1995 started with two 2-0 wins for Ferguson's side. The first coming against Coventry City in the league, this was followed by a visit to Bramhall Lane in the third round of the FA Cup. Another 2-0 win booked a fourth round tie against Wrexham at Old Trafford. January 10 1995 saw Ferguson breaking the British transfer record once again, this time bringing Andy Cole from

Newcastle United in a deal worth £7million. The move for Cole came after United had failed with a bid for Nottingham Forest striker Stan Collymore, who would eventually leave Forest for United's rivals Liverpool. The £7million transfer saw United paying Newcastle £6million in cash and £1million rated winger Keith Gillespie moving in the opposite direction. Many were shocked at Kevin Keegan's decision to allow his striker to move to United, including the Newcastle faithful. Cole had been at St James Park for two-and-a-half seasons and in that time had scored 68 goals in 85 appearances for Newcastle. The first fixture following the transfer saw United travelling to St James Park but it was agreed as part of the transfer that neither player would take part in the fixture. The game finished 1-1, with United opening the scoring through Mark Hughes, the Welsh striker suffered an injury in the process and would be out of action for the next month. Paul Kitson equalised for Newcastle, the man who had first opportunity to replace Cole in the Newcastle attack.

On January 22, United welcomed league leaders Blackburn to Old Trafford. Blackburn came into the game with a five point lead over United but an 80th minute Cantona goal gave United the 1-0 win that cut Blackburn's lead to two points. That Cantona goal would prove to be his last in the 1994/95 season. Three days later Cantona and his team-mates travelled to Selhurst Park to face Crystal Palace, the game finished 1-1 but when asked about this game I don't think anyone will remember the result. They will remember it for the most controversial event in Manchester United's and English footballs history. What happened that night at Selhurst Park was a season defining moment for Manchester United. It started when Cantona was shown a red card for kicking out at Palace defender Richard Shaw. As the Frenchman was leaving the pitch, he was subjected to verbal abuse from the Palace fans. The main abuse came from 21 year-old Matthew Simmons and Cantona reacted to Simmons by launching into a kung-fu kick and trading blows with his hands. United reacted quickly to events, fining Cantona £20,000 and suspending him from first-team duties for the remainder of the season. The Football Association would later extend the suspension to eight months. Meaning the Frenchman would also be suspended for the first two months of the following season. Cantona pleaded guilty to common assault at Croydon Magistrates Court and received a 14-day prison sentence. Cantona was bailed pending appeal, on appeal the sentence was reduced to 120 hours community service. The community service would spent coaching kids at United's training ground.

Despite the loss of their talismanic Frenchman, United won their next three league games and won through to the next round of the FA Cup with a 5-2 win over Wrexham at Old Trafford. The third of the league games was a 2-0 win over Norwich that took them to the top of the table but they wouldn't remain their long, losing their next league game 1-0 against Everton and moving back to second in the Premier League standings. Ferguson's side won through to the semi-finals of the FA Cup with two home victories over Leeds United and Queens Park Rangers, the semi-finals would see United facing Crystal Palace in early April 1995. The highlight of Andy Cole's first season in the red of United came on March 4 as United beat Ipswich Town 9-0 at Old Trafford. Cole scored five of United's nine goals on a day when everything went right for both United and Cole. After signing for the club in January, Cole finished with 12 goals in his first 18 appearances for Manchester United. The rout of Ipswich was followed by a 1-0 over Wimbledon thanks to an 84th minute winner from captain Steve Bruce. A victory that took United back to the top of the league but once again the lead was short lived as United hit a sticky patch in their league campaign. Of the next six league games, United only won two games, losing one and drawing the other three, all three draws were 0-0, this highlighted United's lack of killer instinct in the absence of Cantona. In the FA Cup, United booked their place in the final but needed a replay to do so. The first semi-final against Crystal Palace ended in a 2-2 draw after extra-time. United won the replay 2-0 with goals coming courtesy of centre-backs Bruce and Pallister. The semis against Palace was the first meetings between the two since the Cantona incident and there was clearly still a lot of bad blood between the sides both on and all the pitch. Prior to the replay a Crystal Palace fan was killed as both sets of supporters clashed while on the pitch Roy Keane saw red after several rash challenges on the United midfielder. The last coming from Gareth Southgate and Keane reacted by stamping on Southgate.

After a two-week break United returned to action in the league against Coventry City, a 3-2 over the Midlanders meant United kept alive their hopes of winning a third successive title and a second successive double. Leaders Blackburn had faltered in recent games and the win over Coventry reduced the deficit to five points and United had a game in hand. The next game for United was against Sheffield Wednesday and former Blackburn defender David May scored the only goal of game to cut the gap between his current and old team to two points with two games to play. United played Southampton on May 10 knowing nothing more than a win would take to the race for the Premier League title to the final day of the season. They made a disastrous start to the game, falling behind to a 5th minute goal from Simon Charlton, Cole equalised after 21 minutes. But United were still being held at 1-1 late into the second-half, meaning Blackburn had the champagne on ice until an 80th winner from Denis Irwin gave United a 2-1 win and took the title race to the last game of the season. The final day of the season saw both United and Blackburn playing away from home. United at West Ham and Blackburn travelled to Anfield to face Liverpool. On paper, United looked like having the easier game but fell behind to a 31st minute Michael Hughes strike and despite equalising in the 52nd minute through Brian McClair, United couldn't find the winner with Cole missing two guilt-edge chances.

The draw wasn't enough for United to retain the title and Blackburn would lift the title despite losing their game against Liverpool. After losing the title, Ferguson and United now had to focus on the FA Cup final against Everton. Despite losing out on the league title to Blackburn, United went into the FA Cup final confident of defending the trophy and winning the oldest cup in competition in the world for the third time under Ferguson. They were facing an Everton team that had just escaped relegation and hadn't won a trophy for eight years. United went into the final missing three of their most important players and three players who had scored 41 goals between them in the 1994/95 season. Those three men were Cantona (suspension), Kanchelskis (injury) and Cole (cup-tied). The final saw promising performances from three players who had broken into the first-team squad and would become prominent players in United's history. Those three were Gary Neville, Nicky Butt and Paul Scholes. Neville and Butt started the game and Scholes was a second-half substitute. Everton took the lead on 30 minutes through Paul Rideout as he headed in the rebound after a shot from Graham Stuart cannoned back off the crossbar. The rest of the game saw United dominating the attacking play as they looked to get back in the game, though they couldn't find a way past Neville Southall in the Everton goal. Ferguson and the United players had to watch as Everton captain Dave Watson lifted the FA Cup and left United empty handed for the first time since the 1988/89 season.

Chapter Six: You Can't Win Anything with Kids

Following the disappointment of double failure in the 1994/95 season, Alex Ferguson reacted by selling three senior players and deciding not to replace them with new players coming into the club. Instead Ferguson promoted a number of young players from within the club. Several of these players had played a number of games in the previous season and would become more prominent first-team players in the coming seasons. The first player to head out of the exit door in the summer of 1995 was Paul Ince, who was sold to Italian side Internazionale for £7.5million. Within 24 hours of Ince leaving the club it was announced that Mark Hughes would be following Ince out of the exit door. Hughes was sold to Chelsea for £1.5million. Despite the arrival of Cole in January, the sale of Hughes came as a shock to everyone in the game especially with Cantona suspended for the first two months of the season. The third one to go was Andrei Kanchelskis, who soon after the sales of Ince and Hughes, handed in a transfer request which was accepted by the club. There was interest in the winger from Liverpool and Bryan Robson's Middlesbrough, Kanchelskis would eventually sign for Everton in a £5million deal. Though complications over the contract meant that the move wasn't completed until a few days into the 1995/96 season. On August 6, Cantona headed back to France and informed Manchester United of his intention to quit English football. Cantona was frustrated at the terms of his ban and fearing that he would face fresh disciplinary action after United had been censured by the FA after fielding Cantona in what the club defined as a friendly match. Despite recently signing a new three year contract, Cantona had requested for his contract to be terminated but after a meeting with Ferguson in Paris, Cantona was persuaded to return to Manchester and training with his team-mates.

Despite the sale of three senior figures within the Old Trafford dressing-room, United approached the start of the 1995/96 season with no new major signings and many experts and fans alike were starting to question Ferguson's judgement in letting these players leave and not replacing them with new signings. Ferguson knew though the talent he had within the club and trusted the young players that would be known as the Class of 92. We had already seen the talents of Nicky Butt, Paul Scholes and Gary Neville, whilst also having seen David Beckham in glimpses. The final member to graduate was Phil Neville, who despite making his first-team debut the previous season, the 1995/96 season would be his breakthrough season. Despite the loss of a lot of experience in Hughes, Ince and Kanchelskis and the promotion of these young talented players. This United squad still had a lot of experience in it. The likes of Schmeichel, Bruce, Pallister, Irwin, Keane, McClair and the returning Cantona would all be there to help Ferguson guide his young players through the ups and downs of a Premier League season. The opening day of the Premier League season saw United travelling to Villa Park on August 19. Ferguson named both Neville brothers, Butt and Scholes in his starting line-up, while Beckham was a half-time substitute for Phil Neville. By the time Beckham entered the pitch at the start of the second-half, United were three nil down and while their performance improved in the second-half they could only get a consolation goal from Beckham. The performance and result prompted former Liverpool defender Alan Hansen, a pundit on BBC's Match of the Day to state you can't win anything with kids. Four days after the defeat to Aston Villa, United welcomed West Ham United to Old Trafford and United earnt the first three points of their season with Scholes opening the scoring in the 50th minute in a 2-1 win. United added to the win over West Ham with a 3-1 win over Wimbledon at Old Trafford and followed these home wins with away wins at Blackburn (2-1) and Everton (3-2). The four wins on the bounce meant when United entered the UEFA Cup at the second round stage they were second in the Premier League table, behind Newcastle on goal difference. United had been drawn against Rotor Volgograd in the UEFA Cup with the first-leg finishing in a 0-0 in Russia, meaning Volgograd could knock United out with a scoredraw at Old Trafford in the second-leg. The return leg took place two weeks later and United were trailing 2-1 before a late equaliser from goalkeeper Schmeichel. This goal was not enough and Ferguson's side were knocked out of Europe on the away goals rule.

There was also disappointment in the League Cup as United were knocked out at the first hurdle by York City. The tie was lost in the first-leg as York inflicted a 3-0 defeat on United at Old Trafford. Ferguson's boys won the return leg 3-1 but were knocked out 4-3 on aggregate, meaning that only two months into the season and United were left with just the FA Cup and Premier League title to play for. After the disappointment of exiting the UEFA and League Cups in the space of a few days, United bounced back with wins over Manchester City, Chelsea and Middlesbrough in the month of October. Following these wins United had played eleven games of their league campaign and sat second behind early pacesetters Newcastle United. The month of October saw the return of Eric Cantona to the United first-team. The Frenchman's return came in a 2-2 draw with Liverpool at Old Trafford on October 1. Cantona was soon involved as he created a goal for Nicky Butt after just two minutes. Cantona then equalised from the penalty spot in the 71st minute. November and December saw United hitting some patchy form and losing ground on Newcastle. The first fixture of November was a visit to Arsenal, which the hosts won 1-0. United reacted to the disappointment of losing to Arsenal by beating Southampton and Coventry City, scoring four goals in both of these wins. The next five games though yielded just 3 points for Ferguson and his men. The two results that really hurt United and their fans were back-to-back defeats to Liverpool and Leeds United. These results meant on Christmas Day 1995, United sat ten points behind leaders Newcastle but had an opportunity to cut that gap in their next league fixture against Newcastle. United prevailed in the league encounter with Newcastle thanks to a 2-0 victory with former Newcastle striker Cole scoring the opening goal after just six minutes. Midfielder Keane added a second for United on 53 minutes. The win cut the gap to seven points at the top of the table and United finished off 1995 with a 2-1 victory over Queens Park Rangers with Cole once again on the scoresheet. Following two victories at the end of 1995, United started 1996 disappointedly, failing to win any of their first three games. The first of those games was a visit to White Hart Lane and Tottenham Hotspur on New Year's Day. Tottenham beat United 4-1, that game saw French defender Willian Prunier playing his second and last game for United after signing a trial contract as cover for the injured Gary Pallister. The following game saw United starting their FA Cup campaign with a home game against Sunderland in the third round. Ahead of the game, the FA Cup looked like it might be United's only hopes of silverware in the 1995/96 season. Another trophyless season for Ferguson and United would raise question marks over the manager's decision to let three senior players leave the club prior to the start of the season. In the tie with Sunderland, United were 2-1 down and staring at another cup exit at the first hurdle but enter Cantona to salvage a two-all draw and force replay at Roker Park. Ferguson took his side to Roker Park for the replay and saw his team come away with a 2-1 victory with goals from Scholes and Cole. The winning goal was struck in the dying stages of game and setup a fourth round tie with Reading. The fourth round tie was played at Elm Park and United strolled to a 3-

0 victory. Meanwhile in the league a draw with Aston Villa and a 1-0 victory over West Ham meant Ferguson and his side sat third in the table after 24 games. They were level on points with Liverpool but nine points behind Newcastle who also had a game in hand on both United and Liverpool.

The month of February was a good one for Ferguson and his players as they picked up four wins out of four in the league, closing the gap on Newcastle at the top and progressing to the quarter-finals of the FA Cup thanks to a 2-1 victory over Manchester City. The month started with a 4-2 win over Wimbledon at Selhurst Park. This was followed by three successive home games, two in the league and the FA Cup game with City was sandwiched between these games. The league encounters were against Blackburn and Everton respectively. Blackburn had been struggling to find their championship winning form of the previous season and were sixth in the table. United beat Blackburn 1-0 thanks to a Lee Sharpe goal and after dispatching City in the cup they beat Everton 2-0. The two home wins had seen United cut the gap at the top to six points and while Newcastle had a game in hand, the two teams were due to meet at the beginning of March. Before that United faced Bolton Wanderers and beat their North-West rivals 6-0. The win over Bolton which included goals from Beckham, Scholes (2) and Butt not only bolstered United's goal difference but also closed the gap on Newcastle to four points ahead of the two sides encounter at St James Park in the first league fixture of March. You could call March 1995 the month of Cantona as the Frenchman was the only United player to score in the league as his goals led Ferguson's men to three wins and a draw as they finished March top of the table. The three wins were all by one goal to nil and would prove to be a crucial period in the race for the Premier League title in the 1995/96 season. The first Cantona winner came in the crucial top of the table clash with Newcastle. The game was dominated by Newcastle especially in the first-half and United had Peter Schmeichel to thank for keeping them in the game as the Dane made a handful of fine saves to keep Newcastle at bay. Then Cantona struck the winner after 52 minutes and United held out for the one nil win that closed the gap on Newcastle to just a single point. The next game for United was the FA Cup quarter-final which saw them facing Southampton at Old Trafford, the tie finished 2-0 in United's favour with Cantona once again finding the back of the net along with Lee Sharpe. The win setup a semi-final Chelsea and meant United and Ferguson were just one game away from their third successive FA Cup final. A 1-1 with QPR briefly sent United top of the league on goal difference but they were second again once Newcastle played and won their game. The next two games saw United welcoming both Arsenal and Tottenham to Old Trafford and once again Cantona was the match winner in both games. The win over Arsenal on March 20 1995 took United back to the top of the league and they would end March three points in front of Newcastle but the Geordies did have two games in hand on United.

Now top of the league, United had their eyes on a third Premier League title in four seasons and were also looking to add the FA Cup and a complete a second double in three seasons. United's place in the FA Cup final had been confirmed on the last day of March with a 2-1 victory over Chelsea at Villa Park. The tie was won thanks to two goals in four second-half minute from firstly Andy Cole then David Beckham. Villa Park is a ground that traditionally United enjoy playing at with the exception of the opening day loss that now seemed like a distance memory with Ferguson and his kids top of the league and looking forward to an FA Cup final against rivals Liverpool. Before that though United were looking to wrap up the title in the remaining six games of the season. The title race between United and Newcastle would go down to the last game of the season. Four wins and a loss in the previous five league games meant United went into their final game of the season against Middlesbrough knowing they just needed to draw to clinch their third Premier League title. Newcastle faced Tottenham and needed a win but could only draw 1-1, meaning United could have lost against Middlesbrough and still won the league. In the end United beat Bryan Robson's Middlesbrough by three goals to nil. Despite at one point in the season being 12 points adrift of Newcastle, United finished four points clear of Kevin Keegan's team as both Ferguson and his players got the better of their counterparts at St James Park in the title run-in. Ferguson got under Keegan's skin so much that Newcastle manager stated he would love to beat Ferguson and United in an outburst on live TV ahead of the final games of the season. Despite the promotion of the likes of Butt, Scholes, Beckham and the Neville brothers into his first-team, United still had the required experience of a title run-in while Newcastle were lacking in this department.

With the title in the bag, United faced Liverpool in the FA Cup final on May 11 1996 at Wembley Stadium. Liverpool had finished third in the league, 11 points behind Ferguson's side. The two North-West rivals were the two top scorers in the Premier League, United scoring 73 goals and Liverpool not far behind on 70 goals. One could be forgiven for expecting a high-scoring encounter given the strengths of both teams attacks. The game though will be one of the most unmemorable cup finals for the neutral fan. The game started at frantic pace with United having several early chances before Liverpool came back into the game but neither Peter Schmeichel or David James were seriously tested in each sides respective goals. The winner came after 85 minutes through United's top scorer Cantona. Cantona made his comeback against Liverpool and scored to level the game at 2-2 and he broke their hearts once again despite being marked out of the game for the most part. The winner came from a David Beckham corner that David James punched clear but his clearance only fell to Cantona on the edge of area, who volleyed the ball back through a sea of bodies and past James into the back of the Liverpool net. The win was United's third in the competition under Ferguson and also meant United had won it nine times in their history. At that time the most by any club. It also meant a second double in three seasons, becoming the first English team to achieve the double double. The season will be remembered as the season when Ferguson put his faith in the talent within the youth ranks at Old Trafford but Cantona was the hero of the season. Scoring several match winning goals in crucial 1-0 wins as United chased down Newcastle. Cantona was named as the Football Writers Player of the Year and finished the season with 19 goals in all competitions.

Chapter Seven: Pursuit of the Holy Grail

After three Premier League titles in four seasons and two FA Cup wins in three seasons, the target for Ferguson and his squad was now to make an impression in Europe and the Holy Grail of the European Cup. Just as it was for Sir Matt Busby, the European Cup, now the Champions League became an obsession for Alex Ferguson. United had barely finished celebrating their double success in 1995/96 season and Ferguson was already preparing for the new campaign. Several senior players left the ranks once again. After almost a decade at the club Steve Bruce was allowed to leave on a free transfer, joining Birmingham City less than two weeks after the FA Cup final success over Liverpool. Another to leave on a free transfer was Paul Parker, the full-back had been suffering with injuries in the previous two seasons and had lost his place in the team to Gary Neville. Peter Schmeichel was the undisputed first-choice keeper but United were in need of an able deputy, Tony Coton had arrived at Old Trafford in the January of the previous season but soon moved to newly promoted Sunderland in search of first-team football, sadly for Coton his career was cut short after breaking his leg in five places and only made ten appearances for Sunderland as the injury brought his playing career to an end. Coton would return to United as goalkeeping coach in 1997 until 2008 when he was forced to retire due to ongoing problems with his knees that restricted his participation in training sessions. United's new reserve keeper would be Dutchman Raimond van der Gouw, who signed on a free transfer from Vitesse Arnham.

Further signings were made in preparation for an assault on the European Cup in the 1996/97 season. These came in the shape of two Norwegians in Ronny Johnsen and Ole Gunnar Solskjaer. Defender Johnsen was signed for £1.2 million from Turkish side Besiktas, while Solskjaer arrived from Norwegian side Molde for £1.5million. Also joining United in the summer of 1996 were Czech Republic winger Karel Poborsky and Dutch midfielder Jordi Cruyff. Both players arrived at United after impressing at the summers European Championships which were held in England. Poborsky was signed from Slavia Prague for a fee of £3.5million, while Cruyff arrived in Manchester from Barcelona in a deal worth £1.4million. One further departure prior to the big kick-off in the Premier League was that of winger Lee Sharpe, Sharpe found himself down the pecking order at Old Trafford, with the emergence of Giggs and Beckham. The arrivals of Cruyff and Poborsky would also add competition for Sharpe and he signed for Leeds United in a deal worth £4.5million. The season kicked off with a return to Wembley in the Charity Shield. Normally a game between the League Champions and FA Cup winners but as United won both they faced league runners-up Newcastle. Goals from Cantona, Butt, Keane and Beckham gave United a four nil victory over Kevin Keegan's side.

Despite starting the season unbeaten, United only managed three victories in their first seven games. That left them fourth in the table behind Arsenal, Newcastle and early pacesetters Liverpool. The signing of Solskjaer had been something of a shock signing by Ferguson, the move came after United and Ferguson missed out on Alan Shearer for a second time, with the England striker opting to join hometown club Newcastle. Upon his arrival in Manchester it was thought by many that the young Norwegian would spend his first season as backup to Cantona and Cole. His young looks and goalscoring exploits earnt him the nickname of the Babyfaced Assassin. Solskjaer debut came in the third league game of the season against Blackburn Rovers. Introduced just after the hour mark, it only took the substitute six minutes to score his first Manchester United goal. It wouldn't be the last time that Solskjaer would make his mark as a substitute. September witnessed the start of United's Champions League campaign, drawn in a group with Juventus, Rapid Vienna and Fenerbahce. Juventus were the clear favourites for the group, having the won the tournament in the previous season and had the talents of Alessandro Del Piero, Antonio Conte, Didier Deschamps and new signing Zinedine Zindane. Juventus were the benchmark for United if they were going to be successful in their pursuit of Champions League glory. The Champions League campaign started with a visit to Turin and Juventus, with the Italians winning the game 1-0 thanks to a 34th minute strike from Croatian striker Alen Boksic. Two weeks later Ferguson saw his side pick up their first points in the group stage with a 2-0 win over Rapid Vienna at Old Trafford, first-half goals from Solskjaer and Beckham gave United the three points. The win over Vienna was the second of five games without conceding a goal for United's backline. Also included in this run of games were a 2-0 win over Tottenham and a 1-0 defeat of Liverpool. The final game of the sequence was their third Champions League group game. United travelled to Turkey to face Fenerbahce and came away with a two nil win with goals from Cantona and Beckham. That result left United with six points from their opening three games in the competition and looking good for qualification for the quarter-finals. The next two league games saw United's defence breached as they conceded 11 goals in heavy defeats to Newcastle and Southampton. A 5-0 defeat to Newcastle and 6-3 reverse against Southampton left many speculating that United's dominance of the early Premier League years may be coming to an end. These defeats away from home were followed by a 2-1 home defeat to Chelsea and also a 1-0 loss to Fenerbahce at Old Trafford. The defeat to Fenerbahce ended United's 40 year unbeaten home record in Europe. After the run of three defeats in the league, United were sixth in the table after 12 games. Newcastle were once again setting the early pace at the top and despite being down in sixth place, Ferguson's side were only six points behind the leaders. All round October 1996 was a poor month for United, with the only positive being a 2-1 win over Swindon Town in the League Cup third round.

November and December saw a recovery for United in the Premier League following the defeat to Chelsea at the start of the November, United played eight games in the two crucial months of the season. Winning five of these and drawing the other three. This run of results saw United going into the New Year second in the table, five points behind Liverpool but the Merseysiders had played one more game than Ferguson's side. There was good news and bad news in the cup competitions domestically and in Europe. A League Cup fourth round exit was suffered at the hands of Liverpool. While in the Champions League following back-to-back defeats against Fenerbahce and Juventus, United went into their last match away to Rapid Vienna knowing they needed to win to progress to the quarter-finals. Ahead of the game, Ferguson's men lay third in the group, a point behind Turkish side Fenerbahce who had to travel to runaway group winners Juventus. Both games finished 2-0, Juventus defeating Fenerbahce and United beating Vienna to book their quarter-final place as group runners-up. Juventus finished the group unbeaten and only conceded one goal. While United finished on nine points and were now through to the last eight of Europe's elite club competition. In the last eight they would face Porto. Before that, United had to concentrate on keeping their title charge on track and also beginning their defence of the FA Cup. The FA Cup third round pitted United against Premier League opposition in the shape of Tottenham Hotspur. The tie was played in front of a crowd of 52,445 at Old Trafford. Goals from Scholes and Beckham gave United a 2-0 win and in the next round they were drawn at home again, this time facing Wimbledon

56

towards the end of January. Wimbledon came away from Old Trafford with a draw meaning United had to travel to London for a replay, which Wimbledon won 1-0. Ending United's hopes of reaching a fourth successive FA Cup final. Following a draw with Aston Villa on New Year's Day 1997, Ferguson's men put together a run of six successive wins that took them to the top of the league. That run of results meant that after 26 games of the Premier League season, United had an amassed a total of 53 points. That meant they were one point ahead of closest challengers Liverpool.

By the time Porto were welcomed to Old Trafford for the first-leg of the Champions League quarter-final tie, United had extended their lead at the top of the Premier League tree to four points over Liverpool, while Arsenal were a further six points back in third having played a game more. United were looking good for a semi-final place after just 45 minutes of the first-leg against Porto, 2-0 up at half-time through goals from May and Cantona, and dominating the game. A further two goals were scored in the second-half through Giggs and Cole to give United a 4-0 win and the United faithful could start thinking about a Champions League semi-final. The other quarter-finals saw Borussia Dortmund earning a first-leg advantage over Auxerre, while the other two games ended in one all draws between Ajax and Atletico Madrid and Rosenborg and Juventus. In the return leg in Portugal, United played out a 0-0 draw to ease through to the semi-finals. Joining Ferguson's men in the last four were Dortmund, Ajax and Juventus. The semi-finals saw United facing German champions Borussia Dortmund with the first-leg to be played in Germany. Despite a shock home defeat to Derby County prior to the first-leg in Germany. United remained top of the pile after 32 league games, holding a three point advantage over second placed Arsenal. Ferguson had to take his men into battle against Dortmund without his number one keeper Peter Schmeichel, missing through injury. Meaning a rare start for van der Gouw. The Dutchman was unable to keep a clean sheet as

United went down one nil as Dortmund found a winner in the last quarter of the game. Schmeichel returned in goal for the return leg but United were facing an uphill battle when Lars Ricken put Dortmund ahead after just seven minutes, that goal put Dortmund two nil ahead on aggregate and United's forward line were unable penetrate the Dortmund goal and the German side booked their place in the final. Ferguson's dreams of adding a second European Cup to one won by Sir Matt Busby were over for another year but United had shown an improved performance having been knocked out of Europe before Christmas in the previous couple of seasons. Despite the disappointment of their European exit, United did go on to win the Premier League for the fourth time in five years. The trophy was lifted by captain Eric Cantona following a final day win over West Ham. Newcastle were once again runners-up to United, this time finishing seven points behind Ferguson's men.

After back-to-back to title wins, Manchester United went into the 1997/98 season looking to make it three successive Premier League title wins and also had their eyes firmly set on success in the Champions League. United's preparations for the new season took a massive hit when talismanic Frenchman Eric Cantona decided to retire from the game at the age of 30 after five seasons at Old Trafford. Cantona decision shocked the world of football but the man himself felt he had done everything he could do in the game and decided to try his hand at acting. As well as losing their star striker, Cantona's decision to retire left Ferguson needing to appoint a new captain. The man chosen for the job was Republic of Ireland International Roy Keane. The man chosen to replace Cantona in United's attack was Tottenham and England forward Teddy Sheringham. Sheringham signed for Ferguson in a £3.5million deal and would make his Premier League debut for United against Tottenham on the opening day of the season. Another new arrival was Henning Berg from Blackburn in a £5million deal, the Norwegian defender joined his countrymen

Johnsen, Solskjaer and Erik Nevland, who had joined earlier in the summer but would struggle for first-team opportunities. The beginning of August saw United facing Chelsea in the Charity Shield at Wembley Stadium. Former United striker Mark Hughes scored the opening goal for Chelsea after 52 minutes but Ferguson's men weren't behind for long, equalising through Ronny Johnsen's first competitive goal for the club. After 90 minutes the match finished at one apiece and was to be decided by a penalty-shootout. United scored all four of their spot-kicks to win the shootout 4-2. The Premier League season kicked off the following week with United and new signing Sheringham visiting White Hart Lane. Despite Sheringham missing a penalty on the hour mark, United came away with a 2-0 win thanks to late goals from Nicky Butt and an own goal by Tottenham defender Ramon Vega. The win over Tottenham was one of five in United's first six league games. In the opening six games, United scored 10 goals and conceded just one and sat on the top of the table with 16 points, three points ahead of second placed Blackburn.

After the opening six Premier League fixtures, United started their Champions League campaign, drawn in Group B with Juventus, Feyenoord and MFK Kosice of Slovakia. Surely United and Juventus would once again be fighting it out for first and second spot in the group. Ferguson's men kicked off their campaign with two wins and six goals against Kosice and more crucially Juventus. In the opening game, Ferguson took his men to Slovakia to face Kosice and came away with a 3-0 win to give them the perfect start in their quest for Champions League glory. The three goal win was courtesy of goals from Irwin, Berg and Cole. Juventus were up next for United and after Juventus also notched a comprehensive win in the opening round, it was important that United won this game if they were going to finish ahead of Juventus in the final standings. United welcomed Juventus to Old Trafford on matchday two and the Italians made the perfect start when Del Piero opened the scoring after just one minute. United hit back before half-time through Sheringham. Juventus midfielder Deschamps saw red after 65 minutes, receiving his second booking of the game. Just three minutes later and United were in front through Scholes and Giggs added a third in the dying minutes. Juventus did pull one back through Zindane but it was United who took the three points and took their place at the top of the group standings after the opening two rounds of games. Prior to the Juventus game, United had been stuttering in the league, with draws against Bolton and Chelsea and a first league defeat of the season coming against Leeds. As well as the defeat to Leeds, United also lost captain Roy Keane to cruciate ligament injury for the rest of the season. In his absence Schmeichel would take the captain's armband. Following the win against Juventus, United beat Crystal Palace and drew two apiece with Derby County. In between these league fixtures, United were knocked out the League Cup against Ipswich Town. The League Cup was the least of Ferguson's priorities and was now being used to reshuffle his squad and blood some of the players on the fringes of the first-team squad. After the league encounter with Derby, United welcomed Dutch side Feyenoord to Old Trafford and recorded another group stage win. After this came two big wins in the Premier League at Old Trafford as United scored thirteen and conceded just one. Beating Barnsley 7-0 and Sheffield Wednesday 6-1. Andy Cole scored five goals in the two games, bagging himself a hat-trick against Barnsley. Ahead of the next fixture which saw United travelling to Arsenal, they sat four points ahead of the Londoners.

Despite the fixture coming early in November, the match against Arsenal could prove to be crucial in the title race. Ahead of the game, United were four points clear of their opponents and a win for Ferguson's side would leave them seven points clear and looking to turn the title race into a one horse race. The game didn't start well for United as they were two nil down just before the half hour mark. Two goals from former Tottenham man Sheringham though made it two apiece at half-time. Arsenal midfielder David Platt had been at United as a youth player in the early 1980's and he grabbed the winner for Arsene Wenger's side in the 83rd minute. The 3-2 win for Arsenal reduced the gap between themselves and United to just one point. The defeat to Arsenal was followed by wins over Wimbledon, Blackburn and Liverpool in the league, scoring twelve goals in the process. While in the Champions League an away win over Feyenoord and a 3-0 win over MFK Kosice made it five wins out of five for United and ahead of the final fixture away to Juventus top spot in the group was already sealed for United. The game with Juventus finished 1-0 to the Italians. Just as in the previous season the two sides had finished first and second in the group but this time Ferguson's men finished above the Italian giants. Further victories over Aston Villa, Newcastle and Everton in the league, meant United put together six straight wins after the defeat to Arsenal but they finished the calendar year of 1997 with a 3-2 defeat to Coventry. Despite the defeat to Coventry United finished the year top of the league, five points clear of second placed Blackburn Rovers. Heading into 1998, Ferguson was eying up a third successive Premier League title, a Champions League quarter-final against AS Monaco to look forward to and would be looking for more success in the FA Cup.

The year kicked off with a 5-3 win over Chelsea at Stamford Bridge in the third round of the FA Cup, the scoreline makes the game look closer than it actually was. United raced into a 3-0 lead at half-time with a quick-fire double for Beckham before Cole made it three on the stroke of half-time. A second for Cole and a strike from Sheringham made it five before Chelsea scored three late goals. After winning their first league game of the calendar year against Tottenham thanks to a double from Giggs, United then went three games without a win with defeats to Southampton, Leicester and a draw with Bolton. There was a win in the fourth round of the FA Cup though, where United beat Walsall 5-1. Ahead of the Champions League quarter-final against Monaco at the beginning of March, United faced a fifth round tie with Barnsley in the FA Cup and looked to keep their title challenge on track. In the FA Cup, United welcomed Barnsley to Old Trafford and the Yorkshire side earnt a replay with a 1-1 draw and Barnsley knocked Ferguson's side out with a 3-2 win at Oakwell. While in the league wins over Aston Villa, Derby and Chelsea meant United went into the first-leg against Monaco with an 11 point lead over Blackburn but their main challengers look like being Arsenal, who despite being 12 points behind United had three games in hand. That lead prompted Manchester based bookmaker and Manchester United fan Fred Done to pay out on any bets made on United retaining their league title. A draw away to Monaco gave United a slight advantage but they would have to guard against conceding an away goal in the return leg at Old Trafford a fortnight later.

Between the first and second leg against Monaco, United failed to win any of their three league games. Falling to a shock defeat against Sheffield Wednesday then drawing 1-1 with West Ham and the final game of the three came against title rivals Arsenal at Old Trafford. Going into this game, Ferguson's men were nine points clear of Arsenal but the Gunners still had those three games in hand. United already dealing with a host of injuries to regular first-teamers and suffered a further blow when Schmeichel picked up a hamstring strain in the game against Arsenal. Despite the injury, the Dane stayed on the pitch and could do nothing to stop Marc Overmars from scoring the winning goal in a 1-0 defeat. The result meant Arsenal now held the advantage in the title race, despite still being six points adrift of United. Arsene Wenger's side still had three games in hand. Schmeichel's injury meant he would once again miss a key European tie after injury ruled him out of the first-leg against Dortmund the previous season. Just as then van der Gouw would step in. five minutes into the second-leg with

Monaco, United were left with an uphill after French striker David Trezeguet scored a crucial away goal for Monaco. That strike meant United would need to score at least two goals to qualify for the semi-finals. Solskjaer levelled the match and tie at one apiece after 53 minutes but United failed to break down the Monaco defence a second time and were eliminated on the away goals rule against a Monaco team they were expected to beat. Wins against Wimbledon and Blackburn following the European exit kept United ahead of Arsenal but the Londoners still had three games in hand on United. Successive home draws against Liverpool and Newcastle meant that the Gunners moved above United and held the title advantage. With United a point behind Arsenal but had played two games more, Ferguson conceded that it would take a major collapse from Wenger's side for United to win a third consecutive Premier League title. Ahead of United's final home game of the season against Leeds United, the title chase was over following Arsenal's 4-0 over Everton the previous day. That result left United seven points behind Arsenal with both teams having two games remaining. With the title in the bag, Arsenal lost their last two games, meaning United would only finish a point behind the Gunners. Following the failure to win a trophy for the first time in three seasons, Ferguson vowed his team would bounce back and promised new signings for the Manchester United fans.

Chapter Eight: The Treble

Following the disappointment of losing out to Arsenal in the Premier League title race and suffering a Champions League exit at the quarter-final stage to Monaco, Ferguson set about strengthening his squad for a renewed attack on all fronts. July had seen the arrivals of Dutch defender Jaap Stam and Swedish International winger Jesper Blomqvist. Stam arrived at Old Trafford from PSV Eindhoven in a deal worth £10.6million. At the time a record fee for a Dutch player and a record fee for any defender. Blomqvist had been part of the IFK Gothenburg team that had finished top of United's Champions League group in the 1994/95 season, the winger impressed Ferguson and arrived at United from Italian side Parma for £4.4million. Blomqvist was brought to United as back-up to Ryan Giggs as the winger had been suffering from a recurring hamstring injury. The arrival of Jaap Stam prompted Ferguson to allow Gary Pallister to return to former club Middlesbrough for £2.5million after nine successful years at Old Trafford. Pallister made 437 appearances at the heart of United's defence and returned to Teeside to finish his career under former team-mate Bryan Robson. Another stalwart of the club to leave in the summer of 1998 was Brian McClair. McClair joined United in the summer of 1987 and in his 11 years at Old Trafford, the Scot made 471 appearances, scoring 127 goals. He joined United as a striker and was top scorer in his first season. Later years saw McClair drop into a midfield role. United handed McClair a free transfer and he accepted an offer to join Motherwell.

In 2001 McClair would return to Old Trafford as Reserve team manager after a spell as assistant to Brian Kidd at Blackburn Rovers. Several years after returning, McClair was appointed as Head of United's youth academy, a role which he held for nearly ten years before leaving in June 2015 to take up a similar role with the Scottish FA. November saw the announcement that another one of United's more experienced and long-serving players would be leaving the club at the end of the 1998/99 season. That of course was goalkeeper Peter Schmeichel. The decision was announced just days before Schmeichel 35th birthday with the goalkeeper citing lack of rest time between games as a major factor in his decision. Saying he needed more time to train between games if he was to be fully prepared for games.

Despite finishing the previous season trophyless, United still appeared in the traditional season curtain raiser at Wembley. Facing Arsenal in the Charity Shield after the Gunners completed the double of league and FA Cup. The match witnessed Roy Keane's first competitive match since suffering the injury against Leeds eleven months earlier. While Dutch defender Stam made his competitive debut for United, fellow new signing Blomqvist missed out with an ankle injury. United started the game stronger but Arsenal eventually ran out 3-0 winners. Inflicting United's first Charity Shield defeat for 13 years. Despite having Cole, Sheringham and Solskjaer at his disposal, Ferguson wasn't completely happy with his attacking options. The Charity Shield saw Ferguson opting for a 4-4-1-1 formation with Scholes deployed behind Cole, with Sheringham and Solskjaer left on the bench. Ferguson was still in the market for a forward and there seemed to be two men on his wanted list, Dutch striker Patrick Kluivert, who had impressed for Holland at the World Cup in the summer of 1998. United agreed a £9million deal with Kluivert's club AC Milan, only for the striker to turn down a move to England after he held talks with Milan officials. Kluivert did eventually leave Milan just a few weeks later, joining Barcelona. While the other man on Ferguson's radar was Dwight Yorke, Yorke's club Aston Villa were reluctant to let their man go and wanted Andy Cole to be part of any deal.

Before the Premier League season kicked off, United had to play the first-leg of a qualifying round in the Champions League, come through this tie and they would be in the group stages of the competition. Drawn against Polish champions LKS Lodz, with the first-leg at Old Trafford. A 2-0 win for United with goals scored by Giggs and Cole put Ferguson's side in the driving seat. The Premier League season kicked off on August 15 with a home game against Leicester. United were still pursuing the signing of Yorke from Villa, despite their reluctance to let him go. Ferguson once again opted to field Cole as a lone striker in the game against Leicester. United looked set to lose the opening day fixture when Muzzy Izzet made it 2-0 to Leicester after 76 minutes. Ferguson reacted by introducing Sheringham and the England striker pulled a goal back only minutes after entering the pitch. A last gasp free-kick from Beckham earnt United a draw. Beckham had become a national hate figure following his sending off against Argentina as England exited the 1998 World Cup. Five days after the draw with Leicester, Ferguson finally got his man when United agreed to pay club record fee of £12.6million for Yorke. Villa were reluctant to let Yorke leave but chairman Doug Ellis felt he couldn't stand in Yorke's way any longer and despite letting Yorke leave accused United of tapping up the striker for just over a year before he eventually moved to Old Trafford. Following the arrival of Yorke, United accepted a bid of £5.5million for Solskjaer from Tottenham. Ferguson didn't want to let the Norwegian leave but couldn't guarantee him a regular starting position but after a meeting with his manager, Solskjaer turned down the move to White Hart Lane. The month of August finished with two 0-0 draws. The first coming against West Ham. This match was Dwight Yorke's debut for

Manchester United, following his move but will be remembered for the abuse aimed at David Beckham from the home crowd, jeered for every touch he made and prior to kick-off stones and bottles were aimed at United team coach. Following the game Ferguson, his players and coaching staff all refused to speak to any media. The second goalless and final game of the month was the second-leg in Poland and the draw ensured United's qualification for the group stages of the Champions League.

Events off the pitch dominated the month of September, United were target of a takeover bid from British Sky Broadcasting. After originally bidding £575million, thought to be their final offer, BSkyB made a final bid of £623.4million following two days of talks with the Manchester United board. United were targeted by BSkyB because they were the richest club in England and one of the biggest clubs in the world. The takeover would be rejected by the Governments Monopolies and Mergers Commission in April 1999. Ruling that the takeover would be anti-competitive and have an adverse effect on football industry as a whole. Meanwhile on the pitch Dwight Yorke made his home debut in a game which will be remembered for demonstrations against the proposed takeover by BskyB. The opponents were Charlton Athletic and United recorded their first three points of the league campaign with Yorke scoring two goals. Also on the scoresheet was Solskjaer (2), who despite looking to set to leave the club weeks earlier was still very much in Ferguson's plans as he looked to utilise the four strikers at his disposal. September also saw wins over Coventry and Liverpool in the league, while a 3-0 defeat to Arsenal meant that United finished the month sixth in the table. Six points behind surprise leaders Aston Villa but United had played one less game than many of their rivals. In the Champions League, United were drawn in Group D with Barcelona, Bayern Munich and Brondby. Containing three of Europe's biggest clubs this group was labelled the group of death. United kicked off their campaign for European glory with two draws, the first coming in thrilling encounter at Old Trafford against Barcelona. The game ended three goals apiece despite United twice leading in the game. Goals from Giggs and Scholes gave United a 2-0 lead at half-time before two goals for Barcelona from Brazilian pair Sonny Anderson and Giovanni levelled the game at 2-2. Just four minutes after being pegged back, Ferguson's men were back in from front from a trademark Beckham free-kick. Though United's lead was short lived as Barcelona were awarded a second penalty when Nicky Butt handled in the area. Butt was sent-off and Luis Enrique converted the penalty to earn a point for Barcelona. The second round of group games, saw United travelling to Munich to face Bayern. Despite falling behind early, United hit back to lead with goals from Yorke and Cole until Giovane Elber struck his second goal of the game in the dying stages, meaning a second successive Champions League draw for United. October saw United picking up five wins out of six games in three different competitions. In three league games in the month United scored fourteen goals as they picked up three emphatic wins. Starting with a 3-0 over Southampton at The Dell. Next up for United in the league were Wimbledon, with United racking up a 5-1 win at Old Trafford, after this came the third group game in the Champions League against Brondby. Brondby were considered the weakest opposition in the group and would hold the key to United's hopes of qualifying for the quarter-finals for a third consecutive season. The game in Denmark saw Schmeichel returning to face his former club and United came away with a 6-2 win as they continued their good goalscoring form. A draw with Derby was a followed by a 2-0 win over Bury in the third round of the League Cup before United finished the month with a 4-1 win over Everton at Goodison Park. Four wins and a draw in five league games had seen United rise to second in the table by the end of October, sitting one point behind leaders Aston Villa.

The goals continued to come in November as they beat Brondby 5-0, and a double from Solskjaer gave United a 2-1 win over Nottingham Forest in the fourth round of the League Cup. This was followed by a 3-2 win over Blackburn before Ferguson's side suffered a shock 3-1 defeat to Sheffield Wednesday. The end of the month saw United travelling to Barcelona in their fifth group game. After victories over Brondby, United were looking to strengthen their position in the group. After the thrilling 3-3 draw at Old Trafford, surely we couldn't expect such a thrilling encounter once again. United fell behind to a first minute goal from Sonny Anderson, Yorke levelled for United after 25 minutes. Then six minutes into the second-half, United were ahead after an almost telepathic link-up between Cole and Yorke. Keane played the ball into Yorke, who let the ball run through his legs to Cole before the pair played a sublime one-two before Cole slotted the ball into the bottom corner of Barcelona's net. Brazilian Rivaldo levelled for Barcelona before Yorke netted his second of the game, meaning just as at Old Trafford, United led 3-2 going into the final quarter of the game. Only for Rivaldo to level again and deny United the three points. The point was enough to book United's place in the quarter-finals. The result left United second in the group behind Bayern with the Germans coming to Old Trafford in the final group game. A win for United against Bayern would see them top the group. The game against Bayern came at the beginning of December and was the second of four successive draws for United, these draws were proceeded by defeat to Tottenham in the quarter-finals of the League Cup. The game against Bayern finished in a 1-1 draw meaning the German champions finished top of the group, one point ahead of United. Three draws in the league against leaders Aston Villa, Tottenham and Chelsea were followed by a 3-2 defeat to Middlesbrough at Old Trafford. A Middlesbrough team managed by Bryan Robson and containing Gary Pallister, were three nil up after an hour of play. Goals from Butt and Scholes pulled the score back to 3-2 but United couldn't find a further goal

70

and lost the game. United responded to the defeat by Middlesbrough with a 3-0 win over Nottingham Forest and earned a point at Stamford Bridge with a 0-0 draw in the final game of 1998. Heading into 1999, United were in a strong position with the possibilities of three trophies. Third in the league table, four points behind leaders Aston Villa, a Champions League quarter-final against Italians Inter Milan and a tie against Middlesbrough in the third round of the FA Cup to look forward to.

The first fixture of 1999, saw United welcoming Middlesbrough back to Old Trafford for the second time in a number of weeks. This time in the third round of the FA Cup, you would have to say that this competition was third on the list of priorities for Ferguson and United but it was still a competition they wanted to win. Just as in the league encounter between the two, Middlesbrough took the lead through Andy Townsend just after half-time. Cole levelled for United before two late goals from Irwin and Giggs sealed a 3-1 win and United's spot in the fourth round draw. Where they were drawn at home against Premier League opposition again, this time in the shape of rivals Liverpool. Before that tie United had two league games against West Ham and Leicester. United scored ten goals in these two league encounters, beating West Ham 4-1 and Leicester 6-2. The win over Leicester included a hat-trick for Yorke and two for Cole. United's sixth goal in the win over Leicester was a rare strike for Dutch centre-back Jaap Stam. So next up for United was the FA Cup tie against Liverpool at Old Trafford. Liverpool took the lead after just three minutes through Michael Owen and despite creating numerous goalscoring opportunities it looked like United weren't going to score. That was until the 88th minute when Yorke scored from a Beckham free-kick, then in the second minute of stoppage-time super-sub Solskjaer struck the winner for United and knocked out rivals Liverpool. Chelsea were now the league leaders and the win over Leicester had seen United cut the gap to two points. A 1-0 win over Charlton on the last day of January, meant United went top of the league for the first time in the season. February consisted of six games for Manchester United, five in the Premier League and a fifth round tie against Fulham in the FA Cup. United picked up five wins and one draw, one of the victories came in the FA Cup as they beat Fulham 1-0 with Cole scoring the winner after 26 minutes. Prior to the win over Fulham, United started the month with league games against Derby and Nottingham Forest. A 1-0 win over Derby, put United four points clear of second placed Chelsea, though Ferguson's side had played one more game than their title rivals. Next came a record breaking day against struggling Forest as United recorded an 8-1 win. The win is the biggest away win in the history of the Premier League and contained four goals in ten minutes from substitute Solskjaer. United were already 4-1 up and in a commanding position in the game when Solskjaer entered the game as a 71st minute substitute. Solskjaer grabbed the first of his four goals after 80 minutes. The win consolidated United's four point lead at the top of the table and the seven goal winning margin added to an already superior goal difference. Following the cup win over Fulham, United welcomed Arsenal to Old Trafford and Yorke missed a chance to give United the lead from the penalty spot. Arsenal took the lead just after half-time through Anelka only for Cole to level the game at 1-1 after 60 minutes and that's the way the game finished. The draw with Arsenal was followed by a 1-0 win over Coventry and 2-1 defeat of Southampton. The month ended with United four points ahead of Chelsea and a further seven in front of Arsenal, who had both played one less game than Ferguson's men.

March started with the Champions League quarter-final first leg against Inter Milan. The first leg saw United welcoming the Italians to Old Trafford. Dwight Yorke proved to be the match winner in this one with two first-half strikes that gave Ferguson's side a 2-0 advantage going into the second leg in Milan. This game was followed by the quarter-final tie in the FA Cup, where United faced

Chelsea at Old Trafford. The game finished in a 0-0 draw which meant United had to travel Stamford Bridge for the replay four days later. Again goals from Yorke won the game for United with the first strike coming after just four minutes. The win over Chelsea setup a semi-final with Arsenal. Back in the league United finished the month with wins over Newcastle and Everton. Sandwiched in between these league victories was the return leg against Inter. Despite holding a two nil advantage from the first-leg, the tie was still on a knife-edge, United had to guard against being too defensive and inviting Inter onto them, whilst they didn't want to go too attacking in search of an away goal. Inter looked to have got themselves back in the tie when Nicola Ventola scored after 63 minutes, United held firm and the tie was put to bed when Scholes netted after 88 minutes. The 3-1 aggregate win over Inter setup a semi-final against Inter's Italian rivals and old foes of United, Juventus. Now reaching the business end of the season, Ferguson had navigated his side to the semi-finals of both the FA Cup and Champions League, and held a four point advantage over Arsenal at the top of the Premier League with eight league games left to play. The countdown to the end of the season began with United still in with a chance of winning all three major trophies. Eight league games left and a two legged semi-final in the Champions League and an FA Cup semi-final. United had a maximum of fourteen games left in the season and if they played all fourteen this Manchester United team would have a chance of being forever remembered. The first of United's remaining eight league games came against Wimbledon at Selhurst Park and finished in a 1-1 draw, Beckham equalised just before half-time after Jason Euell had opened the scoring for Wimbledon after five minutes. There was then a break from league action as United faced Juventus in the first-leg of the Champions League semi-final before facing Arsenal in the FA Cup semi-final at Villa Park. The first leg against Juventus took place at Old Trafford with United looking to press home an early advantage in the tie. The Italians were looking to reach their fourth final in a row, having lifted the trophy in the 1995/96 season but finished as runners-up in the previous two finals. Juventus were the superior team in the game and led through a 25th minute Antonio Conte goal. United looked like drawing a blank despite feeling unlucky not to be given a penalty and having a goal ruled out for offside. If Juventus could hold on it would be the perfect away performance but in the second minute of stoppage time Giggs struck a crucial equaliser. Juventus still held the advantage having scored an away goal but at least Ferguson could take his side to Italy level in the tie.

Next up was the semi-final against Arsenal at Villa Park. Both teams were looking to complete a domestic double of Premier League and FA Cup. For United it would be a third such double and for Arsenal it would a second successive double. Going into the tie you felt that whoever came out on top would hold the advantage in the title race. Going into the game, Ferguson's side held a one point advantage over Arsenal and had a game in hand on Arsene Wenger's team. The semi-final went into extra-time as it finished goalless with Keane having a goal disallowed for United. No goal could be found in extra-time, meaning the two sides would have to return to Villa Park and do it all again four days later. Ferguson made several changes for the replay, with Sheringham and Solskjaer replacing Cole and Yorke, while on the wing Blomqvist came in for Giggs. The deadlock was broken 17 minutes into the replay when a Beckham effort beat England colleague David Seaman in the Arsenal goal. Half-time was reached with the score still at 1-0 but Arsenal levelled after 69 minutes through Bergkamp. On 74 minutes the tie seemed to be turning in Arsenal's favour as Keane was sent off for a second yellow card. With the game looking set for extra-time, Arsenal were awarded a penalty following Phil Neville rash challenge on Ray Parlour. Bergkamp stepped up looking to score his second of the game and book the Gunners a second successive FA Cup final but Schmeichel saved not just the penalty but maybe United's season. Defeat in this tie and it would be very difficult for United to keep their season going. Arsenal looked to make the most of the extra man advantage but it was United who won the tie with a wonder strike from Giggs. Arsenal midfielder Patrick Viera played the ball into space on the half-way line where Giggs picked it up and went on a run where he took on all of the Arsenal back four before firing the ball into the roof of David Seaman net. One final booked, now Ferguson and his team were focused on booking a spot in the Champions League final.

Before the second-leg in Turin, United welcomed Sheffield Wednesday to Old Trafford. Goals from Solskjaer, Sheringham and Scholes secured a 3-0 win and perfect preparation for one of the biggest games in United's history. United looked to have blown the tie in the first ten minutes, as two goals from Italian International Filippo Inzaghi gave Juventus a 2-0 lead on the night and a 3-1 advantage on aggregate. Driven by an inspirational performance from captain Roy Keane, United were level on the night and in the tie after 34 minutes. Keane struck United's first goal, rising in the area to head home from a corner. Yorke drew United level, meeting a cross from strike partner Cole to head home. Yorke almost made it 3-2 moments later as he hit the post following good work once again by Cole. Only a minute after United had levelled, Keane was booked for a challenge on Juventus influential midfielder Zidane. The booking ruled Keane out of the final should United make it. The centre-back pairing of Johnsen and Stam had to be on guard at all times as Juventus threatened the United goal. United were now playing on the counter, with Cole missing a chance and Irwin hitting the post. Within minutes of entering the pitch as a substitute for Blomqvist, Scholes also had his name taken by the referee and he like Keane would miss the final. The tie was sealed in United's favour on 83 minutes by Cole who slotted home after a run from Yorke. Yorke ran clear as Juventus pushed forward, and despite being brought down by Juventus keeper Peruzzi the referee allowed play to continue and Cole slotted home the loose ball to book United's place in the final. In doing so they became the first English team to reach the final in 14 years. In the final they would face Bayern Munich for the third time in competition that season. With their place booked in both the final of Champions League and FA Cup, the priority was now to wrap up the Premier League title.

The first of the remaining six league games came against Leeds United at Elland Road and United came into the game two points behind Arsenal but had two games of in hand with the first of those coming in the game against Leeds. After falling behind, Andy Cole earnt a point for United, though the point meant they stayed second in the league they still had a game in hand on their title rivals. Following the draw with Leeds, United played Aston Villa at home and won the game 2-1. Before a 2-2 draw against Liverpool, which saw former United midfielder Paul Ince scoring an 89th minute equaliser. After that game, United had three games remaining and sat three points behind Arsenal but still had a game in hand. A 1-0 win over Middlesbrough courtesy of Yorke's 29th goal of the season, put United back on top of the table. Both Arsenal and United had two games remaining and an identical goal difference. Two days after United's win over Middlesbrough, Arsenal faced Leeds at Elland Road. A winner from Jimmy Floyd-Hasselbaink gave Leeds a 1-0 win and put United in the driving seat with two games remaining, four points from those two games and United would be Premier League champions again after losing the title to Arsenal the previous season. The following day Ferguson took his team to Ewood Park to face a Blackburn team managed by former United player and coach Brian Kidd and on the brink relegation. The game finished 0-0, meaning United needed to match Arsenal's result on the final day. With both teams playing home games, United facing Arsenal's North-London rivals Tottenham and Arsenal welcomed Aston Villa to Highbury. Three games left in Manchester United's season that could go down in history or would want to be forgotten by everyone involved. First of those three games was the final game in 1998/99 Premier League season. United welcomed Tottenham to Old Trafford, Tottenham would be looking to spoil United's championship party, but knew if they did so they would be handing the title to arch rivals Arsenal. Goals either side of half-time from Cole and Beckham secured the win for United as they completed what could be the first leg of a famous Treble. It was never an easy day for Ferguson and his team as they fell behind when Les Ferdinand struck the opening goal after 24 minutes. The goal for Tottenham came against the run of play as United dominated the early stages but couldn't find a way past Ian Walker in the Tottenham goal. Finally United were level minutes before half-time as the ball was moved from left to right and found Beckham on the right-hand side of the penalty area, who hit a swerving shot into the top corner of Walker's net. Still 0-0 at Highbury but United knew they needed to a second goal to be certain of the title. The start of the second half saw the introduction of Cole, replacing former Tottenham man Sheringham. Cole had only been on the pitch a matter of minutes when his match winning moment came. Gary Neville played the ball forward from the right flank, Cole controlled the ball with his first touch before lobbing over Walker. The game at Highbury remained 0-0 until Kanu netted for Arsenal after 66 minutes. Despite the best efforts of Scholes, who was denied on a number of occasions by Walker, United couldn't find a third goal and it was a nervy finish. When the final whistle blew, Ferguson ran onto the pitch to celebrate with his players. With a fifth league title in seven seasons sealed, Ferguson and his team now turned their attention to the FA Cup final against Newcastle six days later.

Suspension in the Champions League final for both Keane and Scholes ensured they were certain to start the FA Cup final against Newcastle. While others were rested completely or given a certain amount of time on the pitch with the Champions League final in mind. Two regular starters who had to settle for a place on the bench against Newcastle were Yorke and Stam. Newcastle started the game the brighter and United suffered a blow after only nine minutes when Keane had to be withdrawn with an injury suffered in a challenge with Gary Speed. His replacement Sheringham had only been on the pitch a few minutes when he opened the scoring after playing a beautiful one-two with Scholes before slotting past Newcastle keeper Steve Harper. Newcastle had plenty of possession but it was United who enjoy the better attacking play and added a second goal through Scholes on 52 minutes. The goal came when Solskjaer played the ball into Sheringham, who laid the ball off for Scholes and he hammered home to make it 2-0. That's the way it finished as United made it a double but the biggest game was still to come in the search for an unprecedented treble.

Following a semi-final and quarter-final in the past two seasons. Ferguson had guided United to the Champions League final and was now one step away from adding to Manchester United's one European Cup success in 1968. After success in the Premier League and FA Cup, Ferguson was looking to secure the Treble and forever be remembered in Manchester United's history. In the final they faced Bayern Munich at Barcelona's Nou Camp Stadium. After drawing both their group games with Bayern, surely it was going to be a tight final. The suspension of both Keane and Scholes meant a reshuffle for United in midfield. Beckham was moved inside to partner Nicky Butt in the centre of midfield, while Giggs started on the right-wing with Blomqvist on the left. Bayern took the lead after just four minutes when Mario Basler struck a free-kick 25 yards from goal. United keeper Schmeichel was caught off guard by the effort and remained rooted to spot as the ball went past him into the bottom corner. United dominated possession but couldn't make their pressure pay, with Bayern looking dangerous on the counter. The pace of match was electric but United were failing to create any clear cut chances in the second-half and Basler came close to a second for Bayern when his effort beat Schmeichel but shaved the top of the bar. Ferguson made his first change of the game, replacing Blomqvist with Sheringham and moving Beckham back to the right. But it was still Bayern who were having the better chances and Basler found Bayern substitute Mehmet Scholl, who lobbed an effort over Schmeichel only for the ball bounce back off the post into the arms of the United keeper. Then came United's second change with Solskjaer replacing Cole. With five minutes to go, Bayern once again hit United's woodwork when Carsten Jancker attempted an overhead kick. We reached the 90th minute and it looked like the Treble dream may be over for United, three minutes of injury time was indicated. United earnt a corner for which Schmeichel headed into the box to cause havoc. The ball eventually fell to Giggs on the edge of the area, whose mishit effort, was turned in by Sheringham from eight yards and it looked like United had forced extra-time. But United weren't happy to play for extra-time and forced another corner, this time the keeper stayed back for the Beckham corner. From Beckham's corner, Sheringham rose at the front post to flick on for Solskjaer who made no mistake and rifled the ball into the roof of the net to break German hearts. Only seconds were left and United were crowned European Champions, 31 years on from Sir Matt's triumph at Wembley and on a day that would been the great man's 90th birthday. Ferguson's team would now join Sir Matt boys in the history books and be remembered as one of the greatest English club sides.

Tens of thousands of United fans packed the streets of Manchester as they welcomed home their heroes and got a glimpse of all three trophies as United celebrated a treble that will never be matched by any English club side. The final in Barcelona was Schmeichel's last game as a Manchester United player and what a way for the Great Dane to leave the club. In Keane's absence, Schmeichel was named captain and lifted the trophy alongside his manager. June 1999 saw Alex Ferguson being awarded a Knighthood in the Queen's Birthday Honours list. In becoming Sir Alex Ferguson he became only the eighth manager or player to be awarded such honour.

Chapter Nine: Hat-Trick of Championships

Following the treble success of the 1998/99 season, the aim for Ferguson and his side was now to remain the dominant force in England while aiming to add to the European success that would see them rank alongside some of the greats of the European Cup. A club like Manchester United should have more than two European Cup successes under their belt and may well have done if it wasn't for the Munich Air Disaster which destroyed one of the finest teams the English shores have ever seen. The first job on Ferguson's to do list at the end of the 1998/99 season was to find a replacement for Peter Schmeichel, who had decided his body couldn't deal with the rigors of the English game, signing for Sporting Lisbon on a free transfer. Ferguson first turned to a man who had been a United player in the late eighties and most recently had been playing the last seven seasons for Premier League rivals Aston Villa. That man of course was Mark Bosnich, Bosnich signed on free transfer after his contract at Villa Park had expired. Another summer arrival at Old Trafford was South African midfielder Quintin Fortune, signing from Spanish side Atletico Madrid for £1.5million. It wasn't Fortune's first spell in the English game, having joined Tottenham as a schoolboy but work permit problems saw him leaving White Hart Lane to join Mallorca in Spain. As well as defending their Premier League and Champions League crowns, United also had the opportunity for further trophies through the UEFA Super Cup, Intercontinental Cup and the inaugural FIFA Club World Championship. Their participation in the FIFA competition caused controversy as it saw the club withdrawing from FA Cup and therefore not defending the trophy. This was decided after discussions with the FA, who felt United's participated in the competition would aid there bid to bring the World Cup to England. The FA were in the process of bidding for 2006 World Cup and offered United the opportunity to withdraw from the FA Cup for one season to play in the competition. FIFA had scheduled the competition for early January in Brazil. Meaning that United would not only have to postpone Premier League games but also a third round FA Cup tie and Ferguson feared a backlog of fixtures when they returned from Brazil. Ferguson felt that it would be impossible for his team to complete for all the trophies, stating we can't play in the FA Cup if we're going to play in Brazil.

Manchester United kicked off their 1999/2000 season on the first day of August in the traditional curtain raiser of Charity Shield. The game played at Wembley Stadium saw United taking on Arsenal and the Gunners struck the first blow of the season with a 2-1 win despite Beckham opening the scoring from a 30-yard free-kick. Beckham's effort struck the underside of the bar and despite initially being awarded to Yorke who had followed up to knock the rebound in, replays showed the ball had already crossed the line. A Kanu penalty and Ray Parlour strike gave Arsenal the first silverware of the season. United kicked off their defence of the Premier League with four wins and a draw in their opening five league games of the season. Despite the good results, Ferguson had problems with his goalkeepers, Bosnich started the season as first-choice but suffered an injury 21 minutes into the third game of the league campaign, a 2-0 win over Leeds. Meaning Raimond van der Gouw was promoted to the number one position and youngster Nick Culkin elevated to the first-team bench. United had an early chance to avenge their Charity Shield defeat when they visited Arsenal in the fourth game of the season. A double from captain Keane gave United a 2-1 win following an opening goal from

Swedish International Freddie Ljungberg. After five games of the league season, United sat top of the table on 13 points, three points ahead of Aston Villa and Arsenal. United had to fit in the UEFA Super Cup tie against Lazio and this sandwiched between two league games. Meaning Ferguson opted to leave several first-team players out of the game and withdraw others at half-time. The game came two days after they had played Coventry and two days before they were due to play Newcastle. United failed to sparkle in the game and lost out 1-0 to the Italians. The Newcastle game was won 5-1 with four goals for former Newcastle striker Andy Cole. Further additions were made to the squad at the end of August and beginning of September, with two players arriving from Italy to bolster United's backline. The first to arrive was Italian goalkeeper Massimo Taibi as Ferguson looked to bolster the competition for the number one spot. Taibi arrived from Italian side Venezia for a reported £4.5million and signed a four-year contract at Old Trafford. The other new arrival was that of versatile French defender Mikael Silvestre, arriving from Inter Milan for £4million. Both men were handed their debuts as United visited Anfield on September 11 and came away with a 3-2 win. Despite going into a two goal load thanks to two own goals from Liverpool defender Jamie Carragher, United were forced to hold on against their rivals after Andy Cole received a second yellow and an early bath on 73 minutes. The defence of the Champions League saw United drawn in a group with Marseille, Dinamo Zagreb and Sturm Graz and started their campaign in frustrating style, failing to score against Zagreb at Old Trafford as the game ended in a 0-0 stalemate. United got their campaign on the right track though with wins over Sturm Graz and Marseille. The second game of the group saw Ferguson taking his side Austria to face Graz and coming away with a 3-0 win. With goals coming from Keane, Yorke and Cole all coming in the first-half of the game. Next up in the Champions League were Marseille at Old Trafford, where United needed two late goals from Cole and Scholes after trailing to a first-half opening goal from Marseille striker Bakayoko. That result left United top of the group after three games. Despite a man of the match award in his debut against Liverpool, new signing Massimo Taibi only made four appearances after a host of mistakes in games against Southampton and Chelsea. The game against Southampton which ended in a 3-3 saw Taibi allowing a shot from Matt Le Tissier to dribble under his body when the score was 2-1 to United. His next and final game for Manchester United came at Stamford Bridge as United were humiliated 5-0. The first minute of the game saw Taibi rushing off his line to cut out a cross and collided with team-mate Irwin, leaving Gustavo Poyet to head in to an open goal. It was a disastrous day for United in a game that saw Nicky Butt seeing red after 23 minutes, for kicking out at Denis Wise after the Chelsea man had clattered into Butt and the fourth goal was an own goal by United defender Henning Berg. A second successive defeat came in a 3-0 reverse at Villa Park in the League Cup third round, a game which saw Bosnich returning between the posts against his former side. A 3-1 reverse against Tottenham on October 23 1999, saw United dropping to third in the table. By the end of November United were back on top of the Premier League tree with wins over Aston Villa, Leicester City and Derby County and through to the second group stage of Champions League despite a defeat to Marseille. Defeat to Marseille in fourth game of the first group stage saw United drop to second in the group but wins against Zagreb and Graz in the final two group games meant United finished top of the group on 13 points. The second group stage was a new addition to the Champions League in the 1999/2000 season after the competition was expanded to 32 teams. The second group stage consisted of four groups of four, with the top two qualifying for the quarter-finals. United were drawn with Valencia, Fiorentina and Bordeaux.

United kicked off the second group phase with a game against Fiorentina in Florence. Ferguson's side made the worst possible start to the group as they suffered a 2-0 to the Italians. The last game of November saw United travelling to Tokyo and contesting the Intercontinental Cup against Brazilian side Palmeiras. The Cup was played between the European and South American Champions and the winners were declared the best club side in the World. The match saw a performance from Bosnich that earnt him praise from all quarters as he kept the Brazilian side at bay, especially as they tried to mount a second-half comeback after United had taken the lead in the first-half through Roy Keane. The goal was made by Giggs as he cleverly shimmied his way past the right-back and his cross deceived the Palmeiras goalkeeper, allowing Keane to side foot home at the far post. The victory for United was the first time that a British club side had won the competition and been crowned World Champions. On their return from Japan, United played four Premier League games, winning three and drawing one. The three wins over Everton, West Ham and Bradford City witnessed thirteen goals from Ferguson's boys and the defeat of Everton saw Solskjaer grabbing four goals. The last of these four games was on December 28 and finished in a 2-2 against Sunderland. This would be United's last league game until the end of January as travelled to Brazil for FIFA Club World Championship. December also saw United playing their last Champions League game of 1999 as the competition took a break until March following the second game of the second group stage. This game saw United welcoming Valencia to Old Trafford and United sent the Spanish side home licking their wounds as they inflicted a 3-0 defeat on them. That result meant United were level on points with Valencia on three points but Valencia were above United on goal difference, with both teams one point behind early leaders in the group, Fiorentina. As United prepared to travel to Brazil they sat second in the league table, one point behind Leeds United but had a game in hand and on their return they would have a number of games in hand. United's trip to Brazil gave their rivals an opportunity to open up a gap while they were away.

The FIFA Club World Championship saw eight teams competing for the right to be crowned the inaugural winners of the competition. There were two teams from South America, two from Europe and one each from North America, Asia, Africa and Oceania. They were split into two groups of four with each team playing each other once in the group and the group winners would play in the final, while the second placed teams would play in the third/fourth place play-off. United were drawn in Group B with Brazilian side Vasco de Gama, Mexicans Necaxa and Australian side South Melbourne. United's first game of the competition saw them facing Mexican side Necaxa, an eventful game that finished 1-1, saw a sending-off, two saved penalties and a late equaliser for United as they once again showed their never say die spirit under Sir Alex Ferguson. Already trailing to an opening goal from a Cristian Montecinos free-kick after 15 minutes. They then lost Beckham to a red card after 43 minutes after a high challenge on Jose Milan. After his sending in the 1998 World Cup, this was the second time Beckham had been sent off in a high pressure world event. Raising question marks over the midfielder's temperament. Each side were awarded second-half penalties, with both spot-kicks saved before Dwight Yorke scored a late equaliser for United. Any hopes United had of winning the inaugural competition were ended in their second game. This was against Brazilians Vasco de Gama and any hopes United had of winning the game or the competition were ended after a horrendous first-half in which they ended the half three nil down. Two uncharacteristic mistakes from Gary Neville gifted Brazilian striker Romario two goals and left United two down after half an hour. Edmundo added a third for Vasco before half-time, Nicky Butt salvaged some pride for United in the second-half but the defeat left United with no chance of qualifying for the final and best they could hope for was a second place finish in the group and to play-off for third and fourth place. With no hopes of reaching the final, Ferguson rung the changes for the final group game against South Melbourne, giving starts to youngsters Higginbottom, Wallwork and Greening. A 2-0 win for United wasn't enough to make the play-off for third and fourth place as they finished third in the group and went home disappointed with not just their results but also knowing they could have performed a lot better.

Almost a month after their last league game, United returned to Premier League action on January 24 against Arsenal at Old Trafford. United were lacklustre and had to thank Teddy Sheringham for rescuing a point for Ferguson's men. Sheringham equalised after Ljungberg had put Arsenal in front. That result left United three points behind leaders Leeds but Ferguson's men had played two less games than their rivals from across the Pennines. Before the end of January United were back on top of the table thanks to a 1-0 win over Middlesbrough at Old Trafford. In a game Ferguson's men dominated but they had to wait until the 87th minute to secure the three points thanks to a strike from Beckham. With United returning to Champions League on March 1, they were looking to strengthen their position at the top of the league before that return to European action with five games in February. These five games saw United winning three, drawing one and losing another included a 1-0 win over Leeds that gave Ferguson's side a six point advantage over the Elland Road side. The build-up to that game was dominated by talk of a training ground bust-up between Ferguson and Beckham, which prompted Ferguson to leave Beckham out of the matchday squad but Beckham was in the stands at Elland Road. Manchester United's defence of the Champions League resumed in March with the final four games of the second group stage. Three wins and a draw meant that United topped the group, three points ahead of second placed Valencia. The three wins came against Bordeaux home and away and Fiorentina at Old Trafford. With United's place in the quarter-final secured they were drawn against Real Madrid. Meanwhile United continued to lead the Premier League in March with a draw against

Liverpool and three wins against Derby County, Leicester City and Bradford City. The win over Bradford, which was 4-0 left United seven points clear of Leeds but the Yorkshiremen would have an opportunity to close the gap the following day. The first of April 2000 saw United making fools of West Ham with a 7-1 victory at Old Trafford. That result put United into a ten point lead at the top of the table and included a hat-trick for Paul Scholes. Next up for United was a visit to Spain and the first-leg of the Champions League quarter-final against Real Madrid. United kept Madrid at bay thanks to a superb goalkeeping display from Bosnich and looked to have earnt an advantage with a 0-0 draw at the Santiago Bernabeu Stadium. Between the first and second legs, United edged closer to back-to-back Premier League titles with successive wins over North-East teams Middlesbrough and Sunderland. A 4-3 win at the Riverside Stadium and 4-0 win at Old Trafford over Sunderland would have filled United fans with confidence ahead of the second-leg against Real. United's defence of the Champions League came to an abrupt end though as they were outplayed by Real Madrid at Old Trafford. Real raced into a 3-0 lead shortly after half-time thanks to a disastrous own goal from captain Roy Keane and two fine strikers from Real forward Raul. Some individual brilliance from Beckham and a Scholes strike from the spot brought United back into the tie but they were out of Europe as they lost 3-2 on the night and went out by the same score on aggregate.

Despite the Champions League disappointment, United went into their next league game away at Southampton in the knowledge that a win would secure back-to-to titles for the third time since the Premier League began in 1992. United were 3-0 up within the first half an hour with goals from Beckham, a Francis Benali own goal and Solskjaer. Despite confirming another Premier League, everyone associated with Manchester United will feel it was a season of what could have been. After failing to impress in FIFA World club Championships and falling at the quarter-final stage in their defence of the Champions League. Surely Ferguson and his players would look ahead to the following season with an attitude of we must improve if we are challenge for the major honours once again. There were obvious areas in his squad where Ferguson would look to strengthen. Despite signing Bosnich and Taibi, both had failed to fill the hole left by Schmeichel. Taibi was only at the club a matter of months before returning to Italy firstly on loan then in a permanent transfer, while Bosnich had put in several impressive performances but injuries and inconsistent form meant he wasn't the answer for Ferguson. The season finished with four wins over Chelsea, Watford, Tottenham and Aston Villa as United amassed a total of 91 points to win the Premier League title for the sixth time in eight seasons and eventually finished 18 points clear of second placed Arsenal. Before the season had ended United were already looking to add to their attacking options, agreeing a British record fee of £18.5million pound with PSV Eindhoven for their Dutch striker Ruud Van Nistelrooy, the move was subject to medical after terms were agreed with both PSV and player and Van Nistelrooy was in attendance as United beat Chelsea at Old Trafford. The striker though had been suffering with a recurring knee injury and hadn't played since March and United were concerned with his recent injury problems and wanted to carry out further tests before completing the transfer. After PSV refused United's request for extra tests on Van Nistelrooy's knee, the transfer was cancelled on April 27 2000 and the following day while training with PSV the player suffered a suspected anterior cruciate ligament injury that could rule him out for up to a year. Following the collapse of the Van Nistelrooy move, Ferguson only made one move in the transfer market ahead of the 2000/01 season and that was the capture of French goalkeeper Fabian Barthez from Monaco for £7.8million just one week after the end of the Premier League season. The deal for Barthez was a British record for a goalkeeper and the Frenchman signed a 6 year-deal at Old Trafford. The transfer also put a doubt over Mark Bosnich long-term future with United. Barthez was an integral part of the French national side that won the 1998 World Cup and Ferguson believed he had the character needed to replace Schmeichel. Meanwhile Danny Higginbottom, Massimo Taibi and Jordi Cruyff all left the club in permanent deals. Higginbottom was sold to Derby County for £2million, while Taibi secured a permanent return to Italy in a £2.5million move to Reggina. Cruyff's contract at Old Trafford was up and he returned to Spain with Alaves on a free transfer.

The 2000/01 season started as many of United's seasons have started in the last ten years with a trip to Wembley and the Charity Shield, this time coming up against a Chelsea team that had won the FA Cup in United's absence as defending champions because of their trip to Brazil. The game is classed as a friendly but this was not a friendly occasion as tempers between the two sides flared up on several occasions and Keane saw red for a cynical challenge on Chelsea midfielder Gustavo Poyet on a day when Chelsea beat United 2-0. The Premier League season kicked off a week later and United welcomed Newcastle to Old Trafford. Goals from Johnsen and Cole, his ninth against his former side, gave United a 2-0 opening day win and sent a message to the chasing pack that United weren't going to give up their title easily. This was followed by two draws against Ipswich and West Ham before United recorded back-to-back wins against Bradford and Sunderland, scoring nine goals without reply in a 6-0 win over Bradford and a 3-0 triumph over Sunderland. After the opening five games, United sat top of the league on goal difference. Leicester were second in the table but had scored only four goals in their opening five goals compared to eleven scored by United. Next came the start of United's Champions League campaign, the first group stage saw United drawn with Anderlecht, Dynamo Kiev and PSV Eindhoven. A different competition but the goals continued to come for Ferguson's boys as they opened up with a 5-1 win over Anderlecht that featured a hat-trick from Andy Cole, the first of his goals converted from a Giggs cross saw Cole passing Denis Law's record of 15 European Cup goals for the club. A 3-1 win over Everton followed the win over Anderlecht but the win over Everton was followed by four games without a win as they played out a goalless draw in Kiev and a 3-3 with Chelsea at Old Trafford. This was followed by two defeats in two different competitions, the first came as United visited Holland to face PSV in third game of the first group stage and despite taking the lead from the spot after just two minutes. Scholes converted from the spot after Solskjaer was brought down in the box. The star of the show though was PSV striker Mateja Kezman as the Dutch side won the game 3-1 with Kezman scoring the decisive third goal. Following this Champions League defeat, Ferguson took his team to face Arsenal. Arsenal had been United's closest challengers in the previous two seasons, though Wenger's side finished 18 points behind United in the previous season. The game was decided by a spectacular goal from French forward Thierry Henry, despite United's best efforts they couldn't find a way past Arsenal's defence and suffered their first league defeat of the season.

United bounced back from these successive defeats with three straight wins, this included the return fixture against PSV. That game was sandwiched in between Premier League victories over Leicester and Leeds, both by three goals to nil. Following the defeat against PSV in Holland, United needed to improve their results in the final three games of the group and started with a 3-1 win over PSV and that result left United top of the group with two games to play. The next Champions League game for United was a visit to Belgium and a game against Anderlecht. After beating the Belgium's 5-1 in the opening game, Anderlecht had recovered and were challenging United for top spot in the group and United's position in the group wasn't helped by a 2-1 defeat in Belgium. This defeat was followed by eight straight wins, five in the Premier League, two in the Champions League and a 3-0 win over Watford in the third round of the League Cup. The run was started with a 5-0 win over Southampton at Old Trafford with the goals shared between Cole and Sheringham. Cole scored two and Sheringham grabbed himself a hat-trick, this was followed by the win over Watford in the third round League Cup tie. The fourth game of the run was a crucial 1-0 win over Kiev at Old Trafford, this win sealed United's passage through to the second group stage, finishing second in the group behind Anderlecht. The second group stage saw Ferguson and side drawn against Valencia, Sturm Graz and Greek side Panathinaikos. United kicked off the second group stage with a home tie against Panathinaikos and a 3-1 win over the Greek side maintained their perfect home record in the competition in the 2000/01 season. The game was lit up by a double from Scholes, his second and United's third saw him lobbing Nikopolidis in the Panathinaikos goal from the edge of the area. By the end of November United sat top of the league on 36 points. With 11 wins from their opening 15 games and sitting 8 points clear of closest challengers Arsenal. The final game of November saw United facing Sunderland in the fourth round of the League Cup. Dwight Yorke was the hero before becoming the villain. The striker opened the scoring for United before receiving his marching orders from the referee on 83 minutes. The tie went into extra-time after finishing one apiece in normal time and the winner for Sunderland was scored by Kevin Phillips, ending United's hopes of League Cup success for another season. The final Champions League game before a mid-season break would see United travelling to Austria to face Graz and goals from Scholes and Giggs made it two wins out of two at the start of the second group stage. United's form in December was patchy, as well as the win over Graz, in the Premier League there were three wins over Tottenham, Ipswich and Aston Villa, two draws, three all with Charlton and a one all draw with Newcastle in the final game of the month and the calendar year. They also suffered one defeat, this coming in a 1-0 defeat at home to Liverpool. That game saw Luke Chadwick sent off less than ten minutes after coming into the game as a substitute. By the end of 2000, United had played 21 league games in the 2000/01 season, winning 14 of these games and scoring 48 goals. Their closest rivals were Arsenal, who sat eight points behind United. January was a decent one for United with five wins and one defeat. The defeat came against West Ham in the fourth round of the FA Cup, 1-0 at Old Trafford. After beating Fulham in the previous round, many people expected United to win through against the Londoners. The winner came for West Ham from Paolo Di Canio, as he slotted past Barthez with the Frenchman appealing for offside. Ferguson finished the game with four strikers on the pitch but United couldn't find the equaliser. Wins over West Ham, Bradford, Aston Villa and Sunderland in the league saw United extending their lead at the top of the league to 15 points.

February saw the resumption of the Champions League with back-to-back games against Valencia before that though United faced Everton and Chelsea in the league. A one nil win over Everton was sealed by an own goal from Steve Watson. The goal came after a shot from Andy Cole deflected off Watson and looped over the helpless Paul Gerrard in the Everton goal. Cole was heavily involved again when United travelled to Stamford Bridge, his 69th minute goal levelled the game at 1-1 and this was the first of three successive draws for Ferguson's side. The draw with Chelsea was followed by draws home and away against Spanish side Valencia in the Champions League. The first game took place in Spain and finished in a goalless draw, while the return at Old Trafford finished one goal apiece with an own goal from Wes Brown earning a draw for Valencia. The final game of February came in the Premier League as United welcomed Arsenal to Old Trafford, despite being thirteen points behind United, Arsenal were the closet team to United in the league table. Arsenal needed to win the game if they had any chance of reeling United in but Arsene Wenger's side couldn't live with Ferguson's team on the day as

United produced a footballing masterclass and despite Henry levelling the score at 1-1 just after the fifteen minute mark, United steamrollered over Arsenal to reach half-time 5-1 up thanks mainly to a nineteen minute hat-trick from Dwight Yorke. Keane and Solskjaer were also on the scoresheet in the first-half and a late goal from Sheringham sealed a 6-1 win for United and extended their lead at the top of the table to 16 points, surely making it only a matter of time before Sir Alex Ferguson led his side to a hat-trick of Premier League titles. The destruction of Arsenal was followed by draws with Leeds and Panathinaikos both finishing one goal each. The draw with Panathinaikos saw United dropping to second the group table behind Valencia, trailing the Spanish side on goal difference. A 3-0 win over Sturm Graz in the final group game wasn't enough to overhaul Valencia at the top of the group, meaning a tougher draw for United in the quarter-finals. That draw pitted United against Bayern Munich for the first time since the 1999 final. Having already lost van der Gouw to injury, Barthez pulled up injured in the warm-up ahead of United's Premier League encounter with Leicester City, meaning a first-team debut for teenage goalkeeper Paul Rachubka. Rachubka kept a clean sheet as United beat Leicester 2-0 with two late goals from Solskjaer and Silvestre. With both van der Gouw and Barthez struggling with injury, Ferguson signed veteran Scotland goalkeeper Andy Goram from Motherwell. With the upcoming quarter-final against Bayern, Ferguson felt he needed someone with European experience as cover. Barthez returned to the starting line-up as United visited Anfield for a game against Liverpool, the game came just four days before the quarter-final first leg with Bayern and United put on a lacklustre performance as they went down 2-0 against their North-West rivals. Maybe their strong the position in the league prompted complacency and the upcoming tie with Bayern was on the players minds.

The first leg against Bayern took place at Old Trafford and the game looked set to be heading for a goalless draw until an 86th minute strike from Paulo Sergio handed the advantage to Munich. The Brazilian struck at the far post after Steffen Effenberg had headed on a free-kick. United's attempts to overturn the deficit in Munich would not be helped by the absence of Beckham, whose yellow card in the first leg ruled him out of the return. The defeat to Bayern was followed up by league wins over Charlton Athletic and Coventry City. The win over Coventry sealed a third successive Premier League title for United. The hat-trick of league titles for Manchester United made Sir Alex Ferguson the first British manager to win three successive league titles with the same club. The win over Coventry, a 4-2 triumph gave United a sixteen point lead over Arsenal, with the Gunners playing later in the day. A 3-0 loss to Middlesbrough made sure of the title for United but their lead at the top of the table meant it was only a matter of time before United would complete the hat-trick of league titles. The title now sewn up, attention turned to the second leg against Bayern and overturning the one goal deficit from the game at Old Trafford. Already trailing to Paolo Sergio's Old Trafford goal, United fell further behind after just five minutes of the first-half in Munich. Then just before half-time, United's task became almost impossible when Mehmet Scholl made it 2-0 on the night and three zero on aggregate to Bayern. Ryan Giggs managed to get a goal back for United just after half-time but that was it for United and the game finished 2-1 on night and 3-1 to Bayern on aggregate. Ending United's hopes of winning a third European Cup for another season. After the Champions League exit there were five Premier League games before the summer break, the first of these being the Manchester Derby. The match finished in a one all draw with Sheringham opening the scoring for United. The match though will be remembered for an assault by United captain Keane on City midfielder Alf-Inge Haaland. Haaland was a Leeds United player when Keane was injured against them in the 1997/98 and Haaland accused Keane of feigning injury. Of the remaining four games United beat Middlesbrough but then with nothing to play for, United suffered three defeats that meant they would eventually finish ten points clear of Arsenal.

Chapter Ten: Retirement U-Turn

Despite finishing the season as United's top goalscorer and double Player of the Year winner, being named as the player of the season by both his peers and the football writers, Teddy Sheringham left United and returned to Tottenham on a two-year deal. The move came after the striker failed to agree a new deal at Old Trafford with United only offering him a one-year deal. Perhaps another reason for his departure was the impending arrival of Dutch striker Ruud Van Nistelrooy. Despite the collapse of his transfer the previous summer, United had kept a close eye on the Dutchman and a year after his transfer was cancelled because of concerns over fitness, Van Nistelrooy completed a £19million move on a five-year contract. Van Nistelrooy was joined at Old Trafford by Argentinian midfielder Juan Sebastian Veron, who joined in a British record deal of £28.1million on a five-year deal. Despite the Champions League success of 1999, Ferguson's side had failed to kick-on from that and become a dominant force in European football, exiting at the quarter-final stage in the previous two seasons. Ferguson hoped that the signings of Van Nistelrooy and Veron could have a similar impact to the signings of Yorke and Stam in the summer 1998. Despite the arrivals of Van Nistelrooy and Veron, Ferguson had already announced his intention to retire at the end of the 2001/02 season and not take up any other role within club. This news came after talks between the club and Ferguson over a new role within the club had collapsed. Despite the announcement, Ferguson was focused on the job in hand and it would be a fitting exit for the Scot if he could guide United to the Champions League final, which was being held at Hampden Park. Once again United kicked off their campaign with the Charity Shield, facing Liverpool, who had lifted the FA Cup the previous season. The game traditionally played at Wembley Stadium but as the stadium was closed for reconstruction and the game was moved to the Millenium Stadium in Cardiff. This was United's six consecutive appearance in the showpiece season opener but they had failed to win the game since a penalty shootout victory over Chelsea in 1997. This game was no different as Liverpool won the 2-1 thanks to two goals in the opening twenty minutes from Gary McAllister and Michael Owen. Debutant Van Nistelrooy scored a second-half goal United but they couldn't find an equaliser.

The opening game of the Premier League season saw United welcoming newly promoted Fulham to Old Trafford and the Londoners gave United a fright before a double from Van Nistelrooy gave United the opening day spoils. French striker Louis Saha put Fulham in front twice, the opening goal was equalised by Beckham from a trademark free-kick before two goals in two minutes from Van Nistelrooy at the start of the second-half got United's league campaign off to a winning start. This game would turn out to be Jaap Stam last for the club as he was sold to Italian side Lazio for £16.5million before the end of August. The decision came as a shock to the World of football, since Stam's arrival at Old Trafford, the defender had been one of the mainstays of the team when fit. Stam had released his autobiography in the summer and had made several claims about Ferguson, including the Scot had tapped him up while at PSV and that he had instructed his players to dive. Many believed that this was the reason why Ferguson decided to part with the Dutchman, a theory which Ferguson denied and said the offer from Lazio was too good to turn and the club were already in the process of purchasing another centre-back. Another theory was that the sale was part of balancing the books for Manchester United having spent big on Van Nistelrooy and Veron in the summer. Whatever the reasons for letting the defender go, Ferguson has since stated that it was one of the biggest mistakes he ever made as Manchester United manager. Only days after the departure of Stam, Ferguson signed French defender Laurent Blanc from Inter Milan for £2.5million. Ferguson had long been an admirer of the Frenchman and when he heard he wanted away from Inter, Ferguson felt it was too good an opportunity to miss and felt Blanc could bring some organisation to his backline and help the development of Wes Brown. The next two league fixtures saw United strolling past Everton 4-1 before suffering a 4-3 defeat to Newcastle meaning in their first five games of the Premier League they had two wins, two draws and one loss. That left United fifth in the Premier League table on eight points with Leeds leading the way on eleven points.

The Champions League saw United pitted against Lille, Deportivo La Coruna and Olympiacos of Greece in the first group stage starting with a home fixture against Lille. Despite getting their Champions League challenge off to a winning start, United were lacklustre and needed a 90th winner from England captain David Beckham. Beckham scored a scrappy winner for United in a game that he was virtually anonymous. The win over Lille was followed by a 4-0 win over Ipswich Town at Old Trafford before Ferguson and his team travelled to Spain to face Deportivo in their second group game. Barthez was twice forced to keep the score at 0-0 before Scholes opened the scoring for United but two late goals for Deportivo gave the Spaniards all three points with a 2-1 win. After two games in the group, United sat second behind Deportivo. The defeat in Spain was followed by a visit to London and White Hart Lane, 2-0 down after 25 minutes, things got worse for United on the stroke of half-time as Christian Ziege put Tottenham 3-0 up. If United were to get back in the game, they would need an early goal in the second-half and that came within a minute of the restart as Cole met a cross from Beckham to head home and get United back in the contest. United were showing more urgency in the second-half and the score was pulled back to 3-2 when Blanc rose highest to head home a Beckham corner after 58 minutes. There were 72 minutes on the clock when Van Nistelrooy headed home United's third and the score was now level at 3-3. Four minutes later United were in front through Veron, who struck home left footed after some fine play between Scholes and Solskjaer. Three minutes from time Beckham completed the resounding comeback and a 5-3 win for Sir Alex Ferguson's side. After the game, Ferguson was questioned as to what he had said to his players at half-time but he wouldn't reveal this. Ferguson's hairdryer had become famous and many questioned as to whether Ferguson had delivered the hairdryer to his players. Many of his former players have said that there are actually occasions when Ferguson would be calm and just encourage his players to keep going and they would get the reward. This is what made Ferguson one of the greatest managers, his players weren't sure how he would react at half-time and at the end of the game. Many have said they could be three goals down like they were at White Hart Lane and the manager would remain calm, while on other occasions they could come in three or four goals up and Ferguson would give them the hairdryer, asking why they weren't further ahead. This kept his players on their toes and his message didn't wear off after a while like it does with some successful managers.

The defeat of Tottenham was followed by two more away wins at Olympiacos and Sunderland before they suffered successive home defeats. The first came as Manchester United welcomed Deportivo to Old Trafford for the fourth game of the group stage. A 3-2 defeat by Deportivo saw the Spaniards completing a double over United as they were gifted a goal in each half by Barthez. Van Nistelrooy put United in front after seven minutes as his struck his first goal in European competition for his new side. Then two goals in two minutes for Deportivo put the Spanish side 2-1 with the first goal coming after 37 minutes. Minutes later United were level as Van Nistelrooy notched his second goal of the game. But on 70 minutes Barthez came out of his area to slide for the ball but missed the ball completely to leave Diego Tristan with an open goal and score the winning goal for Deportivo. The result strengthened Deportivo's position on top of the group, while United would need positive results in the final games to finish above Deportivo. The defeat to Deportivo was followed a home defeat against Bolton. Ferguson had seen his side take the lead from a first-half free-kick superbly taken by Juan Sebastian Veron on 25 minutes before Kevin Nolan levelled for Bolton ten minutes before half-time. Bolton found the winner on 84 minutes through Michael Ricketts to ruin Ferguson's afternoon and inflict a second successive home defeat on United. This was followed by a 3-0 win over Olympiacos in the Champions League and the month of October finished for United with two 1-1 draws against Leeds in the league and Lille in Europe. The draw against Lille was United's final game in the first group phase and meant that they would finish second in the group behind Deportivo. The two sides finished level on ten points and despite United having a superior goal difference, Deportivo finished top thanks to their two wins over United. The second place finish was enough to book United's place in the second group stage of the competition and saw them being drawn with Bayern Munich, Nantes of France and Portuguese side Boavista. The draw with Leeds left defending champions United fifth in the league after ten games, sitting three points behind leaders Aston Villa. The start of the season was a disappointing one for Ferguson's men in what would be his last season in charge. Of their ten league games, United had lost two games and their league form wouldn't improve in the near future.

November started with two defeats to two of United's closest rivals, first losing to Liverpool in the league at Anfield. Liverpool made it four successive wins against Ferguson and United after racing into a two goal lead before half-time. Beckham pulled one back five minute after the restart, giving United and their fans hopes of earning something from the game. But those hopes diminished just a minute later as Barthez gifted Liverpool a third goal and the score remained at 3-1. Next up for United was a trip Highbury and Arsenal in the third round of the League Cup. The match saw both sides fielding a host of reserve and youth players and Arsenal got the better of United with a 4-0 win. Ferguson's men appeared to get back on track with a 2-0 victory over Leicester City at Old Trafford with the goals coming from Van Nistelrooy and Yorke. Coming in mid-November, the win over Leicester would be the last of the month for United. Following the win over Leicester, United travelled to Munich for the opening game of the second group phase in the Champions League against Bayern. These two sides were viewed as the two strongest teams in the group and the results in the two games could decide the outcome of first and second place in the group. Bayern were the reigning champions and Ruud Van Nistelrooy's 74th minute strike almost gave United the three points but with four minute to go, Silvestre failed to deal with a through ball and Paolo Sergio pounced to level the game and earn Bayern a draw. The draw with Bayern was followed by two results in the league that saw United dropping further down the table, first came a second visit to Highbury in the month of November and a second defeat to the Londoners. Paul Scholes gave United the lead after fourteen minutes in this one and half-time was reached with the score at 1-0 to United. Only three minutes after the restart and Arsenal were level through Swedish International Ljungberg, with the game level at 1-1, Barthez handed Arsenal the lead when his clearance went straight to fellow Frenchman Henry who had a simple finish to give Arsenal the lead. Ferguson was already fuming on the bench and his mood wasn't made any better when Barthez spilled a through ball to gift Henry a second and Arsenal a third goal and the three points. Next up was

.

another London side in the shape of Chelsea at Old Trafford. Despite errors in recent games, Barthez kept his place in the side ahead of Roy Carroll, who had joined in the summer from Wigan Athletic. A 3-0 defeat was inflicted on United by Chelsea in a game in which the Londoners completely dominated. The defeat was United's fifth in 14 league games, having lost just six in the previous season. In the Champions League there was better news as United strolled past Portuguese champions Boavista at Old Trafford, a double from Van Nistelrooy helped United to a three nil win with Blanc also scoring. But a return to Premier League action didn't bring a positive result as United suffered yet another home defeat this time to West Ham United. The three successive league defeats to Arsenal, Chelsea and West Ham left United ninth in the Premier League table, eleven points behind leaders Liverpool, having played a game more than the Merseysiders. United's problem was conceding goals, having conceded 27 in their fifteen league games. Only West Ham and Leicester at the bottom end of the table had conceded more than United.

With the Champions League now taking a break until February, Ferguson and his team could concentrate on getting their challenge for a fourth straight Premier League title back on track. They started that quest with two resounding home wins against Derby and Southampton, scoring 11 goals in the process. First came Derby and a 5-0 win and then United visited Middlesbrough and came away with a 1-0 win before the visit of Southampton to Old Trafford which resulted in a 6-1 triumph with Van Nistelrooy bagging himself a hat-trick. Next came two away games that both resulted in victory for United, firstly against Everton, a 2-0 win with second-half goals from Giggs and Van Nistelrooy, then a visit to Fulham, which just as on the opening day finished 3-2 in United's favour with Giggs (2) and Van Nistelrooy once again the goalscorers. Since the defeat West Ham, United had put together a run of five straight wins to finish 2001 fifth in the league, having dropped as low as ninth after suffering six defeats in their opening 14 league games. Despite being fifth in the table they were only one win away from the top of the table.

January consisted of five wins out of seven games as United progressed in the FA Cup and continued their recovery in the Premier League to finish the month on top of the table. The month started with a 3-1 win over Newcastle, that win was United's sixth straight win the league. That run had seen United back in contention in the title race having been written by Ferguson himself just a month earlier. The win over Newcastle came courtesy of goals from Van Nistelrooy and Scholes (2) as they moved up to second in the table. Next up was the third round of the FA Cup and a visit to Villa Park to face Aston Villa and former United goalkeeper Peter Schmeichel. Three goals in five minutes gave United a 3-2 win having fallen two nil behind. Van Nistelrooy capped his first FA Cup appearance for Manchester United with two goals to salvage the win for United having started the game sat on the bench. After falling behind and looking like heading out of the competition at the first hurdle. Ferguson called on Van Nistelrooy and the comeback was started by Solskjaer on 77 minutes before two goals from the Dutchman in two minutes and United were through to the fourth round. The win over Villa was followed by a league victory over Southampton that took United to the top of the table for the first time in the season. James Beattie gave Southampton an early lead before goals from Van Nistelrooy, Beckham and Solskjaer gave Ferguson's men a three one win that took them top of the pile. That had looked unlikely just over two months earlier when suffering defeat to West Ham, their sixth defeat of the season had left United ninth in the table. The win over Southampton was followed by a 2-1 home win over Blackburn that featured a record for striker Ruud Van Nistelrooy. Van Nistelrooy opened the score from the penalty spot to score in a record eight consecutive Premier League games, having also scored in the last

Champions League game before the break and the third round of the FA Cup, Van Nistelrooy had scored in ten consecutive games in all competitions. The win against Blackburn was sealed by Roy Keane on 81 minute after Craig Hignett had equalised for Blackburn. The win over Blackburn made it eight straight victories in the league for Ferguson's side and next up they welcomed Liverpool to Old Trafford. Liverpool held the upper hand in recent games between the two great rivals, having won the previous four fixtures including a 3-1 win at Anfield earlier in the season. United dominated the game but couldn't breakdown the Liverpool defence and were struck with a sucker punch on 85 minutes when Steven Gerrard found Danny Murphy who lifted the ball over Barthez in United's goal. The win not only ended United's winning run but also brought Liverpool back into the title race.

The next game on United's fixture list was the fourth round of the FA Cup and a visit to Middlesbrough, having previously been managed by former United midfielder Robson. Middlesbrough were now managed by former United assistant manager Steve McLaren, who had left his position at Old Trafford in the summer. The tie was won by Middlesbrough with two late goals from Noel Whelan and Andy Campbell. Whelan took advantage of a lapse from Blanc to give Middlesbrough the lead. The exit meant United had exited at the fourth round stage for the second year running. After successive defeats to Liverpool and Middlesbrough, United bounced back with a 4-0 demolition of Bolton. February would be a monumental month in the history of Manchester United with the announcement that Sir Alex Ferguson had performed a u-turn on his decision to step down and retire at the end of the season. It has been revealed years after the event that Ferguson's decision to stay was down to his family. Who told him he couldn't retire, that he was still young and healthy enough to carry on doing the job and he would regret the decision if he stepped down now. United were linked with a host of managers from around the world in their search for Ferguson's replacement. With England manager Sven Goran Eriksson rumoured to be the man that the United board had chosen as Ferguson's replacement. Eriksson revealed in 2013 that he had agreed a deal to take the United job and had even signed an agreement to do so. But once Ferguson informed the club of his decision then there was no way that United would let Ferguson go and the Scot agreed a three-year contract extension and once again insisted that once that contract was up he would leave the club completely. On agreeing the new deal, Ferguson stated that the priority at the club was to sort out the club's academy. On the pitch a double from Solskjaer earnt United a 2-0 win over Charlton at The Valley before they resumed their Champions League campaign. The Champions League campaign resumed with an away game against Nantes and United had to be thankful for a 90th minute penalty from Van Nistelrooy to salvage a point after having looked like they were going to crash to defeat in France despite having a hatful of chances to level the game. Before Nantes were welcomed to Old Trafford for the return game, United played Aston Villa and came away with a 1-0 win. Just as in France Nantes took the lead but this time United hit back straight away through Beckham and went on to the game 5-1 with Solskjaer netting a double. The demolition of Nantes was followed by a 2-2 draw with Derby County in the Premier League. After the draw with Derby, United were one point clear at the top of the league, Arsenal were in second and had a game in hand on United.

The draw with Derby was followed by two home games, the first coming against Tottenham in the league and a 4-0 win. After that United welcomed Bayern to Old Trafford and the pair played out a 0-0 in their Champions League encounter. After this United faced West Ham at The Boleyn Ground and came away with a 5-3 win after twice falling behind early on in the game and this win was followed by a 3-0 win over in Portugal over Boavista to confirm Ferguson's side as group winners. Despite finishing level on points with Bayern, United had a superior goal difference and were drawn to face Deportivo La Coruna in the quarter-finals. The Spaniards had defeated United twice in the first group stage. The month of March finished with a defeat to Middlesbrough before a 4-3 win over Leeds United at Elland Road. With five games left of the league campaign, United were second in the league, one point behind Liverpool. While Arsenal were a point further back but had played two games less than United. Focus for Ferguson and United now turned to their Champions League quarter-final with Deportivo as the manager looked to guide his team to the final at Hampden Park. United gained an advantage after the first-leg against Deportivo, a 2-0 win in Spain was United's first away win at this stage in the competition. Beckham put United ahead on 15 minutes with a 30-yard strike before Van Nistelrooy doubled the advantage just before half-time. The win came at a cost though as they lost both Keane and Scholes for the return leg at Old Trafford. Keane was ruled by an injury received in Spain and Scholes already on a yellow card going into the game was booked and would be missing for the second-leg. Between the first and second-leg United paid a visit to Leicester and came away with a 1-0 win. The second-leg against Deportivo was the fourth time the two sides had met this season and was also Sir Alex Ferguson's 100th European game in charge of Manchester United. After going out at the quarter-final stage in the previous two seasons, United were desperate to reach the semi-finals. They completed a 5-2 aggregate with a 3-2 home win that was helped by a double from Solskjaer. Solskjaer stepped off the bench after 21 minutes to replace the injured Beckham, who was victim of a tackle from Pedro Duscher that saw Beckham suffering a broken bone in his foot that ruled him out for the season and made him a major doubt for the 2002 World Cup. Already without Keane and Scholes through injury and suspension, Veron and Butt were combined in the centre of midfield and it was from Veron's free-kick that Solskjaer prodded home to give United the lead. Their first semi-final in three years would see United coming up against German opposition in the shape Bayer Leverkusen. With the first-leg taking place at Old Trafford.

Before that United had to travel to Stamford Bridge for a league encounter with Chelsea. Goals from Scholes, Van Nistelrooy and Solskjaer gave Ferguson and his men a 3-0 win to keep them in the title race. The first-leg result left United needing a win in Germany or a high scoring draw after a 2-2 draw and two away goals for Leverkusen. The match started badly for United when they lost right-back Gary Neville to a suspected broken foot following a challenge from Ze Roberto. Despite the blow of losing Neville, United did take the lead when Solskjaer's shot deflected in off Zivkovic. 1-0 at half-time to United but Leverkusen hit back through Michael Ballack on 62 minutes. Five minutes later and Van Nistelrooy put United back in front, scoring from the penalty spot and Veron saw his chance to extend the lead spurned by Leverkusen keeper Hans Jorg Butt before Oliver Neuville equalised for the Germans. Two away goals for Leverkusen put the Germans in the driving seat for a place in the final at Hampden Park. With three games to play in the league, United sat five points behind leaders Arsenal and would need to win all their remaining games, which included a home game with Arsenal if they were to have any chance of making it four successive league titles. The first of three remaining league games was a visit to Portman Road and Ipswich Town between the first and second-leg with Leverkusen. United earned a 1-0 win over Ipswich but still remained five points behind Arsenal and even a win over the Gunners at Old Trafford may not be enough to overhaul them. Before that came the second-leg in Leverkusen. United welcomed Keane and Scholes back to the starting eleven but were still without Beckham and Neville. Keane opened the scoring for United after 28 minutes, only for Neuville to level for Leverkusen once again on the stroke of half-time. It was a frantic finish as United looked for the winning goal and despite having two efforts cleared off the line couldn't find a winner and their Champions League dream ended at the semi-finals stage as they lost on away goals. After the disappointment of their Champions League, United welcomed Arsenal in the title deciding game at Old Trafford. A Wiltord goal gave Arsenal the win and confirmed them as league champions and meant United were trophyless for the first time since the 1997/98 season. Not only did they finish the season emptyhanded, the 2001/02 season also saw United finishing in their lowest Premier League finish as they eventually finished third behind Arsenal and Liverpool. Ruud Van Nistelrooy finished as United's top goalscorer in his first season, scoring 23 league and 36 in all competitions.

Chapter Eleven: Got our Trophy Back

Manchester United and Sir Alex Ferguson reacted to finishing the 2001/02 season empty handed by breaking the British transfer record for the third time in little over a year. Having twice broke the record the previous summer for the attacking purchases of Ruud Van Nistelrooy and Juan Sebastian Veron. Ferguson broke the record once again for the signing of defender Rio Ferdinand. The transfer of England defender from Leeds United cost United £29.1million, the move for Ferdinand came as Ferguson looked to strengthen a backline that had looked shaky the previous season after the departure of Jaap Stam and Ferdinand was brought in to partner experienced French centre-half Laurent Blanc. The only other new arrival in the summer of 2002 was Spanish goalkeeper Ricardo, brought in to provide competition for Barthez and Roy Carroll. As well as the new arrivals there were several departures of experienced players from Old Trafford in the summer of 2002. Goalkeeper van der Gouw joined West Ham United on a free transfer, while defenders Denis Irwin and Ronny Johnsen both left the club on a free transfers at the end of their contracts. Irwin signed for Wolverhampton Wanderers and Johnsen joined Aston Villa. Following the arrivals of Van Nistelrooy the previous summer and Diego Forlan in January 2002, striker Dwight Yorke had fallen down the pecking order at Old Trafford and left the club, joining Blackburn in £2million deal where he joined Andy Cole who was sold to Blackburn six months earlier. The departure of Irwin meant he was the final player to leave the club of Ferguson's first title winners and though Irwin could still do a job for United, Ferguson couldn't guarantee the Irishman a regular starting place in his team. I'm sure if you asked Ferguson, Irwin would be regarded as one of his greatest signings by the man himself. A player he could rely on to perform to high standards week after week.

Finishing the previous season trophyless meant United didn't compete in the traditional curtain raiser of the Charity Shield and instead played a pre-season friendly against Argentinian side Boca Juniors at Old Trafford, United won the game 2-0 with two goals from Van Nistelrooy and the Old Trafford faithful got their first glimpse of Rio Ferdinand in a United shirt. Before the Premier League season, United had to play the first-leg of a Champions League qualifying round and it wasn't the result that Ferguson wanted. They played Zalaegerszeg of Hungary and travelled to Budapest for the first-leg just three days before the big kick-off in the Premier League. The Hungarians stunned United in the 90th minute with their only effort on United's goal. Despite the defeat, Ferguson was still confident that his team would win though to the group stages. Before the return leg at Old Trafford, United had two Premier League games, starting with West Brom at home on the opening day of the season. United got their league campaign off to a winning start but for long periods it looked like they would draw a blank in front of goal once again. That was until Solskjaer did what he had done many times before, stepping off the bench to score an important goal for Ferguson. The goal for Solskjaer was his hundredth for the club and gave United the 1-0 win that got their league season off to a winning start. Next up was Chelsea and a visit to Stamford Bridge that ended in a 2-2 draw as United came from behind twice to earn a point. With the second equaliser coming from Giggs and he like Solskjaer struck his hundredth goal for the club. Now it was down to the business of overturning the one goal deficit and booking their place in the Champions League group stages. United brushed Zalaegerszeg aside in the second-leg and were ahead in the tie within 15 minutes of the match starting at Old Trafford and never looked back from there as they beat the Hungarians 5-0 on the night and 5-1 on aggregate. The first group stage saw Ferguson's men drawn with Maccabi Haifa, Olympiacos and an immediate rematch with Bayer Leverkusen. Before the group stage started though it was back to Premier League action as United aimed to win the Premier League trophy back.

Before the opening game of the Champions League group stages, United had four Premier League fixtures to navigate and that started with a game against Sunderland. Despite being given the lead by a 7th minute strike from Giggs it turned out to be a bad day for United as they drew the game 1-1 as Sunderland striker Tore Andre Flo marked his debut with a goal. The dying seconds of the game saw Roy Keane sent off as he clashed with former International team-mate Jason McAteer, Ferguson suffered a further blow in defence as he lost Silvestre to injury. After the disappointment of losing the lead and having to settle for a draw with Sunderland, United welcomed Middlesbrough to Old Trafford and a Ruud Van Nistelrooy penalty gave United a much needed win, having drawn their previous two league games. The defeat of Middlesbrough was followed by two league defeats against Bolton and Leeds. The defeat against Bolton came at Old Trafford and was the second successive season that Bolton had beaten United at Old Trafford and Kevin Nolan was the hero on both occasions. It was a game United dominated but couldn't make their dominance pay in front of goal. After the defeat to Bolton, United travelled to Elland Road and a first return to the ground for Ferdinand since his move to United in the summer. Ferdinand couldn't prevent United from going down to another one nil defeat and with just two wins in their opening six league games, United were 10th in the table. After the defeats to Bolton and Leeds, United racked up six successive victories in the Premier League and

Champions League. That started with a 5-2 win over Maccabi Haifa, Maccabi gave United a scare before goals from Giggs, Solskjaer, Veron and Van Nistelrooy made it 4-1 with just short of an hour played. The biggest cheer of the night though was reserved for Diego Forlan as he struck his first goal for the club with an 89th minute penalty. Following his move to United in January of the previous season, Forlan had made 26 appearances without finding the back of the net. The win over Maccabi was followed up with victories over Leverkusen and Olympiacos in the group to leave United looking good for early qualification to the second group stage. Meanwhile in the league wins over Tottenham, Charlton and Everton lifted Ferguson and his side up to fourth in the league table. The three successive wins in the league were followed by successive one all draws with Fulham and Aston Villa. Sandwiched in between those league draws was a trip to Greece and a game against Olympiacos. A 3-2 win for United confirmed their place in the second group stage of the competition. The draw with Aston Villa was followed by a 3-0 defeat to Maccabi. With United's qualification already confirmed, Ferguson took the opportunity to rest several first-team regulars. The defeat to Maccabi was followed by a 2-1 victory over Southampton in which Forlan scored an 85th minute winner, his first strike in the Premier League for United and a 2-0 win over Leicester in the third round of the League Cup.

Next on the agenda for Ferguson and United was a visit to Maine Road for the last ever league Manchester Derby to be played at the ground. This is a day that Gary Neville will want to forget as his first-half mistake led to a goal for Shaun Goater that gave City a 2-1 lead. Anelka had given City the lead after five minutes before Solskjaer struck back for United three minutes later. Goater added a third for City five minutes after the interval and score remained at 3-1 as City registered their first Premier League win over United. Following defeat to City, United bounced back with a 2-0 win over Leverkusen in the final game of the first group stage, that win

114

meant that United topped the group on 15 points and the second group stage saw United drawn with Basel of Switzerland and old foes Juventus and Deportivo La Coruna. Before they started the second group stage, United had Premier League games against West Ham and Newcastle. A 1-1 draw with West Ham was followed by a 5-3 win over Newcastle. The win over Newcastle featured a hat-trick for Van Nistelrooy that put United 4-2 up just after half-time. The win over Newcastle was the start of eight successive wins in three different competitions. Before a mid-season break in the Champions League, United faced Basel and Deportivo, three goals in six second-half minutes gave United the win in Switzerland after they had fallen behind to a first minute opener. Then came a 2-0 win over Deportivo at Old Trafford that made it two wins out of two heading into the Champions League break, the group stage would resume in February with a double-header against Juventus. Sandwiched between the two Champions League group games were league wins over Liverpool and Arsenal and a League Cup win over Burnley. The win over Liverpool was a 2-1 victory thanks to a double from Forlan as he took advantage of a mistake from Liverpool goalkeeper Jerzy Dudek. Forlan pounced to score the opener as Dudek let a Jamie Carragher header slip through his legs, leaving a simple finish for Forlan on 65 minutes. Forlan made it two after 67 minutes. Sami Hyypia reduced the deficit but United held on the three points. Arsenal arrived at Old Trafford as the Premier League leaders but United dispatched them thanks to a goal in each half from Veron and Scholes. The run of eight consecutive victories also saw United beat West Ham 3-0 and Chelsea 1-0 in the fifth round of the League Cup, with Forlan the hero once again. Following the win over West Ham, United went into the Christmas fixtures second in the table, just one point behind leaders Arsenal and a point ahead of Chelsea in third. After eight consecutive wins United suffered back-to-back defeats over the Christmas period against Blackburn and Middlesbrough. These defeats saw Ferguson's side dropping back to third in the table.

2002 was brought to a close with a 2-0 win over Birmingham City at Old Trafford with goals for Forlan and Beckham.

Manchester United made an unbeaten start to 2003, not losing a game until mid-February. That run saw United keep up their challenge for a fourth title in five seasons and progress in the both the League Cup and FA Cup. The year started with three home games in three different competitions, starting with a league game against Sunderland. Sunderland took the lead through a Veron own goal after five minutes and looked like holding on for a vital three points despite their goal being under siege from United's attack. Beckham scored nine minutes from time to level the game before Scholes headed home from close range in stoppage time from United's 32nd attempt on the Sunderland goal. Next up were Portsmouth in the third round of the FA Cup and a 4-1 win for United was sealed by another Scholes goal in the 90th minute of the game. Two nil after 20 minutes through a Van Nistelrooy penalty and Beckham strike. Portsmouth pulled one back through Steve Stone before half-time. Late strikes from Van Nistelrooy and Scholes gave United the 4-1 win. Three days later was the first-leg of the semi-finals of the League Cup against Blackburn. Blackburn fielded ex-United players Cole and Yorke but it was United who took the lead in this one through Scholes before Blackburn equalised through ex-Liverpool trainee David Thompson. The game finished 1-1 to give Blackburn a slight advantage ahead of the second-leg. The draw with Blackburn was followed by six straight wins which started with back-to-back league victories against West Brom and Chelsea before two cup games that saw United progress in both the domestic cup competitions. The win over Chelsea looked like being a draw until Forlan struck a late winner to stun Chelsea. First up in the cup games was the second-leg of the semi-final against Blackburn, former United striker Cole gave Blackburn an early lead on the night to put Blackburn 2-1 up in the tie. Before half-time though, United were in the lead on the night and in the tie thanks to a double from Scholes. Scholes was on target for the sixth successive game and he would be pivotal to any chances United had of lifting silverware come the end of the season. Blackburn were well beaten by United and Ferguson's men deserved the third goal that came from the penalty spot, converted by Van Nistelrooy. A 4-2 win on aggregate for United booked their place in the final at the Millenium Stadium where they would face Liverpool at the beginning of March. After progressing to the final of the League Cup, United welcomed West Ham to Old Trafford in the fourth round of the FA Cup. West Ham were having a bad season in the league and United were in no mood to give the Londoners an easy ride at Old Trafford as they hit them for six on a day when it could be many more. The reward in the next round of the cup for United was a home tie against Arsenal.

Before the next round in the FA Cup, United faced away games against Southampton and Birmingham and a game at home against neighbours Manchester City in the league. Two wins were achieved against Southampton and Birmingham, keeping clean sheets in both fixtures. Beating Southampton 2-0 and Birmingham 1-0 with Van Nistelrooy scoring in both games. Ahead of the cup tie with Arsenal, United welcomed City to Old Trafford in the Manchester Derby. A win for United against City would bring them level on points with Arsenal in the league but United missed their opportunity as Shaun Goater scored a late equaliser with his first touch. Van Nistelrooy had been left with a simple finish on 19 minutes to give United the lead after a cross from Giggs but they couldn't find the crucial second goal and were made to pay when Goater headed home on 86 minutes. Heading into the tie with Arsenal, the two were fighting it out at the top of the Premier League with Arsenal leading the table by three points to United. The tie turned when Giggs missed an open goal on the half-hour mark and four minutes later Edu fired Arsenal ahead. Giggs looked like he had a simple tap-in after rounding both David Seaman and

Sol Campbell but the whole of Old Trafford was left in shock as Giggs fired over the bar. Just four minutes after that miss, Arsenal were ahead as Edu's 25 yard free-kick took a wicked deflection off Beckham and wrong footed Barthez in United's goal. Seven minutes into the second-half the tie was Arsenal's as Wiltord struck another crucial goal at Old Trafford after being played in by Edu. The headlines after game were about David Beckham and a cut above his eye that had been caused by a flying boot kicked by Sir Alex Ferguson. There had been speculation on Beckham's future all season and Ferguson has since said that he and his coaching had been concerned by the lack of intensity in Beckham's game with the speculation regarding his future. Frustrated with the result against Arsenal, Beckham was picked out by Ferguson for criticism in the dressing-room. Ferguson said that Beckham was about 12 feet away from him and as Ferguson moved to towards Beckham he kicked a boot that was on the floor. The boot hit Beckham above the eye and Beckham reacted to have a go at Ferguson but was stopped by his team-mates and told to sit down by Ferguson. In the aftermath of the Beckham and the flying incident, United resumed their Champions League campaign by welcoming old foes Juventus to Old Trafford. Beckham was the star of the show as he created goals for Wes Brown and Van Nistelrooy in a 2-1 win that put United on the brink of another quarter-final in the competition. The win over Juventus was followed by a 1-1 away to Bolton thanks to a 90th minute equaliser from Solskjaer before a trip to Turin for another group game against Juventus. A 3-0 win for United in Turin booked their place in the quarter-final for the seventh successive season as they looked to add to the club's two European Cup successes. Giggs made up for his FA Cup miss with a double on a night when he started the on the bench but he replaced Forlan after just eight minutes and on 15 minutes he applied the finish to a sweeping United counter-attack. Juventus had chances to level the game and French striker David Trezeguet headed an effort against the woodwork before Giggs struck his second on 41 minutes. This

118

was a wonderful solo goal that evoked memories of the FA Cup semi-final goal against Arsenal in 1999. Another substitute, Van Nistelrooy made it 3-0 to United and booked that quarter-final spot with two games still to play in the group.

After the victory over Juventus, United had the opportunity to pick up the first piece of silverware of the season with the League Cup final against Liverpool at the Millenium Stadium. It wasn't the result that Ferguson and United wanted though as goals from Gerrard and Owen gave Liverpool a 2-0 win, meaning Ferguson and his team had to watch as Liverpool celebrated winning the first piece of silverware of the 2002/03 season. Following the defeat in the League Cup final, United played out the final two games of second Champions League group stage, drawing with Basel and losing to Deportivo but United had already done enough to win the group and setup a quarter-final against Real Madrid. Before the first-leg against Real, Ferguson watched his team winning four successive games in the league with wins over Leeds, Aston Villa, Fulham and a four nil win over Liverpool, to gain a little bit of revenge for the League Cup final defeat. After the win over Liverpool, United were level on points with Arsenal at the top of the table with both teams having six league games to play. Arsenal were top due to a superior goal-difference meaning United would have to finish with at least one more point than Arsenal if they were to win a fourth title in five seasons. Next came the first-leg against Real in Madrid, a double from Raul and a Luis Figo goal left United on the brink of a quarter-final exit as Real were inspired by Frenchman Zinedine Zindane. The second-half was only four minutes old when Raul made it three nil and despite Van Nistelrooy pulling one back just three minutes later, the score remained at 3-1 and Ferguson and his side were facing an uphill task if they were to reach the semi-finals for a second successive year. Despite the disappointment of the result in Madrid, United routed Newcastle 6-2 to open up a three point lead over Arsenal ahead of a decisive fixture against the Londoners at Highbury. Avoid defeat in that one and United would hold the advantage in the title race. Newcastle took the lead against United before they hit six goals without reply which included a hat-trick for Paul Scholes. Now to the Arsenal game and Van Nistelrooy put United ahead after 23 minutes and they led 1-0 at half-time but in the second-half, Arsenal hit back with a double from Thierry Henry but just as Arsenal fans were celebrating being ahead in the game United found an immediate equaliser from a Giggs header. The final minutes of the game saw Sol Campbell sent off for an elbow on Solskjaer and game finished two goals apiece, meaning United kept their three point advantage but had played a game more than their title rivals. Ahead of the second-leg against Real, United welcomed Blackburn to Old Trafford. After taking the lead through a Van Nistelrooy strike, United were pegged back when former United defender Henning Berg scored for Blackburn. Scholes though continued his good goalscoring form with a goal either side of half-time to give Ferguson the three points with a 3-1 victory.

Now for the second-leg against Real and a two goal deficit from the first-leg meant United would probably need to keep a clean sheet if they were to have any chance of progressing to the semis. A hat-trick from Brazilian striker Ronaldo ended any hopes United had especially when he put Real Madrid ahead after twelve minutes, Van Nistelrooy did level for United just before half-time but two goals from Ronaldo in the opening 15 minutes of the second-left left United stunned despite equalising for a second time before Ronaldo made it 3-2 to Real. David Beckham had started the game on the bench for United and replaced Veron on 63 minutes with score at 3-2 to Real. Beckham struck two goals to give United a 4-3 win in a game that both teams displayed some of the best attacking football of the season. The win wasn't enough for United as Ronaldo's hat-trick meant United would have to score six goals on the night to progress. With their Champions League exit confirmed, United had just one trophy to aim for if they were to avoid a second successful trophyless season. A 2-0 win over Arsenal's North-London rivals Tottenham gave United a 5 point lead over Arsenal, though the Gunners had a game in hand on United. A Ruud Van Nistelrooy hat-trick helped United to a 4-1 win over Charlton at Old Trafford to leave United in touching distance of winning the Premier League trophy back. That win left United eight points clear of Arsenal but while United had just one game remaining, Arsenal had three to play. Arsenal lost the first of those three games against Leeds to hand United the title. Not many people would expect Leeds to be the ones doing United a favour but they needed the win as they battled against relegation. With Arsenal's defeat to Leeds, United knew they would be receiving the Premier League trophy again at the end of their last league against Everton at Goodison Park whatever the result. United signed off their season with a win thanks to a Beckham free-kick and a Van Nistelrooy strike, his 44th goal of the season. The goal for Beckham would turn out to be his last in what would be his last game for United, as it was for veteran French defender Blanc.

Chapter Twelve: Ronaldo, Rooney and a New Team

The end of the 2002/03 season had already seen the departures of Laurent Blanc and David May from the United ranks. 37 year-old Blanc decided to retire, having postponed his retirement the previous summer, while May was handed a free transfer by Ferguson and joined Burnley. Goalkeeper Fabien Barthez had been dropped by Ferguson following the Champions League exit at the hands of Real Madrid as he finally lost patience with the Frenchman, who made a number of high-profile mistakes during his time at Old Trafford. The Frenchman's contract ran until the summer of 2006 but United agreed a settlement with him to terminate the contract at the end of 2003/04 season. Ferguson's search for a new goalkeeper led him to the United States, signing Tim Howard from New York New Jersey Metro Stars on four-year contract in a £2.3million deal. Another outgoing from Old Trafford was David Beckham as he left United for a move to Spain. There had been speculation on Beckham's future all the way through the previous season and this only heightened once Beckham was struck by a flying boot kicked by Ferguson. Ferguson has since said that Beckham was sold because he felt the England midfielder thought he was bigger than the manager and Ferguson was concerned about Beckham's celebrity lifestyle. For a long time it looked like Beckham would join Barcelona with the two clubs even announcing they had reached a deal. That move though was dependent on the outcome of Barcelona's Presidential elections and it was believed that Beckham had no interest in a move to the Nou Camp. So in stepped Real to hijack the move of their rivals and signed Beckham in £25million deal.

Three more new signings joined Tim Howard at Old Trafford and they came in the shape of Eric Djemba-Djemba, a Cameroonian International joining from French club Nantes. Brazilian midfielder Kleberson and Portuguese teenager Cristiano Ronaldo. The deals for Kleberson and Ronaldo were completed on the same day and despite Kleberson being a World Cup winner and Ronaldo being an unknown teenager, the headlines were about the signing of Ronaldo. 17 year-old Ronaldo arrived in a £12.24m deal from Sporting Lisbon, signing a five-year contract and Ronaldo was handed the famous number seven shirt vacated by the departure of Beckham. Ronaldo wasn't just following in the footsteps of Beckham in wearing the number seven shirt. The number seven shirt is an iconic number for Manchester United, players such as Best, Robson and Cantona had all wore the shirt number before Beckham and Ronaldo. Manchester United had an agreement in place to sign Ronaldo but it wasn't expected that the Portuguese youngster would arrive at Old Trafford until later than he did. The move was hastened when several other big clubs declared an interest in the player and after the player himself impressed several of his future team-mates in a pre-season friendly between United and Lisbon. Sporting won the game 3-1 and Ronaldo created two of the goals. All the talk in United's dressing-room after the game was of Ronaldo and the players urged their manager to sign him. There was one more outgoing at United before the season kicked off and that was the departure of Juan Sebastian Veron to Chelsea. After arriving for a then record fee of £28.1million Veron failed to impress for the majority of his time in Manchester as he struggled with the fast pace of the Premier League, with the majority of his better performances coming in the Champions League.

With summer transfer dealings complete, United started the 2003/04 campaign with the FA Community Shield against Arsenal at the Millenium Stadium. Tim Howard was selected in goal ahead of Roy Carroll, with Barthez not even making the matchday squad. One of the reasons why Ferguson felt he could let Beckham go was the performances of Solskjaer on the right-side of midfield in the second half of the previous season and the Norwegian was selected there for this game. After 90 minutes the game was at stalemate with the score 1-1, both goals coming Frenchmen. Silvestre opened the scoring after 15 minutes, only for Henry to level for Arsenal on 20 minutes. Despite Van Nistelrooy missing in the shootout, United lifted the trophy thanks to a 4-3 win in the penalty shootout. The league season kicked off with a home game against Bolton Wanderers and United ran out 4-0 winners. Despite only being on the pitch for around half an hour the star of the show was Cristiano Ronaldo. Impressing the Old Trafford faithful with his dribbling skills and having a hand in three goals as United extended their lead from 1-0 to 4-0 after the introduction of Ronaldo. Next United travelled to Newcastle and St James Park, coming away with 2-1 victory with goals from Scholes and Van Nistelrooy. Despite his impressive cameo against Bolton, Ronaldo had to settle for a place on the bench once again. The first start for the Portuguese youngster came in United's third league of the season at home to Wolverhampton and United made it three wins out of three thanks to a tenth minute goal from John O'Shea. After three straight wins, Ferguson saw his side suffer their first defeat of the season when they travelled to the South-Coast to face Southampton. United went down to an 88th minute winner from James Beattie. United bounced back in their next two games, scoring seven goals without reply, first beating Charlton 2-0 at The Valley with a double from Van Nistelrooy. The Champions League was now reduced to one group stage, where United would face Panathinaikos, Stuttgart and Glasgow Rangers in two games billed as the battle of Britain. Their Champions League campaign started with a 5-0 win over

Panathinaikos at Old Trafford, the game featured five different goalscorers including summer signing Djemba-Djemba, his first goal in the red of United. Next up for United was the visit of Arsenal to Old Trafford in what turned to be feisty encounter between the two title rivals. Arsenal had skipper Viera sent off for a second yellow card after he reacted to a challenge from Van Nistelrooy. Arsenal players felt that Van Nistelrooy had got their skipper sent off and when Van Nistelrooy missed from the penalty spot in the dying embers of the game, several Arsenal players reacted by shoving the Dutchman and gloating to him over his miss. This was followed by a 4-1 win away to Leicester with Van Nistelrooy bagging a hat-trick before a 2-1 defeat to Stuttgart in Germany. Victories over Birmingham and Leeds made it three successive wins in the league before they travelled to Ibrox to face Rangers and came away with a 1-0 win thanks to a rare strike from Phil Neville. A second league defeat of season came as Fulham visited Old Trafford. After falling behind early, Forlan levelled for United on the stroke of half-time. Before two second-half goals gave the visitors a 3-1 victory. The defeat to Fulham left United two points off the top of the league after ten games, having already lost two games they couldn't afford to lose many more if they were going to retain the title. Arsenal were top and despite only being two points in front of Ferguson's men they were yet to suffer defeat.

Next up was the start of United's League Cup campaign and a third round tie with Leeds United at Elland Road, United needed a Djemba-Djemba goal three minutes from the end of extra-time to seal a 3-2 win and set up a fourth round tie with West Brom. After the extra-time win over Leeds, United enjoyed five successive wins in the Premier League and Champions League. That run saw wins over Portsmouth, Liverpool and Blackburn in the Premier League, while wins over Rangers and Panathinaikos in the Champions League left Ferguson's men in a strong position in the group. The win over Portsmouth (3-0) witnessed a first goal for Cristiano Ronaldo as he scored from a free-kick. The win over Liverpool, came at Anfield and saw Ryan Giggs scoring a double in a 2-1 win with Liverpool's Jerzy Dudek enduring another nightmare against United. The five successive wins were followed by back-to-back defeats in the league and League Cup. The defeat in the league came as United travelled to Stamford Bridge, Chelsea were one of United's rivals for the title and the defeat was United's third in the league. League Cup exit came as United faced West Brom and suffered 2-0 defeat with Ferguson opting to field a mixture of squad players and promising players from the United's academy. December 2003 was a good month for Ferguson and United as they won every game they played to keep themselves in the title race and progress in the Champions League as group winners. Finishing the group on 15 points, three ahead of second placed Stuttgart. While wins over Aston Villa, Manchester City, Tottenham, Everton and Middlesbrough in the league meant United finished the calendar year top of the table. After 19 games, United were one point ahead of Arsenal but having already suffered three defeats, Ferguson's men may have to go unbeaten in the rest of the league season to win the title for a fifth time in six seasons. Tradition dictates that the first fixture of a new calendar year is the third round of the FA Cup and 2004 was no different as United travelled to Villa Park to face Aston Villa in the third round. A second-half double from Scholes cancelled out an opener from Gareth Barry to give United a 2-1 win and setup another away trip in the fourth round, this time to face Northampton Town. Before that though they had important league fixtures against Bolton, Newcastle and Wolverhampton. The cup tie with Villa had seen Ferguson rest some of his first-teamers but they were back as United faced Bolton and came away with a win that extended their lead at the top of the league to three points as both Chelsea and Arsenal dropped points. That three point advantage was cut though as Ferguson watched his side play out a goalless with Newcastle at Old Trafford and

United dropped a further three points against Wolverhampton, losing their place at the top of the league with a 1-0 defeat to the Midlanders.

The defeat to Wolverhampton also saw Rio Ferdinand's last game for eight months after the defender was banned from all football following at missed drug test at United's Carrington training ground on September 23 2003. Ferdinand left the training ground to go shopping and later remembered about the test and tried to return to the training ground to take the test. The England International was told he was too late, he did take the test the next day and passed. Ferdinand even offered to take a follicle hair test, which would provide results for the previous six months. The eight month ban imposed on Ferdinand meant that the defender would out of action for the rest of the season and the beginning of the next, also meaning he would be unavailable for Euro 2004 selection. As well as the ban, Ferdinand was fined £50,000 by the FA and despite an appeal from United and Ferdinand the ban was upheld and Ferguson would be without his record signing until the September of the 2004/05 season. Despite the loss of Ferdinand it was in attack that Ferguson strengthened his squad as he completed the signing of French striker Louis Saha from Fulham in a £12.82million deal, Saha had impressed Ferguson with 15 goals for Fulham in the first-half of the season. The start of January also saw the departure of Barthez after the Frenchman had been frozen out by Ferguson. Barthez secured a loan move to Marseille and would later secure a permanent move back to the club where he had spent three years in the early 1990's. The first game without Ferdinand came as United travelled to Northampton for the fourth round of the FA Cup, a 3-0 win for United booked a fifth round tie with Manchester City. The absence of Ferdinand was felt as United conceded ten goals in their next four games, winning three and losing one. The wins came against Southampton (3-2), Everton (4-3) and Manchester City (4-2) in the FA Cup. The win over

Southampton saw Louis Saha making his Manchester United debut and Frenchman marked the occasion with a goal, Van Nistelrooy was also on the scoresheet as he celebrated signing a new deal with United. The win over Everton saw Van Nistelrooy and Saha grabbing two goals apiece, the Dutchman's strikes were his 100th and 101st for the club. Despite having Gary Neville sent off in the cup tie with City, United dominated the game and strolled into a three nil lead before two late goals for City made the result look closer than the game actually was. Defeat to Middlesbrough midway through February was United's fifth in the league and left Ferguson's side with 56 points after 25. That left them second in the table, five points behind Arsene Wenger's Arsenal side who were yet to taste defeat in the league. A draw with Leeds in the league after the FA Cup tie with City, saw United slipping a further two points behind leaders Arsenal.

United's reward for winning their Champions League group was a first knockout round encounter with Portuguese side Porto. This encounter saw United and Ferguson coming face-to-face with Jose Mourinho for the first time. The first-leg in Portugal was a bad one for United despite taking the lead through Quintin Fortune after 14 minutes. But a double from Fortune's fellow South African Benni McCarthy gave Porto a 2-1 win and United suffered a further blow with the sending off of Roy Keane. Keane was given his marching orders for a stamp on Porto keeper Victor Baia, the sending off was the 11th of Keane's career. Despite scoring the away goal United knew they would have a tough task if they were to win through in the return leg. Before the second-leg United had two games against Fulham one in the league and the other in the cup. The first game was at Craven Cottage in the league and finished in a 1-1 draw with Saha scoring against his former side. Then United welcomed Fulham to Old Trafford in the FA Cup quarter-finals and a double from Van Nistelrooy gave United a 2-1 win, booking a semi-final with Arsenal. Now for the return against Porto, where a late equaliser from Francisco Costinha's stunned Old Trafford and knocked United out of the competition. Scholes had put United ahead after 31 minutes to level the tie at 2-2 and put United ahead on away goals. Scholes thought he had a second on the stroke of half-time but this was ruled out for offside. A decision that was shown to be wrong by Television replays. Costinha's last minute equaliser prompted Mourinho to run down the Old Trafford touchline to celebrate with his team. Out of the Champions League and a nine point deficit to Arsenal in the league, the FA Cup was Ferguson's only realistic hope of ending the 2003/04 season with a trophy. Beat Arsenal in the semi-finals and they would face either Millwall or Sunderland in the final. The semi-final against Arsenal was won by United 1-0 thanks to a Scholes strike on 32 minutes. The victory setup a final with Millwall at the Millenium Stadium and barring a disaster United would end the season with a trophy. The victory also ended Arsenal's hopes of emulating United's treble of 1999. Arsenal did complete their Premier League title victory and finished the league season unbeaten. United in comparison suffered nine defeats and finished third in the table, 15 points behind Arsenal. Big improvement would be required from United in the 2004/05 season if they were to mount a stronger challenge for the Premier League and that would be helped by the return of Rio Ferdinand once he had served his eight month ban. The season ended with the FA Cup final against Millwall at the Millenium Stadium and a 3-0 win for United ensured they wouldn't finish the season emptyhanded. Cristiano Ronaldo headed United in front to grab his sixth goal of a debut season before a second-half double from Van Nistelrooy gave United their 11th triumph in the competition.

Four days after the FA Cup win, United confirmed their first signing for the 2004/05 season. That of Leeds forward Alan Smith in a £7million deal after the Yorkshire side's relegation from the Premier League. Smith a life-long Leeds United supporter had come up through the club's youth ranks and it shocked many when he joined bitter rivals United. Of course he wasn't the first Leeds player to make the move across the Pennine's, following in the footsteps of a certain Eric Cantona and several others before him and of course most recently Rio Ferdinand. The signing of Smith was followed by the capture of Argentinian defender Gabriel Heinze, arriving in a £6.9million deal from Paris St Germain on a five-year contract. Ferguson's policy of signing up and coming young players continued in the summer of 2004 as he signed three teenagers to add to the signings of Smith and Heinze. The first being 17 year-old defender Gerard Pique arriving from Barcelona on a five-year contract. The signing of Pique was followed by the arrival of Italian striker Giuseppe Rossi. 16 year-old Rossi was signed from Parma. Rossi was yet to sign a professional contract with the Italians, meaning United were required to pay Parma minimal compensation. The summer also saw a number of departures including that of another of the Class of 92 graduates, Nicky Butt. After 13 years at Old Trafford, Butt moved to another United, Newcastle in a deal worth £2.5million. Butt made 387 appearances for United, the last coming as a late substitute in the FA Cup final victory over Millwall. Butt was followed out of Old Trafford by Luke Chadwick and Diego Forlan. Forlan was reported to have been sold for a £2million fee and left the club in search of regular first-team football after struggling to adapt to life in the Premier League. After joining United in January 2002, Forlan made 98 appearances for United, scoring 17 goals and will be fondly remembered by United fans for his double against Liverpool. The biggest transfer of the summer was that of 18 year-old striker Wayne Rooney from Everton on August 31. The deal could cost United up to £27million, paying a fee of £20million upfront with the rest of the fee based on appearances and achievements for United and Rooney. Rooney had scored 17 goals in 77 appearances in his first two seasons in the Everton first-team and passed a medical with United despite still recovering from a broken bone is his foot that he sustained in England's Euro 2004 campaign. The signing of Rooney, meant United had two of the most promising teenagers in European football in Rooney and Ronaldo. After a third place finish in the Premier League the previous season, United would have to play a two-legged qualifying round if they were to be in the group stages of the Champions League. Before that the season was kicked off with the Community Shield against Arsenal and the Londoners won the game 3-1 with Smith scoring United's goal on his debut. Ferguson wasn't happy that he was missing both Ronaldo and Heinze as they both represented their countries in the Olympic Games.

The 2004/05 Premier League campaign kicked off with an away trip to one of the teams that were likely to be title challengers along with United, that was Chelsea. The appointment of Jose Mourinho by the Stamford Bridge side would make them stronger and Chelsea enjoyed success in the game due to a strike from Icelandic striker Gudjohnsen, who scrambled home the only goal of the game in the 14th minute following a weak challenge from United goalkeeper Tim Howard. Before the trip to Chelsea, United had played the first-leg of a third qualifying round of the Champions League as they looked to book their place in the group stages. They faced Romanian side Dinamo Bucharest, a 2-1 win in the Romania gave United the advantage and the tie was finished with a 3-0 win at Old Trafford two weeks later. Before the second-leg, United beat Norwich City 2-1 at Old Trafford and drew one goal apiece with Blackburn Rovers. Smith scored in both games and also scored two goals in the home leg with Bucharest as United completed a 5-1 aggregate win and booked their place in the group stages of the Champions League. A day before United completed the signing of Wayne Rooney from Everton, United welcomed the Merseysiders to Old Trafford and played out a 0-0 draw. The game highlighted why Everton were desperate to keep Rooney and why United wanted the teenage striker. Two draws in the following two games made it four consecutive draws for United, both these games finished two goals apiece as first United drew with Bolton away from home and then travelled to France to face Lyon in the opening game of the group stages in the Champions League. Van Nistelrooy scored a double in France as United recovered to earn a point having fallen two goals behind. Monday 20 September 2004 witnessed the return of defender Rio Ferdinand after his eight month ban but it was fellow defender Silvestre who stole the headlines as United marked the return of Ferdinand by defeating Liverpool 2-1 at Old Trafford. Silvestre grabbed two goals as the defeat of Liverpool moved United up to eighth in the league table. The win over Liverpool was followed by a 1-0 win over Tottenham at White Hart Lane with Van Nistelrooy scoring the only goal from the penalty spot.

Tuesday 28 September witnessed Wayne Rooney's Manchester United debut and it was one to remember for the teenage star as he hit a hat-trick as United beat Fenerbahce 6-2 in the second game of the Champions League group stages. Ryan Giggs headed United in front in this one before Rooney took centre stage as he netted his first United goal on 17 minutes following a precision pass from Van Nistelrooy. A second came for Rooney on 28 minutes with a 20 yard strike before he completed his hat-trick with a second-half free-kick in front of the Stretford End. That strike made it four one to United and Fenerbahce got a second before strikes from Van Nistelrooy and David Bellion made it 6-2 to United. That result put United top of the group and although Ferguson would have been pleased with the attacking play, two defensive lapses would have the manager worried. After three successive wins, United fans now had to endure three draws against teams you would fancy United to beat and scoring only one goal in the process. A 1-1 draw with Middlesbrough was followed by another Premier League draw, this time against Birmingham City now managed by former United captain Steve Bruce. This was followed by a 0-0 draw against

Sparta Prague in the Champions League. The draw against Birmingham had left United sixth in the table after nine league games and next they welcomed defending champions Arsenal to Old Trafford. Arsenal had gone through the previous season unbeaten and came into this game unbeaten in 49 league games. Van Nistelrooy missed a chance from the penalty spot to beat Arsenal in their unbeaten season but this time he made no mistake as United ended Arsenal's unbeaten run with a 2-0 win. The opening goal after 73 minutes came when Sol Campbell was adjudged to have fouled Rooney in the area and Van Nistelrooy slotted home the spot kick. Rooney celebrated his 19th birthday by scoring in the 90th minute to give United the 2-0 win. The win not only inflicted defeat on Arsenal for the first time in 49 games, it also saw United close the gap on Arsenal to eight points at the top of the league. A 3-0 win over Crewe Alexandra in the third round of the League Cup booked a fourth round tie with Crystal Palace. The next two league games would see United facing Portsmouth and Manchester City as they looked to build on the defeat of Arsenal but they would lose further ground in the title race as they only picked up one point from these two games to drop down to seventh in the league table. The game against Portsmouth would end in a 2-0 defeat as United failed to take advantage of numerous chances created. United laid siege to the Portsmouth goal but couldn't find a way through and fell behind to a David Unsworth penalty after Ferdinand had fouled Ricardo Fuller. The pattern of the game continued after that as United went in search of a leveller but couldn't find one and Yakuba's deflected shot sealed the points for Portsmouth. It was the same story as United welcomed City to Old Trafford but this time United didn't concede and had to settle for a point. In between these two league games United welcomed Sparta Prague to Old Trafford and ran out comfortable winners, scoring four goals to Sparta's one. Ruud Van Nistelrooy scoring all four for United, former United winger Poborsky was in the Sparta team and was given a red card on 87 minutes after receiving his second booking of the game.

Following the draw with City, United went on a seven game winning run in three different competitions. Starting with a 2-0 win over Crystal Palace in the fourth round of the League Cup, that win setup a quarter-final with Arsenal at Old Trafford, a 1-0 win over Arsenal was the sixth game in this seven game winning run and setup another clash with Mourinho and Chelsea in the semi-finals. Meanwhile wins over Newcastle, Charlton, West Brom and Southampton moved Ferguson's side up to fourth in the table. United faced Lyon on November 23 at Old Trafford and this game marked Ferguson's 1,000 game in charge of Manchester United at Old Trafford. The occasion was celebrated by a rare goal from full-back Gary Neville as a 2-1 win sealed United's qualification for the first knockout round in the Champions League. A 3-0 defeat though to Fenerbahce in the final group, meant United had to settle for second place in the group, finishing two points behind Lyon and would face AC Milan in the first knockout round. Before that though it was time to concentrate on Premier League, a League Cup semi-final with Chelsea and the start of United's defence of the FA Cup. After a 1-1 draw with Fulham, United finished their Premier League fixtures in 2004 with three wins over Crystal Palace, Bolton and Aston Villa. That meant United finished the calendar third in the table though they were nine points behind leaders Chelsea and four points behind second placed Arsenal. 2005 started with a 2-0 defeat of Middlesbrough before three successive 0-0 draws in three different competitions. The first of these goalless draws came as United welcomed Tottenham to Old Trafford in the Premier League. Tottenham felt they should have got the three points though after Roy Carroll scooped an effort from Pedro Mendes away from goal when it appeared to be over the line. Next came Exeter in the FA Cup and the non-league side performed admirably to keep United at bay and earn a replay.

Goals from Ronaldo and Rooney in the replay earnt United a 2-0 win in another hard fought game. Following the first game with Exeter, United travelled to Stamford Bridge for the first-leg of the League Cup semi-final with Chelsea. After the visit to Stamford Bridge, United faced a league fixture against arch rivals Liverpool at Anfield and the match winner for United was former Evertonian Rooney as Liverpool keeper Dudek endured yet another miserable day against United as he let a tame effort from 22 yards into his net. United deserved the 1-0 win despite having Wes Brown sent off for a second bookable offence on 64 minutes. The win over Liverpool sparked a run of eight wins in nine games for United. With the only disappointment coming as Ferguson saw he side suffer an exit from the League Cup as they lost the second-leg of the semi-final 2-1 to Chelsea. The positive run of results saw United progressing to the quarter-finals of the FA Cup without conceding a goal in the replay with Exeter before beating Middlesbrough (3-0) and Everton (2-0). While in the league, the win over Liverpool was followed by a 3-1 over Aston Villa and 4-2 win over Arsenal despite having Silvestre sent off after 69 minutes. The win over Arsenal was sealed by a fine chip from defender John O'Shea in the 89th minute. That win saw United moving up to second in the league table. The three points saw United leapfrogging Arsenal and sitting two points ahead of Arsenal after the full-time whistle at Highbury but United were still eight points behind Chelsea and Chelsea had a game in hand on Ferguson's side. Two days prior to the win over Arsenal, Ferguson allowed midfielder Djemba-Djemba to leave the club after the Cameroonian failed to settle at Old Trafford. He joined Aston Villa in £1.35million deal. The win over Arsenal was followed by 2-0 wins over Birmingham City and Manchester City in the league and the 2-0 win over Everton in the FA Cup.

After the FA Cup win over Everton, United resumed their Champions League campaign with the visit of AC Milan in the first-leg of the first knockout round of the competition. In Milan

United were facing a far more experienced side containing the likes of Maldini, Nesta, Cafu and Seedorf. The game was settled when a mistake from Roy Carroll allowed Milan to score the only goal of the game, that came on 61 minutes when Carroll spilled an effort from Seedorf and Crespo snapped up the rebound to give Milan a 1-0 win. Before the return leg in Milan, United beat Portsmouth 2-1 and drew 0-0 with Crystal Palace. The return leg with Milan finished in the same scoreline as at Old Trafford with Crespo scoring in the 61st minute once again. This time meeting a cross from Cafu to head past Tim Howard in the United goal. Giggs hit a post for United and Van Nistelrooy missed two chances he would normally have buried. Another disappointing exit from the Champions League for Ferguson and adrift of Chelsea in the Premier League title race, left the FA Cup as the only realistic trophy chance for the second season running. Following the defeat to Milan, United travelled to Southampton in the FA Cup quarter-final and came away with a 4-0 win to setup a semi-final with Newcastle. Before that semi-final United beat Fulham 1-0 before dropping points against Blackburn and Norwich without scoring a goal. They drew 0-0 with Blackburn before suffering a 2-0 defeat to Norwich. The defeat to Norwich left United third in the table with six games to play. They sat three points behind Arsenal in second while they were 14 points behind leaders and eventual champions Chelsea. United booked their return to the FA Cup final and an encounter with Arsenal in the showpiece with a 4-1 win against a lacklustre Newcastle side in the semi-finals. Van Nistelrooy was on the scoresheet twice as United strolled into a 3-0 lead. Following the semi-final win over Newcastle, United stuttered to the end of the season with three wins, two losses and a draw. One of the losses came as United welcomed Chelsea to Old Trafford and as Chelsea had confirmed their title win the previous game United's players gave their Chelsea counterparts a guard of honour. These results meant United finished the season third in the table on 77 points, six points behind second placed Arsenal and a further 18 points behind champions Chelsea. United scored the fewest goals of any of the top three sides, one factor in this must been the absence of Van Nistelrooy for much of the season. United's top goalscorer was Rooney in his first season at Old Trafford, scoring 11 goals in the league and 17 goals in all competitions.

United lost the FA Cup final on a penalty shootout against Arsenal in a game they dominated from the start of normal time to the end of extra-time. The closest United came to scoring was when Wayne Rooney hit the post and then later a Van Nistelrooy header was deflected onto the bar. Arsenal goalkeeper Jens Lehmann would be the hero for Arsenal making numerous saves including one in extra-time to deny Scholes before saving from the United midfielder in the shootout to give Arsenal a 5-4 win on penalties. Despite finishing the season third in the league for the second successive season and finishing the season empty handed, there were positives for Ferguson and United as the manager looked to build a new team that would once again be a force in both England and Europe. One of those positives was the goal return of Wayne Rooney following his big money move from Everton, while fellow teenager Ronaldo was also becoming a more consistent performer for United. Improving on his goal return from his first season in Manchester. Another positive was the performances of full-back Gabriel Heinze. Who was voted the club's player of the year by the supporters. Ferguson was still looking to replace Peter Schmeichel who had left the club at the end of 1998/99 season. The latest goalkeepers that Ferguson had tried were Roy Carroll and Tim Howard. At the end of the 2004/05 season Roy Carroll left the club at the end of his contract as Ferguson couldn't assure him he would be first-choice in the coming season. While Spanish goalkeeper Ricardo was also released by the club, leaving Tim Howard as the only recognised first-team goalkeeper. Surely this is a position where Ferguson would be strengthening in his squad ahead of the 2005/06 season.

Chapter Thirteen: Return to the top

There have been a number of takeover bids for Manchester United in Sir Alex Ferguson's time as the club's manager. The first came from Michael Knighton in 1989, Knighton appeared on the verge of a £20million takeover but his financial backers pulled out at the last minute and Knighton had to settle for a place on the board. In 1991 the club took the decision to become a PLC (Public Limited Company) and float on the stock market before receiving a further takeover bid in 1998 from Rupert Murdock's BskyB but that move was blocked by the Monopolies and Mergers Commission after the Manchester United board had accepted an £623million offer. A few years later Sir Alex Ferguson was at the centre of a power struggle for the club with his former horserace owning partners John Magnier and J.P McManus. The Irish pair gradually became the largest shareholders in United through their company Cubic Expression. This was down to a dispute between the pair and Ferguson over the ownership of race horse Rock of Gibraltar. They became major shareholders in an attempt to remove Ferguson from his position as manager and the Manchester United board responded by approaching investors to attempt to reduce the Irishmen's influence in the boardroom. That is where the Glazers come in, The Glazer Family owned several businesses in the United States including American Football side the Tampa Bay Buccaneers. Malcolm Glazer was the figure head of the family but it was son Avram Glazer who was looking at potential investments in

European football. The Glazer family bought their first stake in Manchester United on March 2 2003, buying a 2.9% stake for £9million, purchased through a holding company called Red Football. Over the next few months, the Glazers upped their stake in Manchester United and speculation began to grow that the Glazers or several other interested parties would launch a takeover bid for the club. On November 29 2003 it was reported that the Glazers had purchased up to 15% in the club and had met with chief executive David Gill to discuss their intentions. February 2004 saw the Glazers increase their stake to 16.31% and the Financial Times reported that the family had instructed Commerzbank to explore a takeover bid. They continued to increase their shareholding and by October 2004 were nearing a 30% stake in the club. Once their shareholding reached 30% they would have to launch a formal takeover bid. On May 12 2005, it was announced that Red Football had reached an agreement with J.P McManus and John Magnier to purchase their 28.7% stake in the club. This gave the Glazers a controlling stake of just under 57%, their stake rose to 62% when they purchased the shares of third-largest stakeholder, Scottish mining entrepreneur Harry Dobson. To end the club's PLC status and remove Manchester United from the London Stock Exchange the Glazers would need a shareholding of 75% and on May 16 they went over that threshold and a month later on June 22 2005 they removed Manchester United's shares from the stock exchange for the first time in 14 years. On June 28 2005 a statement was released to announce that Red Football shareholding had reached 98%, prompting a squeeze out of the remaining shareholders. The final valuation of the club was £790million. There was a lot of supporter backlash from Manchester United fans to the takeover by the Glazer family because they had bought the club by borrowing money and plunged United into debt for the first time in decades. Sir Alex Ferguson and David Gill though came out in support of the new ownership in believe that the Glazers would make sure that club continued to run the same as it had been before their takeover.

There were several new arrivals on the playing staff for the 2005/06 season as United looked to mount a stronger challenge for the Premier League after finishing third in the previous two seasons and the club wouldn't want to go a second successive season trophyless. Surely high on the agenda would be a goalkeeper, having let Barthez, Carroll and Ricardo leave the club in recent seasons. So the first signing after the Glazers takeover of the club was Dutch International goalkeeper Edwin van der Sar from Premier League rivals Fulham. The deal was agreed in June and Dutchman agreed a two-year deal to join the club officially on July 1 2005. The transfer of van der Sar was followed up by the signing of South Korean midfielder Park Ji-Sung from Dutch side PSV Eindhoven in a £4million deal. These signings were followed by another goalkeeper in the shape Ben Foster, signing the young Englishman from Stoke City and then loaning Foster to Watford for the season. Meanwhile leaving the club was another one of the Class of 92 graduates, Phil Neville, who left the club to join Everton in search of more regular first-team football. Something that Ferguson could not guarantee him. Another departure was that of Kleberson, joining Turkish side Besiktas for a fee of £2.5million. Kleberson who arrived at the same time as Djemba-Djemba and like the Cameroonian, the Brazilian failed to make an impact at Old Trafford. After champions Chelsea made a flying start to the previous season, Ferguson knew he couldn't afford to let Mourinho's side get away at the top of the table by Christmas and United started their Premier League campaign with three successive wins all too nil as new goalkeeper van der Sar kept three clean sheets against Everton, Aston Villa and Newcastle. Whilst at the other end of the pitch Van Nistelrooy and Rooney were amongst the goals. Van Nistelrooy scoring in all three games and Rooney scoring on the opening day against Everton and also in a 2-

0 win against Newcastle. Prior to their opening Premier League game, United played the first-leg of a third qualifying round for the Champions League against Hungarian outfit Debrecen, the first-leg took place at Old Trafford and finished 3-0 with Rooney, Van Nistelrooy and Ronaldo all on the scoresheet. The return leg finished 3-0 also to give United a 6-0 aggregate win and sealed their place in the Champions League group stages. Following five straight wins at the start of the campaign, Ferguson saw his men go four games without a win, drawing games against City and Liverpool in the league and a goalless draw against Villarreal in the opening game of the Champions League group stages. The draws with City and Liverpool were followed by a 2-1 defeat to Blackburn that left United sixth in the table. After six games United were already ten points behind Chelsea though they did have one game in hand on the defending champions. After the opening draw with Villarreal in the Champions League, United got their first win of the group stages with a 2-1 win over Benfica at Old Trafford thanks to a late strike from Van Nistelrooy after Simao had equalised a first-half opener from Giggs. That victory was followed by Premier League wins over Fulham and Sunderland. The victory over Fulham, which saw van der Sar returning to Craven Cottage for the first time since his transfer to United, finished 3-2 with Van Nistelrooy striking a double as United recovered after falling behind after 90 seconds to a Collins John opener. The victory over Sunderland (3-1) was sealed by a late strike from young Italian striker Giuseppe Rossi. After those three wins, United endured two successive draws. One in the Champions League as they welcomed French side Lille to Old Trafford and the two sides played out a 0-0 draw. It was a disappointing performance from United as they barely threatened a well organised side and had Paul Scholes sent off on 63 minutes following a second yellow card. The Scholes sending off was United's second in three group games following Rooney's sending off in Villarreal. The draw with Lille was followed by another home draw, this time against Tottenham in the

Premier League. United took the lead on seven minutes when Tottenham goalkeeper Paul Robinson spilled a Van Nistelrooy header that was pounced on by Silvestre but Tottenham levelled after 72 minutes through a Jermaine Jenas free-kick. The draw left United fifth in the table. After the draw with Tottenham, United welcomed Barnet to Old Trafford in the third round of the League Cup. Ferguson opted to field a young side against Barnet including Giuseppe Rossi and Gerard Pique, Rossi put United three nil up after 51 minutes in a game that eventually finished 4-1 in United's favour and setup a fourth round tie with West Brom. Next up in the league was a trip to Middlesbrough and it turned out to be a bad day in the North-East as United were humbled 4-1 by Middlesbrough. Ronaldo got United's only goal in the game, Ronaldo's strike against Middlesbrough was United's 1000th in the Premier League, becoming the first team to achieve such a feat. The defeat left United seventh in the table and 13 points behind leaders Chelsea, with the Londoners due at Old Trafford in their Premier League fixture.

Before the visit of defending champions and current league leaders Chelsea, United played against Lille in France and missing the suspended Paul Scholes United rarely threatened the French team's goal and in the end suffered a 1-0 defeat to leave Ferguson's side in danger of exiting the Champions League at the group stages for the first time. United's travelling support let the players know what they thought of their performance by booing them off the pitch and Ferguson said he and his players could have no complaints about their reaction. Chelsea arrived on the 19th anniversary of Sir Alex Ferguson's appointment as United manager but that would have been the furthest thing from Ferguson's mind as he sent out his team against a Chelsea side that were running away with the Premier League for a second season running. It was a nervous afternoon for Ferguson as his team beat Mourinho's by one goal to nil thanks to a first-half header from Scottish midfielder

Darren Fletcher. Ruud Van Nistelrooy missed a chance to make the game safe in the second-half as he blazed over the bar meaning an edgy United had to play the game out with just a one goal lead. The win was crucial for United as it moved them up to fourth in the table, 10 points behind Chelsea with a game in hand and also ended Chelsea's 40 match unbeaten run in the league. The win over Chelsea was followed by a 3-1 win over Charlton Athletic at The Valley with goals from Alan Smith and Ruud Van Nistelrooy (2). In the absence of injured captain Roy Keane, Smith was being used by Ferguson in a central midfield role. Keane hadn't played for the club since the 0-0 draw with Liverpool on September 18, Ferguson stated that Keane was training well in his recovery from injury so when the news broke that Keane had been released by the club on November 18 2005, the footballing world was in shock. The decision to release Keane from his contract brought to an end Keane's twelve and a half year stay at Old Trafford and came amid speculation Keane had criticised a number of the younger players within United's first-team squad. The straw that broke the camel's back with regard to Keane appears to be when the midfielder appeared on United's in house channel MUTV after their 4-1 defeat to Middlesbrough when whatever Keane said was thought too strong for the club to show it. Upon his release from United, Keane joined Celtic and Ferguson thanked the Irishman for his service and wished him well for the future. Without Keane, United played out a goalless draw with Villarreal in their crucial Champions League group game. The draw meant if United were to qualify for the knockout stages of the competition they would have beat Benfica in Lisbon. United prepared for the visit to Lisbon with three wins over West Ham, West Brom and Portsmouth. The win over West Brom came in the League Cup and saw Gary Neville starting his first game since being appointed club captain following the departure of Keane and the win booked a quarter-final with Birmingham City at St Andrews.

Manchester United and Ferguson travelled to Lisbon to face Benfica in the crucial Champions League game that would decide whether or not United would be playing European football in the second half of the season. United knew they needed a win against the Portuguese side if they were to progress while a draw may be enough if Villarreal beat Lille in the other group game. Paul Scholes gave United the perfect start in Lisbon, giving his side the lead after just six minutes but by half-time Benfica were 2-1 in front and that's how the game finished. Meaning Ferguson and his team crashed out of the Champions League in the group stages for the first time and they were out of Europe before Christmas. In the aftermath of their exit, Ferguson refused to answer any questions on his future, saying he had the nucleus of another successful squad but needed time to build that. Without a trophy since the 2004 FA Cup, out of Europe and adrift in the Premier League title race, the only chances of silverware in the 2005/06 looked like being the League Cup or FA Cup. Following their European exit at the beginning of December, United went unbeaten for the rest of the month as their racked up five wins and two draws in their next seven games. That run saw United book a semi-final spot in the League Cup with a 3-1 over Birmingham City at St Andrews. In the semi-final they would face Blackburn Rovers, while in the league wins over Wigan, Aston Villa, West Brom and Bolton and draws with Everton and Birmingham saw United finishing the year second in the table but despite beating Chelsea at Old Trafford they were still eleven points behind the Londoners and facing an uphill task to stop them winning back-to-back titles under Jose Mourinho. After finishing 2005 with a 4-1 win over Bolton, goals were difficult to come by as they faced Arsenal and Burton Albion at the start of 2006. The year started with a visit to Highbury and a 0-0 that meant United slipped further behind Chelsea at the top of the league. While five days later they travelled to Burton in the third round of the FA Cup and were held to a 0-0 draw by Conference side meaning that United would welcome Burton to Old Trafford in the replay ten days later. An early goal from Saha in the replay set United on their way to a 5-0 win and a fourth round tie with Wolves.

Before the replay with Burton Ferguson looked to strengthen his defence with the double signings of Patrice Evra and Nemanja Vidic. A £7million deal was agreed for Vidic on Christmas Day 2005 but the deal wasn't officially completed until January 6 2006. Serbian International Vidic joined from Russian side Spartak Moscow and because the Russian League was on a winter break Vidic was lacking match fitness and it would be several weeks before he made his debut. Evra joined from French side Monaco four days after the arrival of Vidic. Despite Monaco agreeing a fee for Evra with Inter Milan, Evra's preferred move was to Old Trafford and United agreed a £5.5million fee for the left-back. After the draw with Burton United faced another away cup tie, this time facing Blackburn in the first-leg of the League Cup semi-final. United took the lead through Louis Saha on the half hour mark but five minutes later Blackburn equalised through Morten Gamst Pedersen and the game finished 1-1. After successive cup draws, United returned to Premier League action and a Manchester Derby against City. The game saw Patrice Evra making his Manchester United debut but the Frenchman endured a torrid first-half and was replaced by Alan Smith at half-time. By which time United were already 2-0 down and the second-half got worse for United with the sending-off of Cristiano Ronaldo. Despite the sending of the Portuguese star, United began to look more threatening in the final third and pulled a goal back through Van Nistelrooy, only for Robbie Fowler to make it three one on 90 minutes and that's the way it stayed. The defeat to City was followed by the 5-0 win over Burton in the FA Cup replay and that game was followed by two must win fixtures. The first coming against historic rivals Liverpool. Following the defeat to City, United's players would know they couldn't afford to put their fans through another defeat to a rival. Despite being subbed off at half-time versus City, Evra was once again named in the starting line-up by Ferguson as United beat Liverpool 1-0 at Old Trafford. United fans had to wait until the 90th minute to see them win the game with the winning goal coming from an unlikely source. Rio Ferdinand leaping the highest in a crowded penalty area to head home a Ryan Giggs free-kick past Liverpool goalkeeper Pepe Reina. The win over Liverpool was followed by the semi-final second-leg against Blackburn Rovers. Ruud Van Nistelrooy gave United the early advantage, scoring after eight minutes. Blackburn were level though just after the half hour mark through Steven Reid but the game was won by United when Saha struck the winner after 51 minutes. The game finished 2-1 to United as they booked their place in the League Cup final where they would face Wigan Athletic. After booking their League Cup final place, United travelled to the Midlands to face Wolves in the fourth round of the FA Cup. The win over Blackburn had seen the debut of Vidic as a late substitute and the Serbian made his first start as United beat Wolves 3-0 with goals from Kieran Richardson (2) and Saha. The first game of February for United saw them travelling to Ewood Park once again this time for a Premier League clash and the hosts ran out 4-3 winners. With injuries and suspension ruling out several first-team midfielders, Ferguson opted to field Ferdinand in a central midfield role but the England man didn't have the best of nights and received his second yellow on the night and an early bath after 88 minutes. The defeat to Blackburn left United 15 points adrift of leaders Chelsea with 14 games remaining. While their lead over Liverpool in third was only three points having played two games more than the Merseysiders.

With their position behind Chelsea in the league, United were left to concentrate on their upcoming League Cup final and looking to progress in the FA Cup. In the fifth round of the FA Cup they travelled to Anfield to face Liverpool and Ferguson's side suffered the double blow of progress in the FA Cup ended by a 1-0 defeat and losing Alan Smith to a broken leg when blocking a free-kick late on. The Liverpool winner came after 19 minutes when Peter Crouch headed home. United were lacking in attack and Smith was sent on to add an extra attacking dimension but the forward suffered a broken leg and dislocated ankle when blocking a Liverpool free-kick in the dying minutes. After the defeat to Liverpool came the League Cup final against Wigan at the Millenium Stadium and Ferguson opted for Rooney and Saha upfront, leaving Dutchman Van Nistelrooy sat on the bench for the entire game. This decision was vindicated when both Rooney (2) and Saha got themselves on the scoresheet as United ran out 4-0 winners to lift the League Cup for the second in their history. Ryan Giggs was named in the starting line-up as he added a second League Cup winners, 14 years after his first in 1992. The first league game after the League Cup final saw United travelling to Wigan and coming away with a 2-1 victory as United went on a seven game winning run. Van Nistelrooy remained on the bench for first six of these games further fuelling speculation that there was a rift between Ferguson and his striker. Van Nistelrooy was restored to the starting line-up as United beat Arsenal 2-0 and the Dutchman scored winning goals against West Ham United and Bolton Wanderers but Van Nistelrooy was again benched for the final game of the season against Charlton Athletic but he didn't take his place on the bench and Ferguson said after the game that Van Nistelrooy had left the ground three hours before kick-off angered by the managers decision to bench him once again. Without Van Nistelrooy United won the game 4-0 and finished the season second in the league, finishing eight points behind Chelsea. Only a few days after the season ended it was reported that Van Nistelrooy had been at the centre of a training ground bust-up with Ronaldo. Van Nistelrooy allegedly criticised Ronaldo for his tendency to hold onto the ball instead of passing to his team-mates. Which caused a fight between the two after which Van Nistelrooy apparently remarked "Go crying to your Daddy", referring to United assistant coach Carlos Queiroz, who like Ronaldo was

Portuguese and had taken Ronaldo under his wing. This clearly upset Ronaldo as his father had died eight months previously. Van Nistelrooy did apologise to Ferguson for his behaviour in the last few months of the season but the damage had already been done and Van Nistelrooy would soon be packing his bags.

After finishing behind Chelsea once again, the aim was now to push Jose Mourinho's side even harder the following season and of course put in an improved performance in Europe following their disappointing exit before Christmas. Since the arrival of Mourinho, Chelsea had won back-to-back titles and if United were to stop the Londoners emulating their feat of three successive Premier League titles they knew they would have to hit the ground running in the 2006/07 season. After 150 goals in 218 appearances for United, Van Nistelrooy was sold to Real Madrid for £10.2million on July 28 2006. The Dutch striker wasn't the only player to leave United in the summer of 2006, he was joined by Quinton Fortune who left on a free transfer. While French youngster David Bellion was sold to Nice after failing to impress after arriving from Sunderland. While leaving the club on loan was American goalkeeper Tim Howard, joining Everton on a season-long loan after falling down the pecking. Spanish defender Gerard Pique returned to Spain in a season-long loan deal to Real Zaragoza. Another goalkeeper made a season-long loan move as Ben Foster once again moved to Watford after spending the previous season at Vicarage Road. The move for Foster came after United secured the services of Polish goalkeeper Tomasz Kuszczak on a season-long loan move from West Brom. Several academy prospects including Jonny Evans were sent on season-long loans to Belgium side Royal Antwerp. Meanwhile the only incoming permanent transfer was that of Michael Carrick, joining from Tottenham for an initial fee of £13million and United could pay up to £18.6million. Carrick was handed the number 16 jersey vacated by Roy Keane's departure the previous season. Despite the departure of Van Nistelrooy,

Ferguson opted not to sign a new striker, this was down in part to the return to fitness of Ole Gunnar Solskjaer. The Norwegian had been plagued by a knee injury in recent seasons and made a return to United's first-team towards the end of the 2005/06 season having made numerous appearances for the reserves. The summer had seen Wayne Rooney and Cristiano Ronaldo coming head-to-head while playing for their countries in the summers European Championships. Rooney was sent-off and Ronaldo was caught winking at the camera after the incident, prompting suggestions in the media that the pair wouldn't be able to play together anymore and Ferguson could have a problem on his hands. Any such thoughts were dismissed on the opening weekend of the Premier League season as United dispatched Fulham 5-1 at Old Trafford. United came flying out of the blocks and were 4-0 up inside twenty minutes with both Rooney and Ronaldo amongst the goals. United continued their impressive start with a 3-0 win over Charlton, followed by a 2-1 win over Watford and a 1-0 win against Tottenham. The win over Charlton saw Ole Gunnar Solskjaer scoring for the first-team for the first time since April 2003. Following their disappointing exit in the Champions League in 2005/06 season, Ferguson would be desperate to see his side reach the knockout stages as United were drawn in a group with Scottish champions Celtic, Benfica for a second season running and Danish side F.C Copenhagen. United started their campaign with the visit of Celtic to Old Trafford and Solskjaer was on the scoresheet once again as United won the battle of Britain 3-2.

Four successive wins at the start of the Premier League had left Ferguson's men top of the pile but Portsmouth, Everton and defending champions Chelsea were not far away. Next up for United was the visit of Arsenal to Old Trafford. Arsenal had made a stuttering start to the season and were sitting in 17th place before this game with just two points after two draws and a defeat from their opening three league fixtures. Ferguson was forced to hand a debut to Tomasz Kuszczak in place of Edwin van der Sar as the Dutchman was sidelined with a stomach bug. The Polish goalkeeper kept United in the game when he saved a penalty from Gilberto after he had brought down Arsenal striker Emmanuel Adebayor. Adebayor though was the hero for Arsenal as he scored five minutes from time to inflict United's first league defeat of the season. This defeat was followed by a 1-1 draw with Reading as Ronaldo equalised a Kevin Doyle opener. One point from the two games against Arsenal and Reading, left Ferguson's men third in the table, two points behind new leaders Chelsea. United then racked up five successive wins starting with a 1-0 win in Lisbon against Benfica thanks to a strike on the hour mark from Louis Saha. Also included in the run of five successive wins was a 3-0 win over Copenhagen at Old Trafford that gave United three wins out of three in the group stages of the Champions League. While wins over Newcastle and Wigan meant United returned to the top of the league ahead of a fixture against local rivals Liverpool. That game saw Paul Scholes making his 500th appearance in the Manchester United first-team and he marked the occasion by scoring the opening goal just before the 40 minute mark. Rio Ferdinand then sealed the 2-0 win for United on 66 minutes when he brought the ball down with superb control before firing into the roof of the net to score against Liverpool for the second successive season. Following the win over Liverpool, United travelled to Crewe for the third round of the League Cup and came away with a 2-1 win after extra-time with youngster Kieran Lee scoring the winner after 119 minutes of play. A 1-0 defeat away to Copenhagen was sandwiched in between wins over Bolton (4-0) and Portsmouth (3-0) that made it five successive wins in the Premier League as United made the fast start to the season they needed to once again mount a serious challenge for the Premier League title.

United's defence of the League Cup was ended at the fourth round stage as they suffered a 1-0 defeat to Southend United at

Roots Hall. The previous round against Crewe had seen Alan Smith make his first start for eight months after returning from the horrific leg break he suffered against Liverpool in the previous season. Smith was named alongside Ronaldo and Rooney as United travelled to Roots Hall but the trio couldn't help United through to the next round. Smith struggled for regular appearances in the first-team over the next few months, making just one substitute appearance. Despite the disappointment of a League Cup exit at the hands of Southend, United continued their winning run in the league with victories on the road over Blackburn and Sheffield United. These two wins made it seven in a row for Ferguson's men and it meant United had 11 wins from their opening 13 fixtures and sat on top of the league, three points clear of their next opponents Chelsea. Before that fixture against Chelsea at Old Trafford, United travelled to Scotland for their fixture with Celtic in the Champions League. A win for United would have ensured their passage to the knockout stages but they went down to an 80th minute free-kick from Celtic's Japanese star Shunsuke Nakamura, Louis Saha missed two guilt edge chances to savage a point for United, missing the target when gifted a simple chance, when the Frenchman appeared to be offside then Saha missed a last minute spot-kick meaning they would have to wait until the final game to secure their place alongside Celtic in the knockout stages. Now to the Chelsea Premier League fixture at Old Trafford, a win for United would take them six points clear of the defending champions. Louis Saha made up for his misses against Celtic by giving United the lead with a superb piece of skill that saw the Frenchman curling the ball past Chelsea keeper Carlo Cudicini but United were denied by a second half equaliser from Ricardo Carvalho. The Portuguese defender headed a Frank Lampard corner past United goalkeeper Edwin van der Sar. The draw meant United preserved their three point lead at the top of the table and followed up the Chelsea result with wins over Everton and Middlesbrough before facing Benfica in their final Champions League group game. Just as in the 2005/06 season, United's last Champions League group game was against Benfica but this time it was at Old Trafford. Benfica stunned Old Trafford by taking the lead through a Marcos Nelson 25 yard strike, but this prompted a rousing response from Ferguson's team. With centre-half Vidic levelling on the stroke of half-time before second-half goals from Giggs and Saha sealed a 3-1 win and qualification for the knockout stages with a top spot finish above Celtic. The win over Benfica was followed by a win over Manchester City in the Derby by the same scoreline as Rooney, Saha and Ronaldo all found the back of City's net at Old Trafford. Following the win over their neighbours, United were nine points clear of Chelsea though the Londoners had two games in hand on Ferguson's men.

After 11 wins and two draws in the 13 Premier League games since their 1-0 defeat to Arsenal, United suffered their second defeat of the league campaign with a 1-0 defeat at Upton Park against West Ham on December 17 2006. After the defeat to West Ham, United finished the year with three victories in the Premier League with successes over Aston Villa, Wigan and Reading. This meant United finished the calendar year of 2006 with a six point lead over Chelsea after 21 Premier League games. They were looking forward to the start of their FA Cup campaign and had a tie against Lille in the first knockout round of the Champions League to look forward to. A double from Scholes wasn't enough for United on New Year's Day as they travelled to St James Park to face Newcastle and had to settle for a 2-2 draw. This was followed by back-to-back games with Aston Villa, both at Old Trafford, one in the FA Cup and a Premier League fixture the following week. Prior to these games against Villa, United completed the loan signing of veteran Swedish striker Henrik Larsson. Larsson joined from Helsingborg on a three-month loan deal while the Swedish League was in its off season. Larsson made his debut in the FA Cup tie against Villa and was on the scoresheet after 55 minutes but United needed Solskjaer to reprise his super-sub role as he came off the bench and netted a 90th winner for United after former Liverpool striker Milan Baros had equalised for Villa. The 2-1 win setup a fourth round tie with Portsmouth towards the end of January. Villa were back at Old Trafford a week later for the Premier League fixture and this time it was a bit more comfortable for United as three goals in the first-half from Park Ji-Sung, Michael Carrick and Cristiano Ronaldo gave United a 3-1 win and the three points as they continued their quest to regain the Premier League trophy. After the wins over Villa, United travelled to London to face Arsenal at their newly opened Emirates Stadium and United looked like taking all three points back to Manchester until late strikes from Robin Van Persie and Thierry Henry gave Arsene Wenger's side the win to inflict United's third league defeat of the season. Ferguson and his men responded to this defeat with four wins in a row including a 2-1 win over Portsmouth in the fourth round of the FA Cup and three league victories over London sides Watford, Tottenham and Charlton, scoring ten goals without reply. Despite the defeat to the Arsenal, United sat top of the table, six points ahead of defending champions Chelsea with 11 games to play. In the fifth round of the FA Cup United played host to Reading and despite been given the lead by Carrick, United were held to a 1-1 draw and forced to a replay. Before that replay United had the first-leg of their tie with French side Lille in the first knockout round of the Champions League. The first-leg took place in France and United came away with a 1-0 win thanks to a quickly taken free-kick from Ryan Giggs. Lille players protested as they were still assembling their defensive wall but the goal stood and two weeks later another 1-0 win at Old Trafford courtesy of a strike from Larsson in his last appearance at Old Trafford before returning to Sweden. That goal was his first and last strike in the Champions League for United and booked a quarter-final with Roma for his team-mates of the last three months. Before the second-leg United had won through to the quarter-finals of the FA Cup with a 3-2 win over Reading in the replay and faced

154

Middlesbrough at the Riverside Stadium in the quarter-final. The quarter-final tie would be Larsson's last game for United as a Ronaldo penalty earnt United a replay at Old Trafford after Middlesbrough had threatened to knock out one of the favourites to lift the trophy.

Ahead of their quarter-final with AS Roma in the Champions League, United completed emphatic 4-1 wins over Bolton and Blackburn as well as a 1-0 win over Middlesbrough in the FA Cup replay. The semi-finals of the FA Cup would see United face Watford at Villa Park. The first-leg in Italy yielded a defeat for United but Wayne Rooney scored a crucial away goal as United came away with a 2-1 defeat in a game that saw Paul Scholes sent off just after the half hour mark. The goal from Rooney was his first in the competition since 2004 and gave United a fighting chance of overturning the deficit in the return at Old Trafford. Before the second-leg United faced Portsmouth at Fratton Park in the Premier League and suffered another 2-1 defeat to lose back-to-back games for the first time in the 2006/07 season. The second-leg against Roma was pretty close to a perfect night that United could have wished for as they were three nil up on the night within the first twenty minutes. Carrick opened the scoring to level the aggregate score at 2-2 after twelve minutes with a fine curling effort before Alan Smith, making a rare start added second five minutes later, and two minutes after that Rooney finished off a superb team move to make it 3-0 on the night and 4-2 on aggregate. Ronaldo then added a fourth and fifth either side of half-time before Carrick grabbed his second of the night. A strike from De Rossi was no more than a consolation for Roma and the scoring on the night was finished by Patrice Evra when he added a seventh to put United through to the semi-finals with an 8-3 aggregate win and there they would face another Italian side in AC Milan. Next came the semi-finals of the FA Cup and United saw off Watford with a 4-1 win and booked a final against Chelsea and left United fans dreaming that Ferguson could once again lead his team to the treble of Premier League, Champions League and FA Cup. Before the semi-final first-leg at home to Milan United had two league games, winning the first 2-0 against Sheffield United before drawing 1-1 with Middlesbrough. After the draw with Middlesbrough, United had played 34 league games and were three points ahead of Chelsea. After the first-leg against AC Milan at Old Trafford United held a 3-2 lead after a late strike from Rooney gave United the win on a night of superb attacking football from both sides. A Ronaldo header put United ahead after five minutes before two goals in fifteen minutes for Brazilian Kaka gave Milan a 2-1 lead going into the second-half. Rooney levelled on 59 minutes when beautifully played in by Scholes and despite Milan goalkeeper Dida half-stopping the ball it wasn't enough as the ball rolled into the back of the net. United pressed for the crucial winner and had a number of chances thwarted by Dida before Rooney ran onto a Giggs pass and fired past the helpless Dida to send Old Trafford into wild celebrations. A year after going out of the competition in the group stages and many questioning whether this was the end for Ferguson. United were looking good to regain the Premier League, in the FA Cup final and avoid defeat in the Milan and they would be in the Champions League final for the first time since winning the competition in 99. Back in the Premier League, United faced Everton at Goodison Park and despite falling 2-0 down just after half-time they hit back to win the game 4-2 and move five points clear of Chelsea after the Londoners had drawn 2-2 with Bolton. If results went their way in the next round of fixtures, United could seal the title with two games to spare.

Ferguson's hopes of taking Manchester United to a second Champions League under his leadership were ended in Milan as they went down 3-0 to the Italians and missed out on a final appearance against arch rivals Liverpool. Leading 3-2 from the first-leg, United knew they needed to make a strong start to the return game in Milan but the home side were ahead after 11 minutes when Kaka drilled home for his third goal of the tie to level the aggregate scores and put Milan ahead on away goals courtesy of their two goals at Old Trafford. United couldn't live with the movement and passing of a more experience Milan side and fell further behind when Clarence Seedorf struck after thirty minutes. United struggled to threaten Dida in the Milan goal and any hopes United may have had of mounting a comeback were over when Milan scored a third after 78 minutes. Meaning United would need two goals in the final stages just to force extra-time. The European dream was over for another year for Ferguson and Manchester United but this campaign had seen a big improvement on the previous one when they went out in the group stages. Now they had to concentrate on winning the league title and an FA Cup final against Chelsea. Ferguson watched his team move within touching distance of lifting the Premier League trophy once again with a 1-0 win away to neighbours Manchester City. Cristiano Ronaldo's 38th minute penalty gave United the three points that virtually secured the league success United hadn't enjoyed in three seasons since their last success in the 2002/03 season. The win left United eight points ahead of Chelsea and Chelsea had the first of their remaining three games the following day against Arsenal, any slip up from Chelsea would confirm United as champions once again and stop Chelsea from emulating United in winning three successive league titles. Michael Essien struck a 70th minute equaliser for Chelsea against Arsenal but Jose Mourinho's side couldn't find the winner they required to delay United's title celebrations. After three years without a Premier League title, Ferguson's new side had finally delivered on the potential they have shown over recent seasons and now the aim would be to build on this success by retaining their title next season and build on their Champions League semi-final by looking to go a few steps further and win the second Champions League of Ferguson's reign. With the title in the bag and two league games to play, the focus for

United and Chelsea was the cup final and that showed as the pair came head-to-head at Stamford Bridge with both managers selecting a weakened side. The two teams played out a goalless draw and prior to the game the outgoing champions gave the new champions a guard of honour. The final game of United's league was at home against West Ham and United went down to a 1-0 defeat with Argentinian striker Carlos Tevez scoring the goal that saved West Ham from relegation and it wouldn't be his last goal at the ground. The focus for United though was on the trophy presentation, it had been three seasons since United had got their hands on the league trophy and the honour of lifting the trophy was given to captain Gary Neville and vice-captain Ryan Giggs. The pair had played around 25 league games each with Giggs standing in a captain when Neville wasn't on the pitch.

After several years of the FA Cup final being staged at the Millenium Stadium while the new Wembley was being built, this was the first final to be played at the new ground. United were looking to complete yet another league and cup double, while Chelsea were looking to thwart United and savage something from a disappointing season for them. This game isn't likely to be remembered as one of the great FA Cup finals, a cagey affair with both teams looking more concerned about not losing the game rather than trying to win it. United looked slightly more dangerous in the second-half but it wasn't the attacking football that had taken them to the title and game went into extra-time and continued in the same vain as in normal time. With the first FA Cup final at the new Wembley looking set for a penalty shoot-out, Chelsea's Didier Drogba struck the winner with four minutes left to play. Despite the loss the season will be looked on as a successful one for Ferguson's men as they won the Premier League title for the first time in three years, eventually finishing six points ahead of Chelsea. Despite suggestions in the summer that Rooney and Ronaldo wouldn't be able to play together after what had happened at Euro 2006, the pair flourished and were starting to show why Ferguson had brought the pair to the club as teenagers. The pair scored 23 goals apiece in all competitions, while Ronaldo was United's top scorer in the Premier League with 17. The season had also seen the return of Solskjaer when many suggested he may have been close to retirement due to his knee injury. Solskjaer made 32 appearances in all competition with 17 of those appearance coming from the bench and he scored 11 goals in all competitions

Chapter Fourteen: Second Champions League Success

With the Premier League success of the 2006/07 celebrated the focus was now on retaining the league title with Chelsea expected to be the main rivals once again. While also looking to make their mark on Europe again with that in mind Ferguson set about strengthening his current squad with a mixture of promising young talent and International experience. Goalkeeper Tim Howard had already agreed to make his loan move to Everton a permanent one while United did likewise signing Kuszczak on a permanent transfer from West Brom after the Polish goalkeeper had spent the 2006/07 season on loan at Old Trafford. Signing on the same day as Kuszczak were two players that had been identified by Ferguson as two of the best young attacking talents in Europe. These two players were Nani and Anderson, both arriving from Portugal. Nani arriving from the same club as Cristiano Ronaldo, Sporting Lisbon and was already being dubbed as the new Ronaldo. While Anderson joined United from Porto. United paid a combined fee of £30 million for the pair and despite initially having a work permit rejected for Brazilian Anderson, this was awarded on appeal and both players signed five-year deals at Old Trafford. They joined England International Owen Hargreaves in moving to Old Trafford who had completed his move the previous day. 26-year-old Hargreaves had been on Ferguson's radar for a while having failed in an attempt to sign the midfielder from Bayern Munich the previous summer. Hargreaves finally arrived at Old Trafford for a fee believed to be around £17million and signed a four-year contract with Manchester United. With several new arrivals into the first-team squad, Sir Alex Ferguson let several players leave the club in the summer of 2007. Kieran Richardson was sold to Sunderland and he was joined in the North-East of the country by Alan Smith, who joined Sunderland's local rivals Newcastle United in a £6million deal. Smith had struggled for first-team appearances since he return from injury and it was decided best for the player that he was allowed to leave and get his career back on track. Italian striker Giuseppe Rossi had a spell on loan with Newcastle in the 2006/07 season and despite scoring goals for United's reserves had failed to make a mark on the first-team at Old Trafford, was also allowed to leave the club joining Spanish side Villarreal. Another player to leave United for Spanish shores was Argentinian left-back Gabriel Heinze, Heinze was voted player of the season in his first season but injury and the arrival of Patrice Evra had limited his appearances. Liverpool were interested in signing the defender but Sir Alex Ferguson refused to do business with the Merseysiders and Heinze eventually joined Real Madrid. Carlos Tevez had scored on the last day of the previous season at Old Trafford and the United fans would be seeing a lot more of the Argentinian striker at Old Trafford after United agreed a two-year loan deal. Tevez wasn't loaned from a club but from a third party who owned the players economic rights.

The summer break had seen Solskjaer undergo minor surgery on his knee after complaining of discomfort while on International duty. The surgery took place on June 5 2007 and despite being deemed a success, Solskjaer never fully recovered and his retirement from playing was announced on August 27 2007. The first home after his retirement was against Sunderland on September 4 and Solskjaer walked out onto the pitch to a standing ovation before the game and said goodbye to the Manchester United supporters. Solskjaer remained a part of the Manchester United family as he worked towards his coaching badges and he helped coach the first-team strikers for what remained of the 2007/08 season. The season kicked off with a return to Wembley and the Community Shield against Chelsea. United enjoyed a little bit of revenge for their FA Cup final defeat to the same opposition the previous May with a penalty shootout win. Edwin van der Sar was the hero for United as he made three penalty saves as United won the shootout 3-0 after it had finished 1-1 after 90 minutes. After flying out the blocks the previous season, United started the 2007/08 season at a snail's pace as they drew two and lost one of their opening three leagues scoring just one goal. The defeat came as United payed a visit to neighbours Manchester City and despite dominating the game from start to finish they couldn't find the back of City's net and suffered a 1-0 defeat. The result left United with two points from their opening three games and sitting in the relegation zone. Results did pick after this but United were still struggling for goals as they secured 1-0 victories over Tottenham, Sunderland and Everton. The win over Tottenham came courtesy of Nani's first strike for the club but United rode their luck with Rio Ferdinand clearing an effort off the line and Tottenham having claims for a penalty turned down. The three back-to-back one nil wins left United with eleven points from their opening six games and they sat fourth in the table. Arsenal led the way with 13 points and had played a game less than United, while United's next opponents in the league, Chelsea were level on points with Ferguson's side but sat behind United on goal difference.

Before the league encounter with Chelsea, United started their Champions League campaign in Portugal. Drawn in a group with Sporting Lisbon, Roma and Dynamo Kiev, Ferguson's took his side to Lisbon and named two former Sporting players in Ronaldo and Nani in his team. United registered another 1-0 win as they continued to struggle for goals with Ronaldo scoring on 61 minutes as he headed home a cross from Wes Brown. The goal celebration from Ronaldo was subdued as he showed respect to the Sporting fans. The game against Chelsea saw Avram Grant taking charge of the Blues for the first time since the sacking of Jose Mourinho and United piled the misery on Chelsea with a 2-0 win with Carlos Tevez notching his first goal at Old Trafford for United. The win was confirmed when Saha converted an 89th minute penalty. The win over Chelsea lifted United to second in the table, two points adrift of Arsenal. The win over Chelsea was United's fifth in a row after a difficult start to the season. This was followed by a disappointing 2-0 defeat to Coventry City in the third round of the League Cup at Old Trafford, the match saw Ferguson handing first-team debuts to Jonny Evans and Danny Simpson. United returned to winning ways when they visited Birmingham City and came away with a 1-0 win and this was followed by a 1-0 win over Roma in their Champions League encounter at Old Trafford. The win over the Italians was followed by yet another clean for United as they breezed past Wigan by four goals to nil. After six league games without conceding a goal, United's backline was finally breached as they visited Villa Park, the goal for Villa scored by Gabby Agbonlahor had given them an early but United hit back through Rooney (2) and Ferdinand to lead 3-1 at half-time. The second-half saw Villa have two men sent off and United grabbed a fourth goal through Ryan Giggs. Following the win over Villa, Ferguson and his team travelled to Kiev for their third group game of the Champions League and made it three wins out of three with a 4-2 win. Ferdinand and Rooney were amongst the goals again, with Ronaldo adding two goals either side of half-time to seal the win. On their return from Kiev it was back to Premier League action and the visit of Middlesbrough to Old Trafford. United once again found the back of their opponents net on four occasions to register back-to-back 4-1 league victories. The win over Middlesbrough was United's last fixture of October 2007 and after the win United were level on points with Arsenal at the top of the table, the two teams were also level on goal difference with the Gunners sitting above United on goals scored and the two sides were due to face each other in the first fixture of November. The encounter with Arsenal was at the Emirates Stadium and after the game the state of play at the top of the table remained the same as the two early pacesetters played out a 2-2 draw. United led twice in the game but were pegged almost immediately by Arsenal on both occasions and the game saw Arsenal defender William Gallas scoring for both teams. After the draw with Arsenal, United had two home games starting with the visit of Dynamo Kiev in the Champions League, a 4-0 win confirmed United's spot in the first knockout round. That game saw Gerard Pique scoring his first United goal to give them the lead before strikes from Tevez, Rooney and Ronaldo. A 2-0 win over Blackburn saw United moving three points clear at the top of the Premier League with Arsenal playing the following day, the win came courtesy of two goals in the space of two minutes from Ronaldo. This took his tally for the season to ten goals and meant that the Portuguese International had 26 goals in 51 games for club and country in 2007 after this game. The last league fixture of November saw United suffering a one nil defeat to Bolton with Nicolas Anelka scoring an early goal, the game also saw Ferguson sent to the stands after a disagreement with referee Mark Clattenburg, Ferguson felt several decisions hadn't gone his sides way. The defeat meant United finished the month three points adrift of Arsenal at the top of the Premier League table. Ferguson saw his team get back to winning ways three days later as they defeated Sporting Lisbon 2-1 to make it five wins out of five in the Champions League group stages.

The win over Sporting was followed by victories over Fulham and Derby at Old Trafford in the league before finishing off their group stage campaign with a 1-1 draw in Rome. That saw Ferguson's men finishing top of the group on 16 points after five wins and a draw and they were joined in the knockout phases by Roma. Next came a visit to Anfield and rivals Liverpool. A 1-0 win for United courtesy of a first-half strike from Carlos Tevez that left the Merseysiders outside the top four and nine points behind United, this was followed by a 2-1 win over Liverpool's Merseyside rivals Everton and a 4-0 win over Sunderland on Boxing Day before ending the year with a 2-1 defeat away to West Ham. 2007 was finished with United second in the table, two points behind leaders Arsenal while Chelsea were a further four points behind United. 2008 started with four wins without conceding a goal and scoring 11 goals including six in one game. The strong United defence was built on the partnership of Rio Ferdinand and Nemanja Vidic at the heart of the defence. The pair played 96 games combined for United in the 2007/08 season with Ferdinand making 51 appearances and Vidic 45. The performances of the pair as a combination probably curtailed the progress of several of the younger defenders in United's squad because Ferguson felt he couldn't split the pair up they were that good together. The other mainstays of the United defence were goalkeeper van der Sar, left-back Evra and Wes Brown filled in at right-back for the majority of the season due to the absence of captain Gary Neville with a long-term ankle injury. The first win of 2008 was a 1-0 victory against Birmingham, Carlos Tevez scoring a first-half winner. This was followed by a visit to Birmingham's neighbours Aston Villa in the third round of the FA Cup and United came away with a 2-0 win to book a home tie against Tottenham in the fourth round. The third win of the New Year was the one that saw United hit six goals without reply and on the receiving end were Newcastle United. Newcastle had recently sacked Sam Allardyce and Harry Redknapp had turned down the job, Newcastle fans probably thought things couldn't get any worse for them. They were destroyed on the day and Ronaldo helped himself to his first hat-trick in a Manchester United shirt. Newcastle reached half-time at 0-0 but once the first goal went in, they collapsed under United's pressure and Ronaldo was joined on the scoresheet by Carlos Tevez (2) and Rio Ferdinand. The win sent United to the summit of the Premier League and was followed by a 2-0 away win over Reading with goals from Rooney and Ronaldo. Next came the fourth round of the FA Cup and the visit of Tottenham to Old Trafford, despite falling behind to a Robbie Keane opening goal, United won through 3-1 with goals from Tevez and Ronaldo (2). The reward in the fifth round would be another home tie against Premier League opposition and Tottenham's North London rivals Arsenal but before that it was back to the Premier League and the battle at the top of the table with both Chelsea and Arsenal looking to challenge United for the Premier League crown.

United defeated Portsmouth two nil in their next Premier League game but would drop points in their following two league fixtures. First of those fixtures came at White Hart Lane against Tottenham and Ferguson needed a last gasp strike from Carlos Tevez to take a point from this game. Dimitar Berbatov had given Tottenham the lead after 21 minutes. The Tevez strike was the last kick of the game and was harsh on the hosts as Tottenham put in an impressive all-round display. The result meant that Arsenal moved above United at the top of the table. This game took place just four days before the 50th anniversary of the Munich Air Disaster, which saw United lose eight of their players along with staff of club and journalists covering Manchester United. United's next home game was against Manchester City and the club would remember those lost as they always do on the nearest home game to February 6. This would be an emotional occasion with United wearing 1958 style shirts. They had no sponsor on them and players lined up wearing numbers one to eleven instead of their usual squad numbers. Sir Alex Ferguson was joined by City manager Sven-Goran Eriksson in laying a wreath either side of the centre circle before both sets of supporters impeccable observed a minute's silence. The emotions of the day appeared to get to Manchester United's players as City led 2-0 at half-time. Michael Carrick scored a 90th minute goal but United struggled to make an impact on the special occasion. Following that defeat came a break from Premier League action with the fifth round FA Cup tie against Arsenal. United outclassed their North London opponents with a 4-0 win in which Wayne Rooney opened the scoring and put in impressive performance. Darren Fletcher (2) and Nani were also on the scoresheet. The win setup a quarter-final home tie with Harry Redknapp's Portsmouth side, before that tie though it was back to Premier League action and the first knockout phase of the Champions League against French side Lyon. The first leg against Lyon played in France came after the 4-0 win over Arsenal and Ferguson's side came away with a 1-1 draw as Carlos Tevez scored a crucial away goal. Karim Benzema gave Lyon the lead and was heavily linked with a move to Old Trafford after the game. Back in the Premier League, United scored eight goals in two away games before welcoming Lyon to Old Trafford for the return leg. The first of those away wins was at St James Park against Newcastle and after hitting six past the Magpies at Old Trafford, United continued to punish the Newcastle defence with a further five goals, Rooney and Ronaldo both striking twice, making it five goals in two games against Newcastle for Ronaldo. After the win over Newcastle, Ferguson took his side to Craven Cottage to face Fulham and came away with a 3-0 win that featured an Owen Hargreaves free-kick that gave United the lead after 15 minutes. The win saw Ferguson's side move within one point of leaders Arsenal. Next up was the return against Lyon and Cristiano Ronaldo struck his 30th goal of the season to book United's progress to the quarter-finals of the competition with a 2-1 aggregate win. The French side set out to frustrate United and it was working until the Portuguese star broke the deadlock on 41 minutes. Lyon were more attacking after the break and struck the base of United's post but one goal on the night was enough for United to book a quarter-final against Roma.

Progression in the Champions League was followed by the FA Cup quarter-final with Portsmouth. Fighting out at the top of the league with Arsenal and Chelsea, through the Champions League quarter-finals. Ferguson and his team were looking to repeat the famous treble of 99. Redknapp had enjoyed cup success over Ferguson with both Bournemouth and West Ham and brought his Portsmouth team to Old Trafford looking to knock United out of the oldest cup competition once again. On a day when Ferguson used three goalkeepers including defender Rio Ferdinand. United dominated the game, having a Michael Carrick effort cleared off the line and Patrice Evra struck a post. Kuszczak replaced van der Sar at half-time and after 76 minutes the Pole was sent off when Portsmouth were awarded a penalty after he brought down Milan Baros. The goalkeeper was sent off despite the fact that both Anderson and Rooney had got back on the goal-line. Ferdinand took over in goal but had no chance when facing the Portsmouth penalty taken by Sulley Muntari. Despite the disappointment of an FA Cup exit, the trophy was always third on the list of priorities for Ferguson as he looked to defend their Premier League crown and win a second Champions League title. Redknapp and Portsmouth would go on to win the FA Cup. Before the Champions League quarter-final with Roma United had four league fixtures and they racked up four wins without conceding a goal. These four wins started with a 1-0 win away to Derby before three home wins over Bolton, Liverpool and Aston Villa. The four games saw United scoring ten goals including three against Liverpool as they outclassed a Liverpool side that went down to ten men on the stroke of half-time after Wes Brown had headed United in front ten minutes earlier. Goals from Ronaldo and Nani completed the win for United and this was followed with a 4-0 over Villa that saw Rooney striking a double, while Ronaldo and Tevez were also on the scoresheet. After the win over Villa, United had played 32 of their scheduled 38 league games and sat on top of the league on 76 points. In second place now were Chelsea, five points behind United, while Arsenal sat six points adrift of Ferguson's men in third.

April would be a crucial month for United as they continued their double assault on the Premier League and looking to become the Kings of Europe for a second time under Sir Alex Ferguson. They faced the quarter-finals of the Champions League and if they won through against Roma, would be contesting the semi-finals over two games towards the end of the month. While they also had four Premier League fixtures to navigate, including facing Arsenal at Old Trafford and Chelsea at Stamford Bridge. April Fool's day 2008 saw United facing Roma in the first-leg of the quarter-final, United travelled to Rome and two crucial away goals from Ronaldo and Rooney saw United put one foot into the semi-finals as they also kept the hosts at bay. Ronaldo headed United in front from a Paul Scholes cross on 39 minutes as United went in 1-0 up at half-time. The hosts rallied after the break but couldn't find a way through the United defence and past van der Sar when they did so. Rooney bundled home a second on 66 minutes to give United a 2-0 away win and barring disaster at Old Trafford the following week, United would be throgh the semi-finals. On their return from Rome, United faced another away day, this time to Middlesbrough and had to settle for a 2-2 draw despite taking the lead through Ronaldo. Middlesbrough struck back to lead the game two one before Rooney levelled on 74 minutes. United's place in the Champions League semi-final was confirmed with a 1-0 win over Roma at Old Trafford with Tevez striking the only goal of the game to complete a 3-0 aggregate win and book a semi-final against Barcelona. After confirming their semi-final place in the Champions League, United welcomed Arsenal to Old Trafford. Ahead of the game, United sat three points clear of Chelsea and six points ahead of Arsenal, the Gunners would need a win to stay in the title race. It was a game that the visitors dominated but it would be United that would eventually take the three points to extend their advantage on Chelsea to five points and all but end Arsene Wenger's hopes of winning the Premier League title. The game reached 0-0 at half-time but the Arsenal fans who made the trip to Old Trafford would have been asking themselves how as their side dominated the opening 45 minutes. Only two minutes after the restart Arsenal did the take the lead through Adebayor, though the Arsenal forward appeared to handle the ball before it hit the back of United's net. Six minutes later, United were level when Owen Hargreaves ball into the box was judged to have been handled by William Gallas. Ronaldo hit home the penalty but was forced to take the spot-kick again as his first attempt was ruled out for encroaching and Ronaldo duly slotted home the second spot-kick. 0n 72 minutes, Hargreaves scored the winner from a 25 yard free-kick after Patrice Evra had been fouled. The 2-1 win and three points meant after 34 games United had a five point lead over Chelsea and Arsenal were a further nine points adrift of the defending champions.

With four games left in the league and a semi-final with Barcelona still to play, United had a maximum of seven games left to play and if they played all seven games they would be in with a chance of completing a Premier League and Champions League double in a year that marked the 50th anniversary of the Munich Air Disaster. The first of the remaining four league games was at Ewood Park against a Blackburn Rovers team managed by former United striker Mark Hughes. Carlos Tevez scored a crucial last minute equaliser for United after Roque Santa Cruz had given Blackburn the lead after 21 minutes. That point would leave United three points ahead of Chelsea with three games to play for both sides. The next Premier League fixture would see them facing each other at Stamford Bridge. A win for United in that fixture would virtually seal the title with two games to play while a defeat to Chelsea would see the two team's level on points but United had a superior goal difference to their rivals. Before that game though both teams had Champions League semi-final first-legs to navigate. United travelled to Barcelona and the Nou Camp for their first-leg. A cagey game ended 0-0, Barcelona dominated the game but failed to test Edwin van der Sar in United's goal and it was United who had the best opportunity with a first-half penalty. United were awarded the spot-kick when Argentinian defender Gabriel Milito was adjudged to have handled the ball but Ronaldo couldn't take the opportunity as he sent his spot-kick wide of the post. A 0-0 draw was a pleasing result for United but they would have to be wary of the Barcelona away goal in the return game at Old Trafford six days later. With the possibility of United facing Chelsea in the Champions League final, the two met at Stamford Bridge on what could be prove to be a crucial game in the race for the Premier League title. United held a three point advantage over Chelsea and had an 18 goal advantage on goal difference. German Michael Ballack gave Chelsea the lead on the stroke of half-time before Wayne Rooney took advantage of a Ricardo Carvalho error to level the scores on 57 minutes. Ballack scored a second for Chelsea when he struck 86th minute penalty after the officials awarded the spot-kick for a Michael Carrick handball. The three points for Chelsea saw the two teams draw level on points but United's superior goal difference meant if they won their last two league game against West Ham and Wigan then United would be Premier League champions again. Before those final two league games is was the second-leg against Barcelona as United looked to book their place in the Champions League final to be played in Moscow. If United could overcome Barcelona they would be in the final of the competition for the first time since lifting the trophy at the Nou Camp in 99. In a game once again dominated by Barcelona, the deciding moment of the game came after 14 minutes when a spectacular strike from Paul Scholes gave United the lead. Scholes effort came from 25 yards and was a fitting goal to take United to the final. Not just for the quality of the strike but also that fact that the strike came from a man who missed out on playing in 99 final due to suspension. The win guaranteed that the final would be an all English affair for the first time in the competition with Chelsea and Liverpool due to play their second-leg the following day. It would be Chelsea who would win through and be facing United in

Moscow on May 21 2008. Before that it was a matter of sealing the back-to-back Premier League titles for United. Win their last two league games and that would be achieved, the first of those came against West Ham at Old Trafford and Ronaldo gave United the perfect start scoring after just three minutes of the game and on twenty minutes he would make it 2-0 with his 30th league goal of the season. Two minutes after that former Hammer Tevez rifled in a 25 yard effort to make it 3-0. Dean Ashton pulled one back for West Ham before Nani was given his marching orders after an altercation with Hammers defender Lucas Neill but that couldn't stop United as another former Hammer Michael Carrick struck in the second-half to make it 4-1. Chelsea would beat Newcastle two days later to ensure that the title race would go down to the final day of the Premier League for the time since United edged out Arsenal in 99.

United travelled to Wigan on the final day of the season knowing they would need nothing less than a win to guarantee that they were champions of England for the 17th time. Wayne Rooney was named in the starting line-up despite concerns over his fitness and the England striker would be heavily involved in both goals as United won the game 2-0 and secured the Premier League title. Wigan started the game aggressively, closing United players down at every opportunity and the hosts felt they should have had a penalty on 24 minutes for a handball by Rio Ferdinand but referee Steve Bennett didn't agree. He did though point to the spot at the opposite end after 33 minutes for a foul by Emmerson Boyce on Wayne Rooney. Ronaldo converted the spot-kick to score his 31st goal of the Premier League season, equalling Alan Shearer's record for a 38 game season. Ryan Giggs stepped off the bench to equal Sir Booby Charlton's record of 758 games for the Manchester United first-team and Giggs marked the occasion with the second goal of the game. Giggs goal came ten minutes from time when he slotted past Chris Kirkland in the Wigan goal after a slide-rule pass from

Wayne Rooney. Chelsea conceded a last minute equaliser to Bolton, meaning United won the league by two points and lifted the Premier League title for the tenth time and became champions of England for the 17th time. Leaving them just one behind Liverpool's record of 18 league titles. One of Ferguson's aims when he first arrived in Manchester was to overhaul Liverpool as the kings of English football and he was just one title away from drawing level with their North-West rivals. Another aim of Ferguson was to add to their one European Cup wins, after winning the trophy in 99 he now had the opportunity to win his second and United's third European Cup in the final against Chelsea.

After going head-to-head with Chelsea for the Premier League crown, they faced their Premier League rivals in Moscow with the aim of completing a league and European cup double. A win for United would be their third European cup triumph while Chelsea led by Avram Grant were looking to win the competition for the first time. After the opening twenty minutes had seen both sides feeling each other out. The final came to life on twenty minutes when an aerial collision between Scholes and Claude Makelele saw both men receive a yellow card and left the Manchester United midfielder with a bloody nose. Six minutes later though Scholes combined with Wes Brown before the right-back crossed for Ronaldo to head United in front and score his 42nd goal of the season. United had chances to add to the one nil scoreline before the half-time whistle but couldn't take advantage. Chelsea then got a big slice of luck as Lampard equalised, a speculative shot from Essien took deflections off both Ferdinand and Vidic before falling kindly for Lampard to slot the ball home. The equaliser gave Chelsea the impetus and the Londoners looked more likely to win the game. With 13 minutes left on the clock, Drogba curled a 25 yard effort against the United post. With three minutes of normal time to play, Giggs replaced Scholes and set a new record of appearances for Manchester United. The game went into extra-time and United thought they had taken the lead ten minutes into extra-time but John Terry somehow headed off the line after Patrice Evra carved out an opportunity for Giggs. Four minutes before the end of extra-time Drogba saw red for a slap on Vidic after a melee that came after Chelsea felt Tevez had been unsporting in returning the ball after a break for players receiving treatment following cramp. So the game finished one apiece and the winner would be decided by a penalty shootout. The opening two penalties were converted by both sides before Ronaldo saw his effort saved by Petr Cech to hand the advantage to Chelsea. Lampard scored before Hargreaves converted his spot-kick, Ashley Cole converted to put Chelsea on the brink of victory, Nani converted for United before Terry threw United a lifeline as he slipped and hit the post. Anderson and Kalou both converted their kicks having both entered the game late in extra-time. Record breaker Giggs calmly slotted home to give United a 6-5 lead and put the pressure on Chelsea striker Anelka. Anelka saw his spot-kick palmed away by van der Sar and United were the Kings of Europe in a year that marked the 50th anniversary of the Munich Air Disaster. Sir Bobby Charlton was in attendance on an emotional occasion for the club as Ryan Giggs and Rio Ferdinand lifted the European Cup for the third time in Manchester United's history.

Chapter Fifteen: World Champions and Level on Eighteen with Liverpool

Following the Champions League success in the Moscow, Ferguson and his Manchester United team had a further two trophies to aim for in the 2008/09 season. By the end of the season, United would have had the possibility of having seven pieces of silverware in the trophy cabinet. Starting with the Community Shield in the traditional curtain raiser at Wembley Stadium at the beginning of August. As well as defending the Premier League and Champions League titles, United would also be aiming to progress to the later stages of both the FA Cup and League Cup. While Champions League success had also brought the opportunity of contesting the European Super Cup and the Club World Cup which would take place in Japan in December. Less than a week after their Champions League success, Ferguson and United agreed to let Spanish defender Gerard Pique return to Spain and Barcelona. Pique joined United from Barcelona in 2004 but failed to make a breakthrough to the United first-team on a regular basis. In the later part of his Old Trafford career this was down to the partnership of Nemanja Vidic and Rio Ferdinand at the heart of the United defence. Pique made 23 appearances for the first-team during in his four years as a Manchester United player and has spoken about everything he learnt in his Manchester United days despite failing to make a real impact on the first-team. Maybe if it wasn't Barcelona and Pep Guardiola that had come in for Pique, he would have stayed at Old Trafford longer and may have challenged the partnership of Vidic and Ferdinand. In July 2008, Ferguson completed the signing of Brazilian twins Rafael and Fabio Da Silva from Brazilian side Fluminense. The deal for the twins was agreed between Manchester United and Fluminense in February 2007 and the pair moved to Manchester in January 2008 but couldn't play for the club until they turned 18 on July 9 2008 and were officially signed on July 1 2008. The pair were signed for the future but Rafael impressed the United coaching staff enough to be included in the first-team squad for the majority of the 2008/09 season and would make 22 appearances. While Fabio would only make two appearances in the first-team. Fabio was named on the bench for United's second league game of the season but his progress was set back by a shoulder injury that required surgery. Fabio finally made his first-team debut in an FA Cup tie against Tottenham but suffered a calf injury shortly after the start of the second-half and wouldn't make his Premier League debut until the opening game of the 2009/10 season.

Despite having the attacking talents of Rooney, Ronaldo and Tevez, Ferguson was being heavily linked with a move for Tottenham's Bulgarian striker Dimitar Berbatov. Berbatov joined Tottenham in 2006 and in his two seasons at White Hart Lane had scored 46 goals in 102 games. After weeks of chasing the Bulgarian, Ferguson finally got his man on the last day of the summer transfer window (September 1 2008). The move came as United's big spending neighbours City (under new ownership) had a bid of £30.75million accepted by Tottenham chairman Daniel Levy and Berbatov flew to Manchester, but the Bulgarian was only interested in signing for United and they agreed a deal with Tottenham and Levy. During United's pursuit of Berbatov, Tottenham threatened to make a complaint to the Premier League but once the sale was completed they dropped their complaint. The transfer also saw United youngster Fraizer Campbell moving to White Hart Lane on a one-year loan deal. Ferguson was delighted with his purchase, claiming that Berbatov was one of the best and exciting forwards in world football. United fans all over the world were excited by the prospect of having Tevez, Rooney, Ronaldo and Berbatov in their team, though all four would rarely play together. Campbell wasn't the only player to exit Old Trafford before the close of the transfer window as Chris Eagles was sold to Burnley while Ferguson also allowed two Frenchman in Mikael Silvestre and Louis Saha to leave the club. Silvestre was sold to Arsenal as he struggled for regular appearances in Ferguson's backline while injury had blighted Saha's time in Manchester and the forward was allowed to join Everton. Before completing the signing of Berbatov, United started their season with a win in the Community Shield to retain the Shield, winning a penalty shootout against FA Cup winners Portsmouth after the game finished 0-0 after 90 minutes. The Premier League season started slowly for United and their attacking players, starting with a 1-1 draw with Newcastle at Old Trafford, this was followed by a 1-0 win at Fratton Park over Community Shield opponents Portsmouth. Both United's goals in the opening two games of the league campaign came from the unlikely source of Scottish midfielder Darren Fletcher. The draw with Newcastle saw Rafael Da Silva coming off the bench to make his first-team debut. After the opening two league games, Ferguson took his team to Monte Carlo aiming to win the European Super Cup against Zenit St Petersburg, Zenit scored goals either side of half-time to take a 2-0 lead. Nemanja Vidic pulled one back for United but they couldn't find the equaliser and Scholes was sent off in the dying stages after collecting two yellow cards. Ferguson and his players had a fortnight to lick their wounds, while many of the United players were on International duty and they would have a new team-mate in Berbatov for their next league game against Liverpool.

New signing Berbatov was handed his debut as United travelled to Anfield to face Liverpool, despite taking the lead through Tevez after just three minutes United came away from Anfield empty handed to leave them with one win, a draw and a defeat from their opening three league games. Tevez gave United lead after finishing expertly from a Berbatov pull back. A Wes Brown own goal and Ryan Babel goal ensured it was the Liverpool fans celebrating in the latest edition of this long held rivalry. After three games, United were sitting on four points in the bottom half of the league table, already six points adrift of their next league opponents Chelsea but United had played a game less than the majority of their Premier League rivals. Before their league encounter with Chelsea, it was the start of United's defence of the Champions League. Drawn in a group with Villarreal, Aalborg of Denmark and Celtic, United started with a 0-0 draw at home to Villarreal, the third consecutive goalless draw between United and the Spanish side. The visitors set out their stall to deny the defending champions and were the happier side at the full-time whistle. Next came the visit to Chelsea in the league, already trailing their potential title rivals by six points, United couldn't afford to lose any more ground. Park Ji-Sung gave United the lead after 18 minutes when Chelsea goalkeeper Petr Cech fumbled a shot from Berbatov, who was still seeking his first goal for United. With just over half an hour of the game gone Edwin van der Sar was lost to injury and Chelsea took advantage through a Salomon Kalou equaliser to hold United to a 1-1 draw. After the draw with Chelsea, United put together a run of six wins in three different competitions starting with a 3-1 win over Middlesbrough in the third round of the League Cup. Ferguson handed starts to 18 year-old keeper Ben Amos and 19 year-old forward Danny Welbeck as well as a first start of the season for Ronaldo after injury. In front of Amos, Ferguson selected a strong defence including Vidic and Wes Brown and also handed a first start to Rafael. Ronaldo gave United the lead on 25 minutes but Adam Johnson levelled for Middlesbrough before late strikes from Giggs and Nani sealed United's spot in the fourth round. The next five wins in the sequence came without conceding a goal, starting with a 2-0 home win over Bolton and a 3-0 win over Aalborg in the Champions League. The game in Denmark saw Berbatov grabbing his first goals in a United shirt as he struck twice in the second-half. The next three fixtures saw United travelling to Ewood Park and securing a 2-0 win before a 4-0 win over West Brom at Old Trafford, United then won their Champions League group game 3-0 at home to Celtic with Berbatov scoring two more goals to give him five goals in his last four appearances. The month of October was finished with a 1-1 draw away to Everton and a 2-0 win over West Ham in the Premier League. After nine league games, United had won five, drawn three and lost one to leave them on eighteen points. This left Ferguson's side sixth in the table, eight points behind early leaders Liverpool, while United had a game in hand on the teams around them in the table.

United welcomed Hull City to Old Trafford in their first fixture of November, the visitors were sitting two points ahead of United before this fixture, a position not many would have predicted at the start of the season. United took the game to their opponents and Ronaldo opened the scoring for United after just three minutes after combining with Berbatov. Hull pulled level on 23 minutes before Carrick restored United's lead on the half-hour mark and Ronaldo got his second of the game to extend United's lead just before half-time. Nemanja Vidic extended the lead to 4-1 for Ferguson's men before late strikes from Mendy and Geovanni gave the United faithful a nervy finish but they held on for the three points. This was followed by a trip to Celtic Park in the Champions League and a Giggs equaliser after 84 minutes gave United a point as they remained unbeaten in the group stages. After the draw with Celtic, United travelled to London to face Arsenal and Ferguson watched his team suffer a 2-1 defeat as Samir Nasri struck twice for an Arsene Wenger side that included Silvestre. Silvestre nearly gifted his old team-mates the lead when his poor backpass fell to

Rooney but the England striker couldn't take advantage. Rafael Da Silva struck his first United goal in the dying minutes but this was nothing more than a consolation and the result saw Arsenal moving above United in the table. After the defeat to Arsenal, United bounced back with two home wins against Queens Park Rangers in the League Cup and Stoke City in the Premier League. United progressed to the quarter-final of the League Cup with a 1-0 win over QPR thanks to a Carlos Tevez penalty before they dispatched Stoke 5-0 in the league. The win over Stoke marked the 50th anniversary of Sir Alex Ferguson's first appearance in the professional game for Queens Park and witnessed Ronaldo scoring his 100th goal in the red of United, coming after just three minutes when the Portuguese star struck a trademark free-kick from 25 yards. Ronaldo completed the scoring on 89 minutes and after goals for Carrick, Berbatov and a first senior strike for young striker Danny Welbeck. After five goals against Stoke, United had endure two goalless draws against Aston Villa in the Premier League and Villarreal in the Champions League.

After two goalless draws against Aston Villa and Villarreal, Ferguson took his men across the City to face Manchester City. United dominated the Derby early on but City came closest to opening the scoring. The deadlock was finally broken on 42 minutes by Wayne Rooney when he followed up a Michael Carrick shot. On 68 minutes Ronaldo was sent off, receiving a second booking in the game as he inexplicably handled from a Rooney corner. Rooney almost it 2-0 with a lob late on but was denied by Joe Hart in the City goal. The three points against City left United third in the Premier League table at the end of November, after fourteen games United had 28 points, they were level on points with second placed Liverpool. Both United and Liverpool were five points behind leaders Chelsea with both the North-West teams having a game in hand on Chelsea. In December United faced eight games in four different competitions. As well the Premier League,

United faced a League Cup quarter-final, their final Champions League group game and the Club World Cup in Japan in the build up to Christmas. The month started with the visit of Blackburn Rovers in the quarter-final of the League Cup, Carlos Tevez was the star of the show as he struck four goals as United won the game 5-3 to book their spot in the semi-finals. After opening the scoring on 36 minutes, the Argentinian striker competed his hat-trick after 54 minutes, his hat-trick strike made it four one to United before late goals from Matt Derbyshire and Benni McCarthy for Blackburn and Tevez's fourth of the game saw the game finish 5-3 and booked a semi-final with Championship side Derby County with the tie being played over two-legs at the beginning of 2009. Next on the fixture list were Sunderland at Old Trafford in the league and a 90th minute winner from Nemanja Vidic gave United a 1-0 win and a crucial three points. Before leaving the country for the Club World Cup, United faced Aalborg in the final group game of the Champions League before travelling to White Hart Lane in the league. Despite taking the lead after three minutes against Aalborg, the Danish side hit back to lead 2-1 at half-time. Wayne Rooney levelled for United minutes after the restart and the game finished 2-2. The point was enough to ensure United topped the group on ten points, finishing one point ahead of Villarreal. The game against Tottenham finished 0-0 despite chances for both sides. A point against Tottenham meant that United left for the Club World Cup and Japan third in the table, after sixteen games they had 32 points. The leaders were now Liverpool and United were six points behind the club who were currently the record holders of the most English league titles. A title win for United would of course bring them level with Liverpool on 18 English to flight titles.

The Club World Cup is a competition that pits the six winners from each of FIFA's continental confederations and gave United the opportunity to call themselves the best club side in the world. The way tournament was organised meant that United didn't enter the competition until the semi-finals, meaning that they would just need to win two games in Japan to win the tournament. LDU Quito of Ecuador (winners of 2008 Copa Libertadores) also entered the competition at the semi-finals and it was expected that United would face the Ecuadorians in the final. Before that though they faced Japanese side Gamba Osaka, who had beaten Adelaide United 1-0 in the quarter-finals. A virus ruled Dimitar Berbatov out of the semi-final game but Ferguson was able to name the experienced trio of Giggs, Scholes and Gary Neville in his starting line-up. United had most of the ball from the first whistle with Gamba Osaka looking to counter and catch United short at the back, but United were 2-0 by half-time with both goals coming from Ryan Giggs corners, firstly picking out Vidic before finding Ronaldo on the stroke of half-time. Gamba pulled the score back to 2-1 on 74 minutes before United replied with a further three goals through Wayne Rooney (2) and Darren Fletcher to make the score 5-1 after 79 minutes. Two late goals for Gamba gave the score some respectability for the Japanese but it was United who would be contesting the final three days later against LDU Quito. After coming off the bench to score twice in the semis, Rooney was restored to the starting line-up and formed an attacking trio with Tevez and Ronaldo. With Gary Neville and Ryan Giggs having to settle for a place on the bench, Rio Ferdinand was named as captain by Ferguson and United dominated the game from the start but couldn't find a way past Quito goalkeeper Jose Francisco Cevallos. Cevallos made a series of saves to deny Rooney, Tevez and Park Ji-Sung. Vidic saw red after 49 minutes for appearing to elbow Claudio Bieler but this didn't stop United and they eventually took the lead on 73 minutes when Wayne Rooney finished neatly, Quito failed to muster any serious efforts on van der Sar's goal and United were crowned World Champions. Wayne Rooney finished the competition with three goals, making him the competitions top scorer and was named as player of the tournament. The success meant that Ferguson and United had picked up four pieces of silverware in 2008 after adding the Community Shield and the Club World Cup to the Premier League and Champions League triumphs at the end of the 2007/08 season.

On their return from Japan, United faced two Premier League games in the space of three days before the end of 2008. That started with a Boxing Day trip to Stoke City. Stoke is traditionally looked as a difficult place to go especially in the winter months so Ferguson probably couldn't have picked a tougher fixture for his United side on their return to the country. United made the perfect return to domestic action with a 1-0 win thanks to a Carlos Tevez strike seven minute from time. The three points brought them within touching distance of the Premier League pacesetters and United had games in hand. The final fixture of 2008 saw United coming up against Middlesbrough at Old Trafford and another 1-0 win kept them on the coattails of both Liverpool and Chelsea. A Berbatov strike gave United the three points against a resilient Middlesbrough, the win left Ferguson's side seven points adrift of leaders Liverpool and four behind Chelsea with two games in hand on both teams. Liverpool's position at the top of the table, meant that United could be fighting it out with the club they were looking to draw level with on eighteen championships apiece. January 2009 would be another busy month for Ferguson and United with nine fixtures in the Premier League, FA Cup and League Cup. The month started with the third round of the FA Cup and a trip to Southampton and St Marys Stadium. Before the game was played, the fourth draw was made and United knew if they could beat The Saints they would face a home tie against Tottenham. United ran out three nil winners against Southampton with goals from Danny Welbeck on his FA Cup debut, Nani, who converted a penalty after David McGoldrick handled the ball while he was part of a defensive wall from a United free-kick and Darren Gibson wrapped up the win with the third after combining with fellow substitute Wayne Rooney. Next up was another away cup tie as United travelled to Championship side Derby County for the first-leg of the League Cup semi-final and suffered a 1-0 defeat. Despite losing, United would still be confident of making it to the final. After the two away cup ties, United faced three league games that started by welcoming title rivals Chelsea to Old Trafford. A win for United would cut the deficit to second place Chelsea to one point and United would still have two games in hand. Ferguson and his side turned up the heat on opponents Chelsea and leaders Liverpool with a 3-0 win over Chelsea. United went ahead on the stroke of half-time when Vidic headed home after Berbatov had flicked on a Ryan Giggs corner. Rooney converted a Patrice Evra cross after 63 minutes to make it 2-0 and Berbatov finished off the scoring to move United closer to their title rivals and Ferguson's men still had two games in hand. January saw Ferguson entering the transfer market once again, signing Serbian midfielder Zoran Tosic and Belgium defender Ritchie De Laet. Tosic arrived from Partizan Belgrade and United also agreed a deal to sign his team-mate Adam Ljajic, with Ljajic due to join the following January but this deal was cancelled towards the end of 2009. While De Laet joined United from fellow Premier League team Stoke City. Both these moves were completed before the Chelsea fixture, though both players were seen as signings for the future and wouldn't feature in the first-team in the short-term.

The win over Chelsea was followed by two more wins and clean sheets in the Premier League as they beat both Wigan and Bolton 1-0. The win over Wigan came courtesy of a Wayne Rooney first minute strike while the win over Bolton came thanks to a 90th minute strike from Berbatov. After these two wins though not at their fluent best, United were now ten games unbeaten in the league since the 2-1 defeat away to Arsenal and in those ten games, United hadn't conceded a goal. Meaning a clean sheet against West Brom in their next league game would see van der Sar setting a new Premier League clean sheet record. A clean sheet against West

Brom would see van der Sar surpass the previous record held by Petr Cech. Before that though, United faced two important cup ties against Derby and Tottenham. Derby came into the second-leg of the League Cup semi-final with a 1-0 lead but United were still clear favourites to reach the final. A 4-2 win on the night, gave United a 4-3 aggregate win and United appeared to be coasting on the night with three goals in the first 35 minutes with Nani, John O'Shea and Carlos Tevez all finding the back of the net. The two teams exchanged two late penalties before Giles Barnes struck his second on the night for Derby to give the final scoreline a better look for Derby. It was United though who would be contesting final against Tottenham at Wembley Stadium on March 1 2009. Next up were Tottenham in the fourth round of the FA Cup at Old Trafford. Tottenham took an early lead through Roman Pavlyuchenko before two goals in two minutes from Paul Scholes and Dimitar Berbatov settled the tie in United's favour and the fifth round saw United facing Derby County again just weeks after knocking them out of the League Cup. Now came the game that could see United and Edwin van der Sar set a new record for clean sheets in the Premier League and a trip to The Hawthorn's to face West Brom. Berbatov gave United the lead after 22 minutes and United's cause was helped when West Brom's Paul Robinson saw red after 40 minutes, Tevez doubled the lead just before half-time. Second-half goals from Vidic and Ronaldo (2) secured a 5-0 win and the clean sheet needed to clinch the record. Once the full-time whistle blew, van der Sar had gone a total of 1,032 minutes without conceding in the Premier League, the previous record held by Cech stood at 1,025 minutes. A clean sheet in the next league game against Everton would see the Dutchman passing the English league record of 1,104 minutes without conceding, set by Reading keeper Steve Death in 1979. That record was passed as United finished the month with another 1-0 win. Five wins in the month, meant United had now overhauled both Chelsea and Liverpool at the top of the Premier League table. They had now all played 23 games and United sat five points clear of both Liverpool and Chelsea.

February started with another Premier League clean sheet and another 1-0 win this time against West Ham at Upton Park. Before the game against West Ham, Liverpool had returned to the top of the league having played twice since United defeated Everton but the 1-0 win over West Ham courtesy of a Ryan Giggs goal saw United restore their two point lead over Liverpool and United had a game in hand. The win over West Ham was followed by another away game, this time against Derby in the fifth round of the FA Cup. A 4-1 win for United over their Championship opponent's setup another away tie in the quarter-finals against Fulham. Next up was United's game in hand against Fulham. The game originally postponed because of United's involvement in the UEFA Super Cup gave Ferguson and his team the opportunity to open up a five lead once again at the top of the league. United started the game well and opened the scoring on 12 minutes when Carrick picked out Scholes on the edge of the from a corner, a sublime volley from Scholes was kept out by Fulham goalkeeper Mark Schwarzer but the ball spun back over the line and into the net. The lead was doubled on the half-hour mark by Berbatov before a returning Wayne Rooney made it 3-0 on 63 minutes. Rooney had missed the last seven games with a hamstring strain. The next game for United saw them facing Blackburn at Old Trafford, a win would open up an eight point lead on Liverpool, with the Merseysiders not in action until the following day but Ferguson had one eye on the resumption of United's Champions League defence which saw them travelling to Italy for the first-leg of first knockout phase again Inter Milan three days after the fixture against Blackburn. Ferguson opted to rest van der Sar and Vidic against Blackburn but this didn't stop United collecting the three points thanks to strikes from Rooney and Ronaldo. Rooney opened the scoring on 23 minutes before Roque Santa Cruz levelled for Blackburn. Ronaldo settled the game on the hour mark scoring with a dipping free-kick from the left-hand side of the penalty area. Despite chances for Ronaldo, Park Ji-Sung and Rooney, United couldn't find the breakthrough against Inter Milan in the San Siro though they would have been the happier of the two teams coming away from the 0-0 draw.

Next up was Tottenham at Wembley Stadium and another chance to pick some silverware for Ferguson and his Manchester United side. Van der Sar hadn't played any part in United's run to the final and was rested again by Ferguson, with the manager opting for Ben Foster ahead Kuszczak. While Wayne Rooney missed out with a virus and Berbatov wasn't selected to play in the showpiece against his old team-mates. Opting for a blend of youth and experience, Ferguson selected Scholes and Ferdinand alongside the youth of Welbeck and Gibson. The game was played at a good tempo with both teams having opportunities to score but neither side could find the breakthrough and the winner would be decided by penalties. Giggs scored United's first penalty, hitting ball off the upright but scoring, Jamie O'Hara saw his effort saved by Foster before Tevez made it 2-0. Successful penalties were exchanged before Darren Bent sent his effort wide of the goal, leaving Anderson with the penalty to win the cup and he converted as United won the League Cup for the third time, all under the management of Sir Alex Ferguson. With the League Cup secured alongside the Community Shield and the Club World Cup, United were still looking to add the Premier League title, FA Cup and Champions League crowns to their season's haul. The first game after the League Cup final saw United travelling to Newcastle in the Premier League and despite falling behind early to a goal that ended van der Sar's long run in the league without conceding a goal. United were back in the game after 20 minutes through a Rooney equaliser before Berbatov got a second-half winner for Ferguson's men. Next up United looked to book their place in the semi-finals of the FA Cup with an quarter-final win at Craven Cottage. United ran out 4-0 winners thanks to two first-half goals from Carlos Tevez and second-half strikes from Rooney and Park Ji-Sung. The semi-final against Everton would be a record breaking 26th FA Cup semi-final appearance for Manchester United. Next on the agenda for United were Inter Milan in the second-leg of the first knockout stage of the Champions League. Inter were now managed by former Chelsea manager Jose Mourinho and the Portuguese manager had experience of knocking United out of the Champions League with Porto but this time it was United who came out on top, after dominating the first-leg, United were confident of progressing and thanks to goals from Nemanja Vidic and Cristiano Ronaldo they did. Both goals came after four minutes of each half and gave United a 2-0 aggregate win against the Italians who they also beat on their way to winning the competition in 99. In the quarter-finals they would face Mourinho's former side Porto.

Back in the Premier League it was time for United to go head-to-head with title rivals Liverpool at Old Trafford. United came into the fixture seven points clear of their rivals with a game in hand. United started the game well and were 1-0 up after 23 minutes when Ronaldo converted a penalty won by Park Ji-Sung but the lead wouldn't last long as five minutes later Spanish striker Fernando Torres took advantage of a Vidic error to level. Liverpool were ahead at half-time after Evra tripped Gerrard in the box and the Liverpool skipper converted the resulting penalty on the stroke of half-time. The match went from bad to worse for Vidic and United when the Serbian defender was sent off on 76 minutes after hauling Gerrard down on the edge of the area. Liverpool scored from the resulting free-kick and added a fourth to leave Liverpool trailing Ferguson's men by four points but United still had that game in hand and were still seen as favourites to win a third consecutive Premier League title and draw level with Liverpool on 18 English top flight league titles. Another defeat followed in their next league fixture as they suffered a 2-0 defeat away to Fulham and had both Paul Scholes and Wayne Rooney sent-off to finish the game with nine men. These back-to-back defeats to Liverpool and Fulham had seen United's lead at the top of the Premier League reduced to one point but they still had a game in hand on Liverpool. After an International break United's first fixture of April saw them welcoming Aston Villa to Old Trafford. The game was played on Sunday April 5 2009 and the day before the game Liverpool beat Fulham 1-0 to move above United. Despite taking an early lead through Ronaldo, United were staring at a third straight league defeat with an hour on the clock. Ronaldo got his second of the game to level the game after 80 minutes and setup a frantic finish. Enter 17 year-old Italian striker Frederico Macheda, who signed his first professional contract on his 17th birthday in August 2008 and had spent much of his time in the under-18s, shortly before getting his call-up to the first-team, the Italian had scored eight goals in as many games for the reserves. Macheda replaced Nani just after the hour mark and his match winning moment came on 90 minute as he turned on the edge of the area before curling an effort into the Aston Villa net that took United back to the top of the league. In the Champions League quarter-finals it was Porto with the first-leg taking place at Old Trafford just three days after the win over Aston Villa, Macheda was rewarded for his winner in that game with a place on the bench once again. It turned out to be a disappointing night for the defending champions as they conceding two away goals and had to settle for a draw. Porto took the lead after four minutes but Rooney equalised on 15 minutes, Carlos Tevez looked to have sealed the win five minutes from time only for Porto to level in the dying minutes and hold the advantage of two away goals going into the second-leg in Portugal. Before that game United travelled to the North-East to face a struggling Sunderland side and Macheda proved to be the hero for United once again. Scholes gave United the lead but Kenwyne Jones levelled for the hosts. Macheda was again the hero only a minute

191

after entering the game when he diverted a Michael Carrick shot into the Sunderland goal. Ferguson took his side to Portugal knowing a win was needed if United were to continue their defence of the Champions League. The deciding moment of the game and the tie came after six minutes when Ronaldo struck a stunning 40 yard effort, the win setup an all English semi-final with Arsenal.

With their place in the Champions League semi-final confirmed, next on the agenda for United was an FA Cup semi-final with Everton at Wembley Stadium. United have never failed to reach an FA Cup final once they got through to the semis under Ferguson but this time the competition was third on the list of priorities after the Premier League and Champions League. Ferguson opted to play a weakened side, something he was criticised for later but Ferguson put his decision to protect first-team regulars down to the state of the Wembley pitch. The only first-team regulars to start the game were Rio Ferdinand, Nemanja Vidic and Carlos Tevez. With Ferguson giving further opportunities to Welbeck, Macheda and Darren Gibson as well as fielding both the Da Silva twins. United dominated a poor game but failed to create any clear goalscoring opportunities either in ninety minutes or extra-time, the game would be settled by a penalty shootout and it was Everton's former United goalkeeper Tim Howard who would be the hero. He saved spot-kicks from Ferdinand and substitute Berbatov as Everton won the shootout 4-2 and ended United's hopes of finishing the season with five trophies. Back in the Premier League, Liverpool moved above United on goal difference after a 4-4 with Arsenal but United had two games in hand with the first of those coming the following day against Portsmouth at Old Trafford. The game against Portsmouth saw Ferguson name a team containing nine changes from the semi-final against Everton and despite starting the game slowly, Wayne Rooney converted a Ryan Giggs cross to put United ahead after nine minutes. United carried on creating chances but had to wait until the 82nd minute to seal the three points when Paul

Scholes, playing his 600th game for United played the perfect through ball for Carrick to score and confirm a 2-0 win and United's place back at the top of table. Next up was another home game for United, this time welcoming Tottenham and before the game United knew they had dropped behind Liverpool on goal difference once again following their defeat of Hull City. Darren Bent and Luka Modric took advantage of two lapses in defence from United to leave Ferguson's men trailing 2-0 at half-time. Ferguson opted to replace Nani with Tevez at half-time and United got a goal back twelve minutes into the second-half through a controversial penalty won by former Tottenham midfielder Michael Carrick, Ronaldo converted the penalty. With Tevez, Rooney, Ronaldo and Berbatov all the pitch, United didn't have much option but all-out attack and after 67 minutes Rooney levelled for United and a minute after drawing level, United were ahead when Ronaldo's diving header met a cross from Rooney and three minutes after that United were 4-2 up when Rooney's shot crossed the line despite the best efforts of Jonathan Woodgate. The turnaround was complete when Berbatov stuck a fifth goal in 22 minutes to give them the 5-2 win and the three points put United three points in front of Liverpool with five games to play. The comeback brought back memories of the 5-3 turnaround against the same opposition in 2001 when United were 3-0 down at half-time at White Hart Lane.

Following the comeback against Tottenham, United welcomed Arsenal to Old Trafford in the first-leg of the semi-finals as the two English sides fought for a place in the Champions League final. England were guaranteed to have an team in the final for the fifth year running but would it be United taking their defence to the final. United started the game well but missed opportunities through Rooney, Ronaldo and Tevez before the opening goal came from the unlikely source of John O'Shea. The defender rose highest in the 17th minute to head home a corner, after the goal United continued to dominate and saw a 30 yard shot from Ronaldo cannon off the crossbar before Ryan Giggs making his 800th appearance for the club had a goal ruled out for offside. United would take the 1-0 lead to the Emirates Stadium the following week. Before that they travelled to the Riverside Stadium, Middlesbrough and United came away with a 2-0 win as Ryan Giggs and Park Ji-Sung strikes either side of half-time settled the game in United's favour. Taking a 1-0 lead to the Emirates, United were 3-0 up on aggregate within 11 minutes of starting the second-leg. Arsenal started the game the better but United took the lead on the night from their first attack when Ronaldo put in a deep cross and Arsenal defender Kieran Gibbs slipped to allow Park Ji-Sung to slot home after eight minutes. Three minutes later Ronaldo struck a 40 yard free-kick to put United 2-0 up on the night and 3-0 up in the tie. The two away goals for United meant that Arsenal would need to four goals to reach the final. The hosts continued to dominate possession but couldn't break through the United defence and just after the hour mark a breakaway from United saw Ronaldo scoring his second and United's third and barring disaster United would have the chance to become the first team to regain the European Cup since the inception of the Champions League. In the final United would face a rematch with Barcelona after knocking the Spanish side in the semi-finals on their way to lifting the trophy the previous season. Before that final, United had their eyes on the Premier League title and a record equalling 18th top flight title. And next up on that quest was a Manchester Derby as City made the short trip to Old Trafford, again Liverpool had gone above United but only on goal difference and United still had two games in hand including this one. There were few shots on target in the game but United got two crucial goals in the first-half through Carlos Tevez and Cristiano Ronaldo. Ronaldo struck the first with a deflected free-kick before Tevez added a second on the stroke of half-time. The only talking point of the second-half came when Ronaldo reacted angrily when Ferguson opted to take the

Portuguese star off. That result left United needing just four points from their three remaining league games to win their third consecutive title. Achieving this feat would a second time for Manchester United under Ferguson. Next on the fixture list were Wigan Athletic and they gained three of the points they needed with a 2-1 win at the JJB Stadium, trailing to a 28th minute strike from Hugo Rodallega and without managing a shot on target in the first-half. Ferguson sent on Tevez in place of Anderson after 58 minutes and it took the Argentinian just three minute to draw United level, back-heeling a deflected shot from Carrick into the Wigan net and Carrick got the winner on 86 minutes to give United the three points and one point against Arsenal in their next game would give Ferguson and Manchester United their 11th Premier League title. Despite missing chances through Wayne Rooney and having a Park Ji-Sung goal ruled out for offside, United played out the draw and at the final whistle, players, Ferguson and his backroom staff all celebrated Manchester United's 18th league title. A feat that drew them level with this season's main challengers Liverpool. The last game of the Premier League season saw United playing against Hull City, the result didn't matter but United won the game 1-0 thanks to a 20 yard strike from Darren Gibson.

With the Community Shield, Club World Cup, League Cup and Premier League already in the trophy cabinet, Ferguson and his team travelled to Rome aiming to successfully defend the Champions League crown they won in Moscow the previous May. United weren't the only ones looking to add to their trophy haul for the season, Barcelona were looking to complete their own treble having already won the Spanish league and cup. United started the better and had several chances in the opening exchanges, with Ronaldo forcing a save from Barcelona keeper Victor Valdes in the second minute. Despite United starting the better, it was Barcelona who took the lead on ten minutes through Samuel Eto'o when his low shot beat van der Sar at his near post. After the goal, Barcelona

195

settled into smooth passing game, dominating possession and restricted United's chances of getting back into the game. The start of the second-half saw Ferguson introducing Tevez in place of Anderson but Barcelona settled back into their passing rhythm. Another attacking change came in the 70th minute with Berbatov replacing Park Ji-Sung but this had no effect on the pattern of the game and the second goal came for Barcelona when Xavi crossed for Messi, he rose impressively to head past van der Sar and clinch the win for Barcelona and Manchester United suffered defeat in the European Cup final for the first time, having won their three previous finals. Despite the disappointment of the final defeat to Barcelona the 2008/09 was a successful one for United and Ferguson. They picked up four pieces of silverware including a third successive Premier League title that brought them level on 18 English top flight titles with Liverpool. They won the League Cup for the third time and reached the FA Cup semi-finals and won the club World Cup in Japan. Veteran midfielder Ryan Giggs was voted the PFA Player of the Year by his fellow professionals. There was plenty of optimism for the future of this team.

Chapter Sixteen: In Search of Number 19

Following the successes of the previous three seasons, United were looking to make it four consecutive league titles for the first time while in Europe they were looking to reach a third consecutive final in the Champions League, having won the trophy in 2008 before losing out to Barcelona the following season. After drawing level with Liverpool on 18 top flight titles, a fourth consecutive league title would move Manchester United onto 19 league titles and see them set a new record. As well as being defending league champions, United came into the 09/10 season as League Cup holders after beating Tottenham on penalties in the previous season. After finishing as the club's top scorer for the last two seasons, Cristiano Ronaldo was allowed to leave the club for a then world record transfer fee of £80million. Six seasons in Manchester had seen Ronaldo scoring 118 goals in 292 games for the club. Picking up honours both individually and as part of one the most successful United teams. During in his time at Old Trafford, United had won three league titles, an FA Cup, two League Cups, a Champions League and the FIFA Club World Cup. While on an individual level he was named World Player of the Year in 2008, while winning United supporters Player of the Year on three occasions and winning both the PFA Players and Young player of the Year awards, including the double in the 2006/07 season. There were strong rumours at the end of the 2007/08 season that Ronaldo would leave United for Real Madrid with United filing a tampering complaint with FIFA over Madrid's alleged pursuit of the player but FIFA declined to take any action with President Sepp Blatter saying that the player should be allowed to leave if he wanted, calling it "modern day slavery". Ronaldo remained at Old Trafford for the 2008/09 with Ferguson stating he wouldn't sell that mob a virus. Ronaldo was eventually sold to Real after the end of 2008/09 season for the world record fee. Ronaldo wouldn't be the only attacking player to leave Old Trafford that summer as Ferguson decided not to take up the option of signing Carlos Tevez on a permanent deal after his two years on loan with the club. The Argentinian ended up signing for neighbours Manchester City as they looked to challenge United at the top of the English game. Following the departures of Ronaldo and Tevez it was obvious that Ferguson would need to bring in new faces and was linked with a big money move for French striker Karim Benzema but he would join Ronaldo in Madrid and Ferguson opted to sign former Liverpool striker Michael Owen on a free transfer. While other new faces at the club were Antonio Valencia, Gabriel Obertan and Mame Biram Diouf. Valencia was signed from Wigan Athletic for an undisclosed fee believed to be in the region of £16million, while Obertan and Diouf were both signed for smaller fees. Valencia was seen as a replacement for Ronaldo and would go straight into the first-team, Diouf and Obertan were seen as signings for the future.

As in many other seasons under Sir Alex Ferguson, United started their domestic campaign with the Community Shield (formerly Charity Shield). This time they faced Chelsea at Wembley and the game finished 2-2 after 90 minutes. At one time the trophy would have been shared after a draw but now was decided by a penalty shootout if the scores level are after 90 minutes. United have won the trophy several times after a shootout in recent seasons. Ben Foster had been the hero when United won the League Cup in a shootout but the English goalkeeper couldn't repeat that feat as Chelsea won 4-1 on penalties. Van der Sar was due to miss the first few months of season with injury and

Ferguson opted for Foster between the sticks ahead of Kuszczak and despite being criticised for both Chelsea goals in the Community Shield, Ferguson kept faith with Foster at the start of the Premier League season starting with an opening day win over Birmingham City. As well as missing van der Sar, United were also missing Ferdinand and Vidic from the heart of their defence. Ferdinand struggled with back and knee injuries throughout the 2009/10 season making only 13 appearances in the league and 21 in all competitions. While Vidic also missed several games throughout the season, making 24 appearances in the league and 33 appearances in all competitions. This meant that Ferguson struggled to name the same back four throughout the season with the only mainstay being French left-back Patrice Evra. After an opening day with over Birmingham, United travelled to Turf Moor to face a Burnley side playing their first home fixture in the top flight for 33 years and their first home fixture as a Premier League club. A volley from Robbie Blake inflicted defeat on United but he wasn't the only hero for Burnley as goalkeeper Brian Jensen saved a penalty from Michael Carrick to deny United an equaliser just before half-time. United bounced back from that disappointment when they travelled to Wigan and came away with a 5-0 win in a game that saw Rooney scoring a double to go past 100 goals for the club. While Michael Owen also notched his first goal for the club. The win over Wigan was the first in a run of eight consecutive victories that saw wins in the Premier League, Champions League and League Cup.

The first league fixture against a possible title contender came in the fourth league game of the season as United welcomed Arsenal to Old Trafford. It was Arsenal who took the lead, five minutes before the half-time whistle thanks to a strike from Russian Andrey Arshavin, firing a 25-yard strike past Ben Foster after being played in by Brazilian Denilson. Arsenal had been denied a penalty in the first-half but United had the opportunity to level when the referee pointed to the spot in the second-half. Rooney stepped to take and score the spot-kick he won after being brought down by Arsenal keeper Almunia. Just over five minutes later, United were in front as Abou Diaby headed into his own net from a Giggs free-kick. Arsenal thought they had levelled five minutes into stoppage time through Gallas but the Frenchman was ruled offside and United made it three wins from their first four league games. A International break came after the win over Arsenal and United's first game after the break came away to Tottenham. This game saw the partnership of Vidic and Ferdinand at the centre of the defence for the first time since the Champions League final defeat to Barcelona but the pair couldn't stop Jermaine Defoe giving Tottenham the lead after 38 seconds. Goals from Giggs, Anderson (his first strike for United) and Rooney, scoring his fifth in five league games at the start of the season gave United the three points. One negative from the game was the sending-off of Paul Scholes for two yellows with the score at 2-1. The three points left United second in the table to an unbeaten Chelsea. After this United were on their travels again as they played in Turkey against Besiktas in their opening Champions League group game of the season and a 77th minute goal from Scholes gave United the three points. The next league fixture on the agenda was the Manchester Derby against a City team managed by former United striker Mark Hughes and containing Carlos Tevez. Rooney netted his sixth goal in six league games after just two minutes but City were level on 16 minutes through Gareth Barry after Tevez pressurised Ben Foster into a mistake. It stayed 1-1 until half-time, four minutes into the second-half Darren Fletcher headed in a Giggs cross but City hit back almost immediately through Craig Bellamy. Berbatov saw two good chances saved by City keeper Shay Given before Fletcher got his second on 80 minutes. With just seconds left of normal time, Ferdinand gifted possession to City and it saw Bellamy getting his second goal and looking like he had secured a point for City. The fourth official had indicated four minutes of extra-time but after the goal celebration for Bellamy's equaliser and substitutes made, the game went into a sixth minute of extra-time and with almost the last kick of the game Michael Owen scored what could turn out to be the most important goal of his Manchester United career after being played in by Ryan Giggs. United were celebrating and City complaining that the game should have finished before the goal came. After the drama of the last-gasp Derby win came the start of United's defence of the League Cup with the visit of Wolves to Old Trafford. Ferguson opted to give game time to some of his younger squad members, with Darren Gibson, Federico Macheda and Danny Welbeck all starting alongside the Derby hero Michael Owen. United were reduced to ten men when Fabio Da Silva saw red for a professional foul. Despite one less man than the opposition, United took the lead through Welbeck shortly after the hour mark after a one-two with Owen. The score remained 1-0 and in the fourth round, United were drawn away to Barnsley.

The three points continued coming for United in the Premier League and Champions League as they beat Stoke and Wolfsburg. The win over Stoke was 2-0 and came thanks to second-half goals from Berbatov and John O'Shea. That win for United and a 3-1 defeat for Chelsea meant United finished the latest round of fixtures top of the table for the first time in the 2009/10 season. United then welcomed German champions Wolfsburg to Old Trafford, despite dominating the game United reached half-time at 0-0 and Wolfsburg took the lead in the second-half before goals from Giggs and Carrick gave United the 2-1 win that made it two wins out two at the start of their Champions League campaign. The winning run was halted as United drew 2-2 with Sunderland in the next league game. In a game that United twice trailed, they needed a late own goal from Rio's brother Anton to earn a point and preserve their unbeaten home record. After the draw with Sunderland, they were back to winning ways with the visit of Bolton in a game that saw Edwin van der Sar playing his first game of the season and United won 2-1. Next up were CSKA Moscow away from home in United's third group game, United went into the game missing Giggs, Evra, Park Ji-Sung, Fletcher and Rooney through injury but won a cagey game thanks to an 86th minute strike from Antonio Valencia. On their return from Moscow, United faced another away day but this time they only had to travel down the M62 to face Liverpool. Rooney was passed fit along with Giggs and Evra, the inclusion of Rooney meant that former Liverpool striker Owen had to settle for a place on the bench. Spanish striker Fernando Torres put Liverpool ahead on 65 minutes, Ferguson replaced Berbatov with Owen and the former Liverpool favourite was welcomed by a chorus of boos from the home crowd. Owen drew a foul from former team-mate Carragher, for which the defender received a yellow card but there were questions as to whether he was the last man and should have been sent off. Both sides did finish the game with ten men as Vidic received a second yellow, the third time in as many matches Vidic has seen red against Liverpool. Then Javier Mascherano received a second yellow but Liverpool added a second goal in the sixth minute of injury time. The defeat and a win for Chelsea against Blackburn, meant United dropped to second in the league. The defeat to Liverpool was followed by two 2-0 wins for United, the first coming against Barnsley in the League Cup, again Ferguson opted for a less experienced side including summer signing Obertan making his first start as goals from Welbeck and Owen setup a fifth round tie with Tottenham. Jonny Evans and Wes Brown had been at the heart of United's defence against Barnsley and that partnership continued against Blackburn with both Ferdinand and Vidic ruled out by injury, United kept a another clean sheet as goals from Berbatov and Rooney gave United the three points. The win also saw Obertan making his Premier League debut and the French winger was involved in the build up to United's second goal. The three points against Blackburn meant that United finished October second in the league table, two points behind leaders Chelsea ahead of a trip to Stamford Bridge in their next league fixture.

Before the Chelsea game though, United welcomed CSKA Moscow to Old Trafford looking to making it four wins out of four in the Champions League. United were still without Ferdinand and Vidic for this encounter as well as missing Berbatov, while Rooney was only on the bench following the birth of his first son. Ferguson paired Owen and Macheda up front and Owen equalised for United before the Russian side opened up a 3-1 lead and it stayed that way until Scholes headed home a deflected cross on 84 minutes. Another deflection came to the aid of United as Valencia struck a long range shot that was going wide until it took a wicked deflection that beat Akinfeev in the Moscow goal. The point was enough to secure United's passage to the knockout rounds. Next came the visit to Stamford Bridge and United were able to welcome Rooney back to the starting line-up but were only able to name Vidic on the bench while Ferdinand was still ruled out. United dominated for large parts of the game and went close through Rooney twice but they would pay for their lack of cutting edge when John Terry headed Chelsea in front fifteen minutes from time and the score remained at 1-0, meaning United fell five points behind Chelsea in the title race. Looking to bounce back in their next league against Everton, Ferguson was still without Berbatov and gave Owen a spot in the starting line-up alongside Rooney and he was able to recall Vidic to his defence. The return of Vidic saw United keeping a clean sheet and picking up the three points thanks to goals from Fletcher, Carrick and Valencia. United suffered another defeat in their next game against Besiktas, with United's qualification already confirmed Ferguson opted to field an inexperienced side that included Obertan, Gibson, Welbeck and Macheda and United went down to a deflected effort from Rodrigo Tello after 20 minutes and the defeat ended their 23 game unbeaten record at Old Trafford in the Champions League. After the defeat to Besiktas, United bounced back with four wins in the league, League Cup and Champions League. This started with a 4-1 win over Portsmouth at Fratton Park, already missing Ferdinand through injury. Ferguson would once again be without van der Sar for a sustained period and this time Ferguson opted for Kuszczak as his replacement, with Berbatov only fit enough for the bench, Ferguson opted for Giggs alongside Rooney in attack and Rooney scored a hat-trick while Giggs added a fourth for United, his 100th Premier League goal on the eve of his 36th birthday. Next United faced Tottenham in the quarter-final of the League Cup and a double from Republic of Ireland midfielder Darren Gibson gave United a 2-0 win and booked a semi-final with neighbours City. United's next league game came away to West Ham and three second-half goals in the space of 11 minutes from Gibson, Valencia and Rooney secured a 4-0 win and kept up the pressure on Chelsea, the win left United two points behind leaders Chelsea after 15 league games. An injury hit United then travelled to Wolfsburg in the final group game, Ferguson had to field Carrick and Fletcher in a three-man defence alongside Patrice Evra, while Owen was selected in attack and scored a hat-trick to give United a 3-1 win and secure top spot in their Champions League group. 2009 was brought to an end with five league games and United suffered two defeats in these last five league games of the year, losing at home to Aston Villa 1-0 and suffering a 3-0 defeat away to Fulham. The defeat to Villa was followed by a 3-0 win over Wolves then United suffered the defeat to Fulham before beating Hull 3-1 and beat Wigan 5-0 in the final game of 2009. After five league defeats in their first 20 fixtures, United lay second in the table heading into 2010. They sat two points behind leaders Chelsea, one positive for United was that of their other 15 league games so far, United had won 14. Ferguson took his team into the 2010, still looking to win a four consecutive title for the first time, still in the League Cup and Champions League and an FA Cup third round tie against Leeds United to look forward to.

2010 started with the FA Cup third round tie against bitter rival Leeds United at Old Trafford, Ferguson opted to rotate his team for this tie, starting the game with team that had an average age of 21 as he included Fabio Da Silva, Obertan, Anderson and Welbeck. Leeds came into the tie top of the table in League One and caused a massive shock coming away with a 1-0 win thanks to a Jermaine Beckford strike after 19 minutes. The loss was the first suffered by Manchester United under the management of Sir Alex Ferguson in the third round of the FA Cup and also the first time United had lost to a lower division side under Ferguson. After the disappointment of their FA Cup exit, United looked to bounce back as they travelled to Birmingham for their first league fixture of the calendar year but needed an own goal from Birmingham defender Scott Dann just after the hour mark to salvage a 1-1 draw. Finally United got their first win of 2010 on January 16 as they welcomed Burnley to Old Trafford. Burnley held United to nil for just over an hour before two goals in five minutes from Berbatov and Rooney and a 90th minute strike from Mame Biram Diouf (his first United goal) gave United a 3-0 win. After the win over Burnley, it was City up next in the first leg of the League Cup semi-final. This was the first time in over forty years that the two Manchester clubs had met in the semi-finals of a cup competition. The first-leg was originally scheduled to take place three days after the loss to Leeds but heavy snow in Manchester caused the postponement of the game despite the fact that the pitch was playable. United took the lead on 17 minutes when Ryan Giggs was left with a simple finish after Wayne Rooney's shot had been saved. City were level shortly before half-time when Tevez converted a penalty that had awarded by referee Mike Dean for a pull by United right-back Rafael on City's Craig Bellamy. Tevez added a second for City in the second-half after United failed to clear a City corner and the hosts would take a 2-1 lead into the second leg. Before the return leg, United welcomed Hull to Old Trafford and took the chance to go above Chelsea with a 4-0 win, although United had played two games more than their title rivals. United set the early pace at the start of the second-leg but it was City who made the better chances as the first-half finished goalless. Seven minutes into the second-half, City won a corner which United cleared to Rooney who beat his marker before playing a cross field pass to Giggs on the right wing, the Welshman's cross eventually fell to Scholes on the edge of area and veteran midfielder hit a low shot into the bottom corner of the net. With 20 minutes left to play, Carrick doubled the lead for United and put them 3-2 ahead on aggregate. Though City were level in the tie five minutes later as Tevez once again scored against United. As the second-leg headed into injury time, the game looked set to go into extra time before United won a corner, which Giggs took short before receiving the ball back and crossing into the six yard box where Rooney headed past Shay Given in the City goal and United were in the final where they would face Aston Villa in a repeat of the 1994 final. United celebrated their League Cup semi-final success with a great away performance against Arsenal, leaving the Emirates Stadium with a 3-1 win and three points. Before the game Arsenal were just a point behind United and looking to challenge United and Chelsea for the Premier League title. Arsenal started well but a man of the match performance from Portuguese winger Nani helped United to the win and a crucial three points. Firstly he beat two defenders before crossing to the far post where Manual Almunia palmed the ball into his own net. Five minutes later, Arsenal had a corner but it was 2-0 to United when a lightening quick breakaway from Nani and Rooney saw the Englishman scoring his 100th Premier League goal. 2-0 at half-time and it was 3-0 shortly after the break thanks to another breakaway and a Park Ji-Sung goal. Despite a late strike from Thomas Vermaelen, United took the three points back to Manchester. This was United last fixture of January and they started February with an emphatic 5-0 victory over Portsmouth at Old Trafford with the visitors being credited with three own goals. The win over

Portsmouth put United top of the league but only for 24 hours as Chelsea beat Arsenal the following day.

After the victory over Portsmouth, United travelled to Villa Park and were happy to come away with a point after having Nani sent off for a two-footed challenge on Stiliyan Petrov after 29 minutes. At the time the score was 1-1 after a James Collins own goal had levelled the score for United. The draw combined with Everton beating Chelsea on the same evening, meant that the gap at the top of the table was down to a point. The following week came the resumption of the Champions League and the first knockout round. The draw took place in December and pitted United against AC Milan and David Beckham. It would be the first time that Beckham faced United since his departure to Real Madrid in 2003. Beckham was on loan at AC Milan from American MLS side LA Galaxy. Beckham started the first-leg on the right side of Milan's midfield as United came away from the San Siro with a 3-2 win thanks to goals from Scholes and Rooney (2). After the victory over Milan, United travelled to Goodison Park to face Everton, Everton had beaten Chelsea at Goodison the previous week and despite going ahead through a Berbatov strike United also suffered a defeat, going down 3-1. The following weekend United would be playing in the League Cup final and because of this their league fixture against West Ham was brought forward and United enjoyed a 3-0 victory with two goals from Rooney and Michael Owen's first league goal since his winner in the Manchester Derby. Despite falling behind to a fifth minute penalty in the League Cup final, United recovered to win the game 2-1 and successfully defend the League Cup. Seven minutes after falling behind, United were level through a Michael Owen strike but the English striker had to be withdrawn just before half-time with a hamstring strain and his replacement Rooney scored the winning goal as he headed home a cross from Antonio Valencia and only minutes after Rooney could have made it 3-1 but struck a post. United won their first piece of silverware of the season and won the League Cup for the fourth time, all coming with Sir Alex Ferguson as manager.

The weekend after the League Cup victory, United faced an away game against Wolverhampton Wanderers. A poor game was decided by a Paul Scholes strike on 73 minutes. The goal was Scholes's 100th Premier League goal and took United two points clear of Chelsea at the top but the Londoners had a game in hand. Rooney missed the Wolves victory through injury but was passed fit for United's next game, the second-leg against AC Milan. Beckham started the game on the bench but entered the game after 64 minutes to play his first game at Old Trafford against United. AC Milan knew they needed two goals without reply to knock United out but it was United who struck first on 13 minutes when Rooney headed home a right-wing cross from Gary Neville. By the time Beckham entered the fray, United were 3-0 up and Darren Fletcher added a fourth in the 88th minute to give United a 4-0 win on the night and a 7-3 aggregate win over the Italians. In the quarter-finals United were drawn against Germans Bayern Munich. With their place in the quarter-finals of the Champions League confirmed, United welcomed Fulham to Old Trafford with Ferguson's men looking to exact revenge for a 3-0 defeat at Craven Cottage earlier in the season and United did just that with a 3-0 win of their own with goals from Rooney (2) and Berbatov. Next up was a league encounter with bitter rivals Liverpool. Win the league title this season and United would be on 19 league titles, taking them one ahead of Liverpool. Liverpool had won the last three league encounters and it looked like it may be four successive wins for Liverpool when Torres put the Merseysiders ahead after five minutes. The lead lasted just seven minutes as United were awarded a penalty. Despite seeing his spot-kick saved by Pepe Reina, Rooney scored from the rebound. The score stayed at 1-1 until the hour mark when Park Ji-Sung headed a Darren Fletcher cross past Reina. The win took United four points clear of Chelsea and two clear of Arsenal, but Chelsea had a game in hand on both United and Arsenal. Next United faced Bolton away and despite a tight first-half, United eventually ran out four nil winners with a double from Dimitar Berbatov. With six league games remaining, United were one point clear of Chelsea at the top of the Premier League. The next round of league fixtures would see United welcoming Chelsea to Old Trafford. Before that though Ferguson would take his side to Germany to face Bayern Munich in the first-leg of the Champions League quarter-finals. United travelled to Germany for the first-leg of the quarter-finals as Ferguson looked to take United to a third consecutive Champions League final. The night started perfectly for Ferguson when Wayne Rooney volleyed United in front from six yards after just 66 seconds, but United would return to Manchester with a 2-1 defeat and have major injury concerns over Rooney for the return leg as well as the upcoming league games. Munich hit an injury time winner through Ivica Olic and it was in the build-up to that goal that Rooney suffered the injury when he went over on his ankle and appeared to be in severe pain. With the return leg the following week it appeared that Rooney would face a race against time to prove his fitness for that game. First up though was Chelsea in what could be a title decider with just one point between the two sides at the top of the table. Without Rooney United struggled for any creativity. Joe Cole put Chelsea ahead after 20 minutes and it was two nil to the visitors when Didier Drogba scored from an offside position, despite protests from United the goal stood. Macheda pulled one back two minutes later for United but they couldn't find the leveller and Chelsea went top of the league, two points in front of United with five games remaining. Reports coming out of United suggested that Rooney would also miss the second-leg against Bayern but he was a surprise name in the starting line-up and United came flying out the blocks and were 2-0 up after seven minutes, putting them 3-2 ahead on aggregate. Nani added a third on the night after 41 minutes but two minutes later and two minutes before half-time Olic struck his second of the tie and a crucial away goal for Bayern. One more goal for Bayern they would head through on away goals and United's position became difficult when right-back Rafael received a second yellow and an early bath after 50 minutes. The sending off of Rafael and the withdrawal of Rooney on 55 minutes invited pressure from Bayern and Arjen Robben got a second goal for Bayern after 74 minutes and United were knocked out on away goals.

After the Champions League exit, United just had the league to focus on and with five games remaining Ferguson's men were two points behind Chelsea. Their next league fixture came at Ewood Park against Blackburn Rovers and despite returning to the team against Bayern, Rooney was once again missing for United meaning a start for Macheda alongside Berbatov. Despite playing the best football, United couldn't find a way past a resolute Blackburn defence and the game finish 0-0 leaving them a point adrift of Chelsea having played a game more. Next up for United was the Manchester Derby. This was the fourth Manchester Derby of the season and a one nil win gave United their third win of the season over City and more importantly kept their title dreams alive. The winning goal came just 17 seconds before end of the scheduled injury time when Paul Scholes headed home a Patrice Evra and we saw Gary Neville celebrating by planting a kiss right on Paul Scholes lips. The win and a 2-1 win for Tottenham over Chelsea left United a point behind Chelsea with three games remaining. Tottenham were the next visitors to Old Trafford in a game that both teams needed the three points, United to keep alive their title dream alive and Tottenham were looking for a top four finish and Champions League football. Despite returning against City, Rooney had picked up another injury, this time a groin strain and was ruled out of the game. The first-half passed by with barely a shot on goal from either side. United won a penalty on the hour mark, which Giggs converted but Ledley King levelled the game up with twenty minutes to go before Nani and Giggs with a second penalty gave United the crucial three points. Before their penultimate game of the season, United knew only a win would be enough to take the title to the last day. United faced Sunderland away after Chelsea had already beaten Liverpool to open up a four point lead. A Nani goal gave United a 1-0 win and the three points that took the title to the last day. Just as in the 2007/08 season United and Chelsea both had a chance of winning the league on the final but this time Chelsea had the advantage going into the last day. They would welcome Wigan to Stamford Bridge while United played Stoke at Old Trafford. It took United almost half an hour to break through the Stoke defence when Darren Fletcher scored as a rebound fell to him and Giggs made it 2-0 before half-time. Second-half goals from Higginbottom (own goal) and Park Ji-Sung made it 4-0 and that's how it finished but Chelsea also beat Wigan (8-0) to finish one point clear of United and deny Sir Alex Ferguson the honour of guiding his team to a fourth successive league crown and that 19th league crown that would move the club above Liverpool and set a new record.

Despite starting the season as United's number one goalkeeper in the absence of an injured van der Sar, by the time we reached the end of the 2009/10 season Ben Foster was seen as third choice behind van der Sar and Kuszczak and was allowed to leave the club just ten days after the end of the season. Foster left Old Trafford in search of first-team football and was sold to Birmingham City for undisclosed fee believed to be around £4million. Foster wasn't the only goalkeeper to leave Old Trafford in the summer of 2010 as young goalkeepers Tom Heaton and Ron-Robert Zieler both left the club on free transfers, joining Cardiff City and Hannover 96 respectively. Ferguson had agreed a deal for Fulham defender Chris Smalling towards the end of January 2010 but the transfer didn't officially go through until the summer of 2010 as United allowed the player to remain with Fulham until the end of the 2009/10 season. Once again the fee wasn't disclosed by either club but United are believed to have paid around £7million for the centre half. Smalling officially became a United player on July 1 2010 and Mexican striker Javier Hernandez become a United player on the same day. The deal for Hernandez had been announced on April 8 2010 after United came to an agreement for the 21 year-old with his club Chivas de Guadalajara. The move for Hernandez was subject to a work permit and United would play a pre-season friendly against Chivas in the build up to 2010/11 season. Hernandez played a half for each side in that game. The final arrival of the summer came with the shock signing of Portuguese player Bebe in a £7.4million deal. The player was signed on the recommendation of Sir Alex Ferguson's former assistant Carlos Queiroz. United agreed to pay the release clause for the player, who only joined Vitoria de Guimaraes five weeks earlier and had signed a five-year deal with the Portuguese side. After a disappointing few years with United, they allowed Serbian midfielder Zoran Tosic to leave the club. Selling him to CSKA Moscow for an undisclosed fee. With all the summer transfer business completed, it was time to get down to the business of football on the pitch.

The competitive action kicked off at Wembley as United once again contested the Community Shield and their opponents were once again Chelsea, who had won the game on penalties the previous season. In a game that pitted two of the biggest title contenders in the last few seasons against each other. United had won three out of the last four Premier League titles and only losing out to Chelsea on a fourth consecutive league title in the previous season (2009/10), United laid down an early marker for a season that would surely see United and Chelsea fighting it out for the major honours once again. Ferguson's team lifted the trophy with a 3-1 win thanks to goals from Valencia, Hernandez striking his first goal in the red of United and the win was wrapped by Berbatov in injury after Kalou pulled one back for Chelsea. The Premier League fixture computer handed United an opening day fixture with Newcastle at Old Trafford, first-half goals from Berbatov and Fletcher put United in control and a third goal came after 85 minutes when Ryan Giggs met a Paul Scholes ball on the volley to keep up his record of scoring in every Premier League season. Next came a trip to Craven Cottage and a 2-2 draw with Fulham, United looked good for the three points when Fulham defender Brede Hangeland put through his own net on 84 minutes but the Norwegian International made amends to equalise for Fulham after 89 minutes. After the draw with Fulham, West Ham visited Old Trafford and were dispatched 3-0 with Rooney scoring from the spot before goals from Nani and Berbatov. After an International break, United travelled to Goodison Park for the first of a Premier League double header against the two Merseyside clubs. Everton dominated the opening exchanges and took the lead on 39 minutes through Steven Pienaar but the lead was short-lived as Fletcher levelled for United just two minutes before half-time. Two minutes after half-time, United were in front when Nani crossed for an unmarked Vidic to head home and Berbatov made it 3-1 just after the hour. United looked to heading for the three points until two 90th minute strikes salvaged a draw for Everton. Leaving United with two home wins and two away draws from their opening four league games of the campaign.

After the draw with Everton, United played out a 0-0 draw with Rangers in the first game of their Champions League campaign as Ferguson looked to take United to a third European Cup triumph under his management and a fourth for the club overall. Ferguson took the opportunity to rest several first-team players in this match against one of the teams he used to play for. There was bad news as winger Antonio Valencia suffered a dislocated and broken left ankle when his studs were caught in the Old Trafford turf during a fair challenge with Rangers defender Kirk Broadfoot. It was expected the injury would rule the Ecuadorian winger out for the rest of the campaign. Up next was the second-half of the Merseyside double header as United welcomed Liverpool to Old Trafford. Dimitar Berbatov was the hero as the Bulgarian scored a hat-trick. Berbatov opened the scoring shortly before half-time when stooping to head home a corner and Berbatov made it 2-0 after controlling a Nani cross and performing an overhead bicycle kick that hit the underside of the crossbar before bouncing into the back of the net. Two goals in six minutes from Steven Gerrard levelled the scores but Berbatov completed his hat-trick on 84 minutes when heading home a cross from John O'Shea. Berbatov became the first United player to score a hat-trick against Liverpool since Stan Pearson in 1946 and the first to do so at Old Trafford since Joe Spence in 1928. Pearson's hat-trick was scored at Maine Road while Old Trafford was being rebuilt after bomb damage in the Second World War. After five league games, United had 11 points and were third in the table, four points behind defending champions and early leaders Chelsea. After successfully defending the League Cup with victory over Aston Villa in the final, Manchester United were looking to become only the second club to win three successive League Cups, after Liverpool achieved the feat in 1983. United started their defence with third round tie away to Championship side Scunthorpe United and Sir Alex Ferguson missed the game as he was watching Champions League opponents Valencia, with Mike Phelan taking over the managerial reigns for game. As usual in the early rounds of the competition, United opted to make a number of changes from their league victory over Liverpool. Scunthorpe took an early lead before goals from two of the players given opportunities scored goals with Darren Gibson equalising before Chris Smalling put United in front. A Michael Owen double and Park Ji-Sung strike put United 5-1 up before a late strike made the score 5-2 and the fourth round pitted United against Wolverhampton Wanderers. The next three league games saw United picking up just three points as they drew

2-2 Bolton, 0-0 with Sunderland and 2-2 with West Brom. After eight league games they had 14 points and sat third in the table, five points behind leaders Chelsea. Meanwhile in the Champions League, two 1-0 wins over Valencia and Bursaspor left United top of their group on seven points, Rangers sat second in the group on five points.

Prior to the Champions League fixture with Bursaspor there was media speculation that Wayne Rooney wasn't willing to sign a new contract with Manchester United and in his pre-match press conference before the game, Ferguson confirmed that 24 year-old striker had expressed a desire to leave Old Trafford. Ferguson stated that he was bemused and disappointed by Rooney's stance who was believed not to be happy by the ambition being shown by United in the transfer market. Rooney wouldn't play in the game against the Turkish side as he had picked up an ankle injury in training. To watch Ferguson in that press conference was like watching a father who had been disappointed by his favourite son. You could clearly tell that he didn't see this coming and while being disappointed with Rooney, he stated that the door was still open for the England striker to sign a new deal and stay at Old Trafford in the long-term. Ferguson confirmed that David Gill had contacted him in the summer to tell that Rooney wouldn't be signing a new deal. Ferguson couldn't believe this news as Rooney had been talking about how he was at the greatest club in the world only months earlier. Just a few days later it was confirmed that Rooney had performed a U-turn and agreed a five-year-contract with Manchester United. On signing the deal, Rooney stated that believed that everyone at the club was 100% committed to maintaining Manchester United's history of challenging for the major honours.

With Rooney's contract sorted, United won their next five games. Starting with a 2-1 over Stoke City at the Britannia Stadium with a double from Javier Hernandez after this United beat Wolves 3-2 in the fourth round of the League Cup. Once again Ferguson rung the changes with Bebe one of those given a first-team opportunity and the Portuguese attacker scored the opening goal but United needed a 90th minute goal from Hernandez to book a fifth round tie away to West Ham. A 2-0 win over Tottenham was followed by a 3-0 win over Bursaspor in Turkey with Gabriel Obertan and Bebe scoring goals after Darren Fletcher opened the scoring just after half-time. These wins were followed by another win over Wolves, this time 2-1 and this time in the league, the game was won by United in 90th minute once again, Park Ji-Sung scoring the late winner this time. The win over Wolves left United with 23 points from their opening 11 games and sitting second in the table, two points behind Chelsea who had played a game less. The next league fixtures saw United playing out two draws, starting with a 0-0 draw with Manchester City at the City of Manchester Stadium, the closest United came to scoring was from a Berbatov overhead kick. Next up was another away game and another draw, this time a 2-2 draw against Aston Villa in a game that United trailed 2-0 before goals from Macheda and captain Nemanja Vidic salvaged a point for Ferguson's team. Next came a 2-0 win over Wigan Athletic in a game that saw the return of Wayne Rooney after a five week absence and his first appearance since agreeing his contract extension. After this it was Rangers at Ibrox and United needed just a point to confirm qualification for the Champions League knockout stages but they took home all three thanks to an 87th minute penalty from Rooney. United would finish the group stages with a 1-1 draw with Valencia to finish unbeaten in the group. After the Champions League win over Rangers, United played host to Blackburn in the league and recorded a 7-1 victory with Dimitar Berbatov scoring five goals for Ferguson's side. United were ahead after just two minutes when Berbatov stuck out a leg six yards from goal to finish after Rooney had flicked on a free-kick from Nani. After being fed by Nani, Park Ji-Sung played a one-two with

Rooney before finishing to make it 2-0. Berbatov got his second when intercepting a poor back-pass. Berbatov completed his second Old Trafford hat-trick of the season to make it 4-0, he started the move in United's half before finishing the move with a effort high into Blackburn's net after a lay back by Nani. Nani then got in on the act to make the score 5-0 after 48 minutes. After 70 minutes, United were 7-0 up and Berbatov had five goals, only the fourth player to score five goals in a Premier League game after Andy Cole, Alan Shearer and Jermaine Defoe. Blackburn defender Christopher Samba scored a late consolation. The next game for United saw their long unbeaten run in the League Cup come to an end as they suffered a 4-0 defeat to West Ham at Upton Park. The game saw former United defender Jonathan Spector scoring twice for the Hammers. After the postponement of their league fixture against Blackpool on December 4 due to a frozen pitch, United went without a league game for two weeks. Allowing both Arsenal and Manchester City to overtake United at the top of the table although Ferguson's men did have games in hand on their rivals.

United's next league game saw them playing Arsenal on December 13 at Old Trafford and a Park Ji-Sung first-half goal gave United a 1-0 win. The win saw United moving to the top of the table, two points above Arsenal and City, with Chelsea a further point back. United still had a game in hand on their rivals. More bad whether saw United's next scheduled league with Chelsea cancelled and rearranged for March 1. Arsenal's game with Stoke was also postponed while Manchester City suffered a defeat to Everton to ensure United were top of the league on Christmas Day for the first time in four seasons. December 19 2010 saw Sir Alex Ferguson become Manchester United's longest-serving manager, passing the previous record of 24 years, 1 month and 13 days previously held by Sir Matt Busby. The first game for Sir Alex Ferguson after becoming the longest-serving manager in the club's history came against Sunderland at Old Trafford on Boxing Day. A double from Berbatov saw United celebrating Ferguson's record with a 2-0 win and the rest of the Boxing Day results saw United staying top of the league, two points clear of City in second but United had two games in hand on their neighbours. Despite City being in second place, Ferguson stated on Christmas Eve that the title race was a three-way battle between United and the two teams from London, Arsenal and Chelsea. The last fixture of 2010 saw United drawing 1-1 with Birmingham City at St Andrews. United led through a Berbatov strike before Birmingham midfielder Lee Bowyer equalised with less than a minute left on the clock. The draw saw United finishing 2010 on top of the table on goal difference from City but they still had two games in hand. January saw the start of United's FA Cup campaign but before that they had two league games against West Brom and Stoke City. Two hard fought victories followed for United as they beat West Brom 2-1 with the opening goal coming from Wayne Rooney, his first strike from open play since March 2010. This was followed by a win over Stoke by the same scoreline with goals from Hernandez and Nani.

The third round of the FA Cup had pitted United against bitter rivals Liverpool at Old Trafford. This was the first time that United had been drawn against Liverpool in the FA Cup in five years and the first time in twelve years that the pair had met at Old Trafford in the oldest cup competition in the world. On that occasion it was two late goals from Yorke and Solskjaer that gave United the win as they went on to lift the cup on their way to the treble. This time it was a goal within the first few minutes that saw United through when Giggs scored from the spot after Berbatov was fouled by Liverpool defender Daniel Agger after just 31 seconds. United travelled to White Hart Lane and had to settle for a 0-0 as they extended their unbeaten league run to 26 games, the club record was 29 games without defeat in the league. Next came Birmingham at Old Trafford in the league and United recorded a 5-0 victory with Dimitar Berbatov scoring his third Old Trafford hat-trick of the season with the other goals coming from Giggs and Nani. After this United travelled to Blackpool for their rearranged fixture and had to stage a comeback to preserve their unbeaten record after falling 2-0 behind in the first-half. Berbatov scored United's first after 72 minutes and two minutes later United were level when Hernandez scored after being released by fellow substitute Giggs. The comeback was complete when Berbatov struck home with left foot on 88 minutes. The win took United five points clear at the top of the table. Arsenal were United's closest rivals, with City six points behind United but City had played a game more while defending champions Chelsea were 10 points behind Ferguson's men. The fourth round of the FA Cup had seen United drawn away to Southampton. Southampton were along with United one of the founders of the Premier League but currently found themselves in the third tier (League One) of English football. Southampton took the lead through Richard Chaplow but this was cancelled out by Michael Owen twenty minutes into the second-half and Hernandez struck the United winner ten minutes later. In the fifth round United were rewarded with a home tie against non-league Crawley Town. Next up United welcomed Aston Villa to Old Trafford looking to equal the club record of 29 league games without defeat and were ahead after just 54 seconds as Rooney controlled a long free-kick from van der Sar over his shoulder before lashing past Brad Friedel in the Aston Villa goal. Rooney got his second and United's in first-half stoppage time, Darren Bent pulled one back for Villa but the two goal lead was soon restored through Vidic. A 3-1 win and United had equalled a club record of 29 league games without defeat. They wouldn't break the record though as they suffered a 2-1 defeat away to Wolves in their next league fixture. The defeat to Wolves came on February 5 2011 and before that the last time this United side had suffered defeat in the league was on April 3 2010 when they lost 2-1 to Chelsea, in a game that would eventually cost them a fourth consecutive league crown. The first defeat of the league season came in the 25th game and left United four points clear of Arsenal and five in front of City who they would face next in the second Manchester Derby of the Premier League season.

Manchester United club captain Gary Neville announced his decision to retire with immediate effect on February 1 2011. Neville was of course a member of the famous class of 92. Neville retired fifth on the list of Manchester United's highest appearance makers after making his debut in 1992 against Torpedo Moscow. Neville was first-choice for Sir Alex Ferguson for over ten years and was appointed club captain in 2005. Neville suffered a broken ankle against Bolton Wanderers in March 2007 and he failed to fully recover from injury and faced competition from Wes Brown, John O'Shea and Rafael for the right-back spot. He made a further 33 appearances for the club after returning from the injury with the last of those games coming against West Brom on New Year's Day 2011.

Wayne Rooney wasn't having the greatest season, going into the second Manchester Derby of the season, Rooney had only netted five league goals before this game against a City team that were looking to challenge United for the league title but Rooney would make his mark on the game to win it for United. Nani had given United the lead just before the half-time break before David Silva equalised as an Edin Dzeko shot found the net off the Spanish midfielder's backside. After the equaliser City looked the better team and more likely to win the game until Rooney struck the winner that shocked everyone inside the ground including Rooney himself and was worthy of winning any game of football. The winning moment came after 78 minutes as Nani's cross from the right flank took a slight deflection which took the ball behind Rooney, who was lurking around the penalty spot but Rooney managed to readjust his body and perform a spectacular overhead kick that flew into the top corner of City net and left Joe Hart with no chance of saving it. The win kept United four points ahead of Arsenal, City were now eight points back and had played a game more than both United and Arsenal. Next was the FA Cup fifth round tie against non-league Crawley Town, the game was decided in United's favour by a rare Wes Brown goal. The defender's strike was only his fifth in 358 games for Manchester United. The reward in the quarter-finals was another home tie, this time against Premier League rivals Arsenal. After the win over Crawley, United resumed their Champions League campaign in France as the played Marseille in the first knockout round first-leg. A tight game with few chances for either side finished 0-0. Meaning only a win would be enough in the second-leg at Old Trafford to take United through to the quarter-finals. Before that though United faced three league games and their FA Cup quarter-final with Arsenal. The first of those three league games, came away to Wigan and United kept their four point advantage at the top of the table with a 4-0 win at the DW Stadium. After dispatching of Wigan with ease, United faced back to back away league games against Chelsea and Liverpool. The match against Chelsea was the one which had originally scheduled for December 19 and despite being put ahead by a 25-yard strike from Wayne Rooney, United suffered only their third defeat of the season (in all competitions). Frank Lampard won the game with a 79th minute penalty for Chelsea and Sir Alex Ferguson's mood wouldn't have been made any better when Nemanja Vidic picked up a second yellow card, meaning he would miss the fixture against Liverpool. After going 29 games without defeat in the Premier League, United suffered another defeat when they travelled to Anfield to face Liverpool. Meaning they had lost three out of their last five games. Dutch forward Dirk Kuyt scored a hat-trick as they beat a United team missing the suspended Vidic 3-1. United remained top of the league despite the defeats to Chelsea and Liverpool but their lead over Arsenal was down to three points and they had played a game more than the Londoners. Next up the two title rivals would meet at Old Trafford in the FA Cup quarter-finals and despite naming a starting line-up that included seven defenders, United had the greater attacking threat and could have won by greater than the two goal margin that they did. Goals from Fabio Da Silva and Wayne Rooney gave United a 2-0 and setup another semi-final with Manchester City after United had beaten their neighbours in the League Cup semis the previous season. After booking their place in the FA Cup semi-finals, in a game that also saw the return of Antonio Valencia as a second-half substitute. Now United welcomed Marseille to Old Trafford looking book their place in the Champions League quarter-finals. Javier Hernandez continued to impress for United in his first season with a double that saw United through. The first came after good work from Giggs and Rooney and Hernandez just had to finish from close range and he made it two with another close range finish before a Wes Brown own goal meant a nervy finish for Ferguson and the Old Trafford faithful but United held on and were drawn with Chelsea in the quarter-finals, a repeat of the 2008 final.

After their two cup wins, United were looking to get back to winning ways in a league fixture against Bolton at Old Trafford. United won the game 1-0 but had to wait until the 88th minute to see Dimitar Berbatov score the winning goal. His first goal since scoring twice in the 3-2 comeback win over Blackpool. The win along with Arsenal being held to a 2-2 draw with West Brom, saw United move five points clear at the top of the table but Arsenal still had a game in hand on United. Next a Wayne Rooney hat-trick inspired a United comeback as they visited Struggling West Ham, the Hammers were fighting against relegation and two first-half penalties both converted by Mark Noble gave them a 2-0 lead. A second-half free-kick curled in by Rooney started the comeback before he powered in a low shot to equalise. The free-kick was scored after 65 minutes and on 73 minutes United were level before Rooney completed his hat-trick as he converted a United penalty after 79 minutes to make it 3-2 and Hernandez added a fourth for United. After the game Rooney was charged by the FA for using offensive, insulting and/or abusive directly into the camera after scoring his and United's third goal. He was banned for two games, meaning he would miss a league fixture against Fulham and the FA Cup semi-final against Manchester City. The win over the Hammers along with Arsenal failing to beat Blackburn moved United seven points clear at the top of the table with eight league fixtures left for United. Ferguson was once again taking his team to London as they visited Stamford Bridge for first-leg of the quarter-finals in the Champions League. Rooney was set to serve a domestic ban but was available for this Champions League game and he scored the only goal of the game, the goal coming after 24 minutes following great work by Giggs and Carrick. Rooney wouldn't be missed in their league encounter with Fulham with goals from Berbatov and Valencia giving them a 2-0 win. Valencia striking his first goal since returning from his horrific injury. After the win against Fulham, United faced Chelsea in their quarter-final second-leg in the Champions League before facing Manchester City in the FA Cup semi-final. After winning the first-leg 1-0, United held a slight advantage over their Premier League rivals. United's advantage was doubled moments before half-time when Hernandez finished from close range and Chelsea's task was made even harder with the sending off of Ramires following a second yellow card. Didier Drogba levelled the scores on the night after 77 minutes but within a minute United's two goal aggregate lead was restored when Park Ji-Sung score after he was found by Giggs and the South Korean made no mistake. That was the way score finished and United progressed to the semi-final where they would face German side Schalke 04. After progressing in the Champions League, United faced City at Wembley looking to book their place in the FA Cup final. Ferguson opted for Berbatov in place of the suspended Wayne Rooney and the Bulgarian missed two golden chances as United dominated the first-half. They were made to pay for those missed chances when Yaya Toure put City ahead on 52 minutes and United's hopes of a comeback were ended when they had Paul Scholes sent off for a high and mistimed challenge on City full-back Pablo Zabaleta. The defeat ended any hopes United had of repeating the treble of 99 but they could still complete a Premier League and Champions League double just as they had in the 2007/08 season. United missed an opportunity to go nine points clear at the top of the table when they faced Newcastle and had to settle for a 0-0 draw. Javier Hernandez was the hero for United in their next league game against Everton when he headed home a cross from Antonio Valencia in the 83rd minute to give United a 1-0 win and keep them six points clear of Chelsea with four games to go. This meant Ferguson and his team needed just seven points from a possible twelve to become champions of England for a record 19th time.

Before they could close in further on their 19th league crown, United faced Schalke in the semi-final first-leg of the Champions League with the final set to take place at Wembley Stadium. United travelled to Germany for the first-leg and came away with a 2-0 win to all but book their place in the final. Barring a disaster in the return leg, Sir Alex Ferguson would guide his Manchester United team to a third final in four seasons. The goals came Giggs and Rooney but the scoreline would have been even better for United if it wasn't for Schalke and Germany goalkeeper Manuel Neuer pulling off a string of fine saves. United's lead at the top had been cut down to three points by the time they faced Arsenal in their fourth to last league game of the season on Sunday May 1 2011. Arsenal's title challenge had all but ended following a 2-1 defeat to Bolton in their previous league game and Chelsea were the only real challengers to United. Both teams had penalty shouts turned down by referee Chris Foy and it was Arsenal who won 1-0 with Aaron Ramsey scoring the winner in the 56th minute. United were still in the driving seat but couldn't afford to drop many more points in the three remaining league games. United's place in the Champions League final was confirmed as they bounced back from the defeat to Arsenal with a 4-1 win over Schalke 04 that gave them a 6-1 aggregate win. Goals from Valencia and Darren Gibson gave United a 2-0 lead half an hour into the game. Jose Manuel Jurado pulled one back on 35 minutes before two second-half strikes from Anderson booked their place in the final at Wembley Stadium. In that final United would have the opportunity to avenge their 2009 final defeat to Barcelona. Before that United would have to navigate their remaining league games to confirm a 12th Premier League title and 19th league crown overall.

For the second season running Manchester United and Chelsea met at Old Trafford with the winner almost being assured of the league title. Coming into the game, United held a three point advantage over Chelsea and had one goal advantage on goal difference. Sir Alex Ferguson stated before the game that a win for United would all but end Chelsea's hopes of retaining the league crown. United wasted no time to exert their authority over Chelsea when Hernandez struck with just 36 seconds on the clock and Nemanja Vidic added a second on 23 minutes, heading in from a Ryan Giggs cross after a short corner. Hernandez spurned two good chances to extend the lead and put the game to bed. Chelsea got a goal back thanks to a Frank Lampard goal on 68 minutes, the goal came against the run of play and United held on for the win to move six points clear of their opponents with two games remaining. A point in their next game again Blackburn and United would be champions again. Despite all the success United had enjoyed under Sir Alex Ferguson they never did things the easy away, and this was no different as they fell behind and Blackburn could have added to their goal before United were given an opportunity to get back in the game and get the point they needed. That came when Blackburn keeper Paul Robinson was adjudged to have brought down Hernandez and Rooney converted the spot-kick for his 11th league goal of season. Both teams played out the game to a draw as neither wanted to risk losing the one point they had. The final whistle blew and United had won their 12th Premier League title under guidance of Sir Alex Ferguson and a 19th league title overall that knocked Liverpool off their perch as kings of English football. Something Sir Alex Ferguson is reported to have said he wanted to do when he arrived in November 1986. The final league game of the season saw United hosting Blackpool and for a second time this season United performed a comeback against the Seasiders as they recorded a 4-2 victory. Park Ji-Sung gave United the lead before goals from Charlie Adam and Gary Taylor-Fletcher gave Blackpool a 2-1 lead after 57 minutes. Four minutes later United were level as Anderson scored before an Ian Evatt own goal and Michael Owen strike gave United a 4-2 win. The three points meant United finished with 80 points, finishing nine points ahead of both Chelsea and Manchester City.

With the Premier League title in the bag, United faced Barcelona in the Champions League final at Wembley Stadium looking to gain revenge for their final defeat to the same opponents in 2009. Barcelona like United were looking to complete a League and European Cup double. Ferguson looked to outplay Barcelona with an attacking approach. Playing two up front after looking to flood the midfield in 2009. Wayne Rooney scored after 34 minutes to cancel out Pedro's opener and United reached half-time drawing 1-1 despite being outplayed by a Barcelona team that was dominating the midfield. Barcelona enjoyed 68% possession and had 22 shots on United's goal compared to United's 4 attempts on the Barcelona goal. Barcelona continued to dominate in the second-half and retook the lead when Messi shot past van der Sar from 20 yards. Van der Sar did his best to keep United in the game, making a string of saves before the third goal for Barcelona arrived through David Villa. United attempted to get back in the game but they couldn't live with Barcelona on the night. As in 2009, they lost to one of the best teams on the planet and you have to feel whatever tactics Ferguson used in those two finals, Barcelona would have won. Facing anyone but Barcelona and United may have had three Champions League successes in four seasons and five European Cups overall

Chapter Seventeen: Head to Head with City

Despite regaining the Premier League title at the end of the 2010/11 season. Sir Alex Ferguson would have been disappointed to see his team fall short in the FA Cup and Champions League. Losing out in the FA Cup semi-finals to neighbours Manchester City and being outplayed in the Champions League final against Barcelona. As well losing the game against Barcelona, that final also saw Paul Scholes and Edwin van der Sar making their final appearances in a Manchester United shirt as they both decided to call time on their playing careers. Van der Sar had confirmed in January that he intended to retire at the end of the season after media reports came out stating that this was the Dutchman's intentions. While Scholes waited until after the Champions League to announce his decision. Paul Scholes joined the United coaching staff after his retirement and Ferguson wanted van der Sar to do the same but the Dutchman wanted to spend time with his family after deciding to retire. Van der Sar was earmarked as a potential replacement for Peter Schmeichel when he left the club at the end of the 1998/99 but the van der Sar had already agreed to move to Italian giants Juventus. Ferguson finally got his man in 2005 and in his six seasons with United, van der Sar made 266 appearances and helped United to eight major honours, including four Premier league titles, a Champions League and a FIFA World Club Cup. As soon as van der Sar announced his intention to retire, Unite were linked with a number of goalkeepers including Manuel Neuer and David De Gea. Danish goalkeeper Anders Lindegaard joined

United in January 2011 but it was expected that Ferguson would make another signing in that department and Lindegaard would be his number two goalkeeper.

As well as losing the experience of both Scholes and van der Sar, Ferguson decided now was the time to allow experience defenders Wes Brown and John O'Shea to leave the club. Both were sold to Sunderland. They joined former United defender Steve Bruce at Sunderland, both Brown and O'Shea came through the join academy at United and both made close to 400 appearances in the United first-team, helping the club to a number of major honours. They were joined in leaving club by Gabriel Obertan and Owen Hargreaves. Despite an encouraging first season at United, when he made 34 appearances and helped the club to the double of Premier League and Champions League, Hargreaves would only go on to make a further 5 appearances and was allowed to leave the club at the end of his contract. Hargreaves must go down as one of Sir Alex Ferguson's most disappointing signings. There were three new arrivals at Old Trafford as Ferguson once again look to launch a quadruple attack on the major honours available to Manchester United. The first of those came with the arrival of defender Phil Jones from Blackburn. 19 year-old Jones joined United having come through the Blackburn Rovers youth academy and had made 40 appearances for Blackburn before his move to Old Trafford for a fee believed to worth £16.5million and signing a five-year-deal with United. Ferguson had reportedly been impressed with Jones commitment and the leadership skills he had shown despite his young age. Ten days after signing Jones, he was joined in the Old Trafford ranks by Aston Villa winger Ashley Young. Young joined for a fee believed to be between £15million and £20million after five seasons with Villa. Atletico Madrid keeper David De Gea was believed to be the number one target to replace the retired van der Sar as Ferguson's first choice goalkeeper and on June 29 2011 Manchester United completed the signing of De Gea. The fee for De

Gea was believed to £18.9million, making him the second most expensive goalkeeper at the time. De Gea joined United having made 85 appearances for the Atletico Madrid first-team after coming through the club's youth system. De Gea helped Atletico win the Europa League in his first season in the first-team and played every league game for the club in the 2010/11 season. United prepared for the 2011/12 season with six pre-season friendlies including a game New York Cosmos at Old Trafford on August 5. This game was a testimonial for the retired Paul Scholes. Scholes played in the game and opened the scoring in a 6-0 win with a trademark 25 yard strike. Two days after the Scholes testimonial, United travelled to Wembley to face Manchester City in the Community Shield. After losing to City in the FA Cup semi-final this was an early opportunity for United to get one over on their neighbours. After finishing third the previous season, City were looking to challenge United for the Premier League title which resulted in Ferguson referring them as the noisy neighbours. The game at Wembley saw Ferguson handing competitive debuts to four players. De Gea started in goal while Ashley Young was also handed a start. Phil Jones and Tom Cleverley both made appearances from the bench. Cleverley had been at United since the year 2000 when he joined from Bradford City as an 11 year-old. Cleverley had been sent out on loan on three occasions to gain first-team experience and was identified by Ferguson as the man who could replace the retired Scholes. At half-time United were 2-0 down to their rivals and Ferguson made three half-time changes. With Jones and Cleverley both making their first competitive appearances for Manchester United. Within thirteen minutes of the restart United were level after goals from Smalling and Nani. Then in the fourth minute of stoppage time, Nani scored his second of the game to secure the first piece of silverware of the 2011/12 season. The winning goal came as Nani charged down a clearance from City defender Vincent Kompany on the halfway-line before sprinting through on goal and rounding Joe Hart in City's goal and sliding the ball into an empty net.

Unite started their defence of the Premier League with five consecutive wins, scoring 21 goals in the process. The opening round of fixtures saw United travelling to The Hawthorns to face West Brom and picking up a 2-1 win with the winner coming thanks 81st minute own goal from Steven Reid after Shane Long had equalised Wayne Rooney's opener. Next United faced Tottenham in their first home league game of the season and despite taking an hour to find the breakthrough, United won the game 3-0 with goals from Danny Welbeck, Anderson and Rooney. Though only two games into the season, United and City were already fighting it at the top of the table. United watched City beat Tottenham 5-1 before their next game against Arsenal at Old Trafford and Ferguson's men responded in perfect fashion with an 8-2 win over their North London visitors. Welbeck opened the scoring just as he had the previous week against Tottenham and within 20 minutes of the opener, United were 3-0 up. Theo Walcott pulled one back on the stroke of half-time for Arsenal. The score stayed at 3-1 until the 64th minute when Wayne Rooney's second goal of the game was the first of three goals in six minutes as Rooney's goal was followed by goals from Nani and Park Ji-Sung to make the score 6-1. Robin Van Persie got another goal back for Arsenal on 74 minutes but an 84th minute Rooney penalty sealed his hat-trick before an 90th minute goal from Young (his second of the game) completed the scoring and the result saw United go top of the table on goal difference. Next United travelled to the Reebok Stadium to face Bolton Wanderers looking to go back to the top of the table after dropping to third in the table after both City and Chelsea had already recorded wins earlier in the day. A 5-0 win took United back to the top with a double from Javier Hernandez and a second successive hat-trick for Rooney. Hernandez opened the scoring after five minutes but Ferguson suffered a blow when he had to withdraw Cleverley following a challenge from Bolton forward Kevin Davies. The hat-trick for Rooney was his seventh for United. The draw for the Champions League group stage saw United drawn with two previous opponents in Benfica and Swiss champions Basel and one new opponent in the shape of Romanian champions Otelul Galati. The opening group game saw United travelling to Lisbon to face Benfica and the game ended in a 1-1 draw with both goals coming in the first-half. Ferguson opted to start with Lindegaard in goal for this game and the Dane made some fine saves but could not stop Benfica taking the lead after 24 minutes through Oscar Cardozo. Three minutes before half-time Giggs levelled as he cut inside from the right and fired in a 20 yard strike. After beginning their Champions League campaign with a draw, United returned to league action with the visit of Chelsea to Old Trafford, meaning the first three home games of the season had been against London sides. Ferguson restored De Gea in goal for this game after opting for Lindegaard in Lisbon. Chris Smalling put United ahead after eight minutes, as he rose unmarked to head in an Ashley Young free-kick. We reached half-time with the score at 3-0 to United after Nani had fired the ball into the top corner from 30 yards and this was followed by a Rooney goal after a good run from Jones. Fernando Torres got one back for Chelsea only a minute after the restart but it was United who came closest to adding to the score as Nani hit a shot against the crossbar that resulted in a penalty as he attempted to gather the rebound. Rooney stepped up to take the penalty but slipped when taking and shot wide. Chelsea's best chance of a second goal came when Torres shimmied past De Gea but shot wide of an open goal. The third round of the League Cup pitted United against Leeds in a game played at Elland Road on September 20 and United left Yorkshire with a 3-0 win in a game that Ferguson handed a first start to 18 year-old defender Zeki Fryers and all the goals came in the first-half through Owen (2) and Giggs. In the fourth round were drawn away to Aldershot Town. Next United travelled to Stoke and dropped their first points of the league season as Peter Crouch levelled for Stoke after Nani had given United the lead. The draw against Stoke was the first time United had failed to beat this opposition in the Premier League after winning there six previous encounters. After the draw with Stoke, United faced Basel in their second group game in the Champions League. Two goals from Danny Welbeck in the space of two minutes looked to have given United control of the game as they looked for their first win in this season's Champions League. Basel fought back though and were level on the hour mark and a 76th minute penalty from Alexander Frei gave the Swiss champions a 3-2 lead and United were looking at taking just one point from their opening two games. A 90th minute Ashley Young header from a Nani cross point rescued a point for United and preserved their 18 month unbeaten home record. Two points from their opening two games, left United third in the group ahead of back-to-back games against Romanian side Otelul Galati.

After successive draws at home and in Europe, United returned to winning ways as Norwich City visited Old Trafford and a rare Saturday 3pm kick-off for United in the Premier League era of Sky Sports coverage. Norwich spurned several good chances especially through Anthony Pilkington and United took the lead on 68 minutes when a Ryan Giggs corner was eventually headed in by Anderson. After United took the lead, Pilkington saw an effort tipped onto the crossbar by Lindegaard who was making his Premier League debut. The win was sealed on 87 minutes when Welbeck scored after exchanging passes with Park Ji-Sung. After the win over Norwich, the majority of Manchester United's first-team were on International duty and when they returned they would face Liverpool at Anfield. United started the better side but Liverpool gradually came into the game and took the lead after 60 minutes when Steven Gerrard scored from a free-kick on the edge of the area after Rio Ferdinand had brought down Charlie Adam.

The goal ensured that this wouldn't be the first 0-0 draw between the two sides but Liverpool's joy was soon over when 10 minutes later Javier Hernandez headed home to level. Both sides looked for a winner but the game would end one goal apiece and one point apiece. The point moved United a point clear of City before their neighbours moved above above them with a 4-1 win over Aston Villa. The Liverpool game though was overshadow by claims that Patrice Evra had been racially abused by Liverpool's Luis Suarez.

The incident that brought the complaint took place as Evra was marking Suarez as Liverpool prepared to take a corner in the 62nd minute. In the 58th minute a foul was given against Suarez as he kicked Evra on the knee. Suarez won the 62nd minute corner and jogged into the penalty area. Now marking Suarez for the impending corner, Evra asked Suarez why he had kicked him to which Suarez responded "because you black" and Evra responds to that by saying "say it to me again, I'm going to kick you". To this Suarez says "I don't speak to blacks", to this Evra says "Ok, now I'm going to punch you". Suarez responds to this by repeatedly calling Evra blackie, he says "Ok, blackie, blackie, blackie. As Suarez is speaking he pinches Evra's forearm and as referee Andre Marriner stops play, Suarez uses the term "negro" to Evra, which prompts an angry reaction from Evra and he tells the referee he has been racially abused. Marriner tries to calm the situation and as the players walked away Suarez puts his hand on the back of Evra's head but the defender knocks his arm back. So Marriner intervenes again, Evra says he does want Suarez to touch him. To which Suarez responds "Why, blackie?" Evra is later booked following an exchange with Dirk Kuyt which results with Evra shoving Kuyt in the chest. Evra is warned to calm down by Ryan Giggs and Evra tells Giggs he's been racially abused. As Evra and his United team-mates return to the United dressing room at full-time, Evra is clearly agitated. Four players, Nani, Valencia, Hernandez and Anderson all testify that Suarez would not talk to Evra because he was black. Valencia and Anderson tell Evra to speak to Sir Alex Ferguson. After Evra speaks with Ferguson they head to the referee's office where Ferguson tells Marriner that his player has been called a racially abused by one of the Liverpool players. Evra proceeds to give his account of events and Ferguson says that Manchester United want to make a formal complaint. Marriner has asked fourth official Phil Dowd to make notes of the exchange and assures Ferguson and Evra that he will include the incident in his official report when he files it with the FA. Liverpool's team administration manager Ray Haughan was in the tunnel and overheard the conversation in the referee's room and goes to tell the Liverpool team management. He tells Damian Comolli and Kenny Dalglish that Ferguson has alleged that Suarez called Evra "a nigger five times". Comolli a fluent Spanish speaker talks to Suarez to get his version of events. Suarez says that nothing untoward has happened, but admits to using the term "negro" in response to Evra saying "Don't touch me, South American". Comolli informs Dalglish of Suarez's comments before Dowd arrives to ask Dalglish and Suarez to come to the referee's room. Dalglish arrives to speak with Marriner and Dowd without Suarez and Marriner tells Dalglish the substance of Evra's allegations and warns the Liverpool manager that a formal complaint has been made before Dalglish leaves. A few minutes after Dalglish has left the referee's room, Comolli arrives to relay his conversation with Suarez to Marriner and Dowd. Comolli says Suarez said "Tue s negro" to Evra. In that English that is "You are black" and Comolli claims there has been a mistranslation and Suarez did not use the term "nigger".

Evra is asked to do an interview by a French journalist working for Canal+. Before the interview proceeds, the journalist can see that Evra is upset and asks him why, to which the defender explains that he has been racially abused. The journalist interviews Evra and Evra says he was abused "10 times". Marriner writes up his match report that evening, including an Extraordinary Incident Report Form where he details allegations against Suarez, using Dowd's handwritten notes. Suarez becomes aware of Evra's allegations on French television and posts messages on his Facebook, personal website and Twitter account saying he is upset by the accusations and he has always respected and respects everybody. One month after the game on November 16 2011, Surez was charged by the FA after an investigation. Suarez was charged with "abusive and/or insulting words and/or behaviour contrary to FA rules, including a reference to the ethnic origin and/or colour and/or race of Patrice Evra". Liverpool later released a statement saying that Suarez would plead not guilty and that Liverpool football club would remain fully supportive of their player. On December 20 2011, the FA concluded a seven-day hearing and handed an eight-match ban to Suarez and fined him £40,000 for racially abusing Evra. On December 31 2011, the FA released their findings in a 115-page report. In it the FA says that Suarez had damaged the image of English football around the world and while finding Evra to be a credible witness. They declared that they had found Suarez's evidence to unreliable and inconsistent with the video footage. Suarez was warned that two similar offences in the future could lead to a permanent suspension. Suarez accepted his ban but reiterated that he felt he had done nothing wrong. Following the draw with Liverpool, United travelled to Romanian to face Otelul Galati in their third game of the Champions League group stages. United were still looking for their first win in this seasons competition after draws with Benfica and Basel. They won the game 2-0 thanks to two second-half penalties from Rooney but had Vidic sent-off. After that win they welcomed City to Old Trafford in the first Manchester Derby of the league season and despite starting the game the better, it would be City who took the lead through Mario Balotelli. The score remained at 1-0 until half-time as United continued to have the better of the play. Two minutes into the second-half United were reduced to 10 ten men when Jonny Evans saw red for a challenge on Balotelli near the edge of the area. Balotelli added a second and Sergio Aguero made it three nil to City after 69 minutes. Darren Fletcher pulled one back on 81 minutes and despite being down to ten men, United pushed for a second goal and came close when a Ashley Young free-kick found Chris Smalling but he was unable to direct the ball towards the net. As United tried to get back in the game in the final minutes, City looked to hit United on the break and scored three more goals to give them a 6-1 win and a five point lead at the top of the Premier League table. The defeat was United's first home defeat since losing to Chelsea in April 2010. United bounced back from the defeat to City with a 3-0 win over Aldershot Town in the fourth round of the League Cup. With goals from Berbatov, Owen and Valencia. The draw for the next round pitted United against Crystal Palace. The return to league action saw United travelling to Goodison Park, a venue that they had struggled at in recent seasons but came away with the three points on this occasion as Javier Hernandez converted a cross from Evra to give Ferguson's side a one nil win. The win over Everton was the first of four wins without conceding a goal. The next one came with a 2-0 win over Otelul Galati that took United top of their Champions League group. The next two league games saw United picking up 1-0 wins over Sunderland and Swansea. The game against Sunderland saw Wes Brown and John O'Shea returning to Old Trafford for the first time. Brown didn't have the best of returns as he deflected a cross into his own net to hand United the three points.

The game against Sunderland was United's 11th league game of the season and after 11 games, they were second in the table, five points behind their neighbours City. Next up was matchday five in the Champions League group stage and United welcomed Benfica to Old Trafford and played out a 2-2 draw with the Portuguese side. Benfica took a 1-0 lead thanks to a third minute own goal from Phil Jones. Berbatov levelled for United on the half-hour mark and on 59 minutes United went ahead thanks to a Darren Fletcher strike. United weren't ahead for long though as Pablo Aimar equalised for Benfica within a minute. The point left United second in the group and left Ferguson's side needing a positive result in their final group game away to Basel. Next up was a home league game against Newcastle United and after a uneventful first-half, United took the lead after 49 minutes when Rooney took a free-kick near the area. Rooney struck the free-kick against the wall and the ball bounced back to him and he hit the ball towards goal again to see it deflect off a defender before hitting Hernandez and ending up in the back of Newcastle's net. Newcastle levelled on 64 minutes when they were awarded a spot kick after Rio Ferdinand brought down Hatem Ben Arfa and Demba Ba converted the penalty and that's the way the scored stayed as United drew a second successive game. After the draw with Newcastle, United welcomed Crystal Palace to Old Trafford for the League Cup quarter-finals. A much changed United side which included the Da Silva twins, Darren Gibson, Macheda and Mame Biram Diouf struggled to break down the defence of Championship side Crystal Palace and the visitors took the lead on 65 minutes through Darren Ambrose. The lead lasted just four minutes as United won a penalty after Macheda was fouled, the Italian took the penalty himself and equalised. Despite increasing pressure from United, the tie went into extra-time and eight minutes into extra-time Glenn Murray scored a second for Palace and the game ended 2-1 and it was Crystal Palace who would go through to the semi-finals. After the League Cup exit at the hands of Crystal Palace, United travelled to Villa Park, a ground where United seemed to enjoy playing, having a good record at the groud whether it be against Villa or in FA Cup semi-finals played at the ground. That good record continued as United came away with a 1-0 victory with defender Phil Jones scoring his first United goal as he converted a cross from Nani. The victory over Villa sent United and their fans into the crucial Champions League game against Basel in high spirits. United needed a point to progress to the knockout round but fell behind to a 9th minute strike from Marco Streller and the situation was made worse for United just before half-time when they lost Nemanja Vidic to what would turn out to be a cruciate knee ligament injury. Despite hoping that the injury would only keep his centre-half out for a few weeks. Ferguson later confirmed that the Serbian was likely to be out for the rest of the season. Alexander Frei scored a second on 84 minutes and despite a second goal in two games for Jones when he scored on 89 minutes. United suffered a defeat that saw them finishing third in a group they were expected to stroll through after appearing in three of the last four finals. The third placed finish would see United dropping into the Europa League (formerly UEFA Cup), playing in the competition for the first time since the 1995/96 season.

After a disappointing few weeks that had seen United knocked out of the League Cup and suffering humiliation in the Champions League by finishing third in their group and now entering the Europa League in the second-half of the season rather than competing for a fourth Champions League success. They looked to finish 2011 on a high note in the five remaining league games of the year. This started with a fixture against Wolves at Old Trafford. United started the better and were two goals up after half-an-hour with goals from Nani and Rooney. Steven Fletcher pulled one back two minutes into the second-half before Nani and Rooney both notched their second goals of the game to give United a 4-1 win. As well as United winning, there was also a defeat for City against Chelsea, meaning that the gap at the top of the league was reduced to two points. The win over Wolves was followed by three wins without conceding a goal and scoring 12 goals at the other end. The first of those came with a 2-0 win over Queens Park Rangers at Loftus Road with goals from Rooney and Carrick. After the win over QPR, United faced another game in London as they played Fulham at Craven Cottage and came away with a 5-0 win with five different goalscorers including Ryan Giggs. A goal for Giggs meant that the Welshman had scored in all 20 Premier League seasons to date. Welbeck, Nani, Rooney and Berbatov were United's other goalscorers. There were two games remaining on United's fixture for 2011 both at home starting with the visit of Wigan Athletic on Boxing Day. Another win and another five goals without reply as United were helped by the sending-off of Wigan striker Conor Sammon with the score at 1-0. Park Ji-Sung had given United an early lead before Sammon received his marching orders. Dimitar Berbatov helped himself to a hat-trick with the other goal being scored Valencia. The win over Wigan and a draw for City away to West Brom saw the two Manchester clubs level on points going into United's last league fixture of 2011. The final game of the year came on New Year's Eve and Sir Alex Ferguson's 70th birthday but it wasn't a happy one for the manager as he saw his side suffer a 3-2 defeat. Injury problems for Ferguson, saw him using Valencia and Carrick in defence, while Rafael and Park Ji-Sung formed an unlikely partnership in the centre of United's midfield. Yakubu struck either side of half-time for Blackburn to give them a 2-0 lead. Berbatov struck twice to bring United level and make it six goals in three games for the Bulgarian and many would have expected United to win the game from here but it was Grant Hanley who struck a winner for Blackburn ten minutes from time and stopped United finishing 2011 on top of the league. The only positive for United fans was the following day, City also suffered a defeat away to Sunderland. The first game of 2012 saw United travelling to St James Park and Newcastle United looking to bounce back from the defeat to Blackburn and keep pace with City at the top of the league. United struggled and suffered a 3-0 defeat with Phil Jones scoring a late own goal. The defeat paired with a 3-0 win over Liverpool for Manchester City left United three points behind their City rivals ahead of an FA Cup third round tie against City.

United suffered FA Cup defeat to City in the semi-finals in the 2010/11 season, City went on to win the cup and United were given an opportunity to knock the holders in the third round. Manchester United had a new signing on the bench, the name of Paul Scholes was on the United team-mate, six months after Scholes had taken the decision to retire. Since his retirement Scholes had been on the coaching staff at Old Trafford and had taken part in some first-team training sessions and several senior players and Ferguson himself felt that Scholes could still make a contribution to the first-team. Though the players didn't know that Scholes was returning to the playing ranks until they saw the midfielder changing into his kit in the dressing-room. Another reason for the return of Scholes was injury and illness to Tom Cleverly and Darren Fletcher. Two players that had been earmarked as potential replacements for Scholes in United's engine room but both had been absent for much of the season. By the time Scholes entered the game in the 59th minute, United were leading 3-1 and City were down to ten-men following the dismissal of captain Vincent Kompany after 12 minutes for a two-footed on Nani. By the time Kompany saw red United were already 1-0 up after a 10th minute goal from Rooney. Welbeck made it two for United on the half-hour mark and Rooney got a second before half-time to give United a 3-0 lead over the tem-man City. The third goal came as United were awarded a spot-kick, Rooney saw his penalty saved but headed the ball home on the rebound. City hit back in the second-half with two goals but were unable to get the equaliser that would force a replay. Scholes showed he hadn't lost any of his passing ability in his 30 minutes on the pitch but was someway short of the required fitness levels. United's reward for the victory over their rivals was another away trip to another bitter rival in Liverpool. United earnt their first league win of 2012 with a 3-0 win over Bolton. United created a number of first-half opportunities and Wayne Rooney saw a penalty saved for the second consecutive game but Scholes opened the scoring for United on the stroke of half-time when he stroked home a cross from Rooney. Welbeck and Carrick goals in the second-half completed the three goal win. The next two games for United would see them travelling to two of their rivals, firstly meeting Arsenal in the league and Liverpool in the FA Cup. Looking to complete a league double over Arsene Wenger's side following their 8-2 win at Old Trafford earlier in the season, United took the lead the on the stroke of half-time as Antonio Valencia met a Ryan Giggs cross at the far post. Arsenal improved after the break and despite missing a chance to level, Robin Van Persie did so on 71 minutes but it would be United who took the three points as Valencia ghosted through the Arsenal defence to setup up Welbeck who lashed home the winner. The win gave United their 18th win in 40 Premier League encounters with Arsenal. As United faced Liverpool in the fourth round of the FA Cup, the focus was on United left-back Patrice Evra as United played at Anfield for the first time since the Evra-Suarez affair. Suarez wasn't involved in the game as he was still serving his eight-game ban, but the Anfield faithful let Evra know their feelings towards him. After the draw in that Premier League game it was Liverpool who got the better of this cup tie to end United's hopes of progressing in the competition. United hadn't won the FA Cup since beating Millwall in 2004 and hadn't reached the final since they faced Chelsea in 2007. United went into the game without Rooney, Jones and Nani who had all picked up knocks against Arsenal while Rio Ferdinand was only fit enough for a place on the bench. Where he was joined by Berbatov and Hernandez as Ferguson opted for Welbeck to lead his attack following recent goals against City and Arsenal. Also on the bench were youngsters Michael Keane and Paul Pogba. Daniel Agger put Liverpool in front after 21 minutes before Park Ji-Sung levelled on 39 minutes. The winner for Liverpool came on 88 minutes through Dutchman Dirk Kuyt. United made it three wins out of four in January with a 2-0 win over Stoke with both goals coming from the spot. As Hernandez and Berbatov both netted penalties either side of half-time. The 2-0 win for United and a 1-0 defeat for City away to Everton, meant that the two city rivals were once again level on points but City had the superior goal difference that kept them top of the league.

Sir Alex Ferguson took his side to Stamford Bridge in the first fixture of February looking to make it four consecutive league wins after the back-to-back defeats to Blackburn and Newcastle at the beginning of 2012. Stamford Bridge hadn't been a happy ground for United and Ferguson in the last decade and they looked like coming away nothing again as they fell three goals down after 50 minutes. Chelsea's three goals came in a fifteen minute spell either side of half-time. United found their way back into the game courtesy of two spot-kicks awarded by referee Howard Webb and Wayne Rooney got over his recent penalty woes to convert both. Before substitute Hernandez headed United level on 84 minutes but they had to thank keeper De Gea as he twice saved United in the final minutes to earn the point. In the aftermath of the game, United would look on it as a point gained but ultimately it could be viewed as two points dropped. Next United faced another rival in Liverpool and a game that saw Evra and Suarez coming face-to-face for the first time and the positive result in the game was overshadowed by what happened before the game kicked off. As before every Premier League fixtures the two teams lined up to shake hands and Suarez refused to shake hands with United captain on the day Evra. The game reached 0-0 at half-time and there was an apparent bust-up in the tunnel at the interval. United won the game thanks to a Wayne Rooney double in the space of three minutes at the start of the second-half. Suarez gave Liverpool hope with ten minutes to play but United held on for the three points and the win moved United to the top of the league if only for 24 hours with City in action and winning the following day. The game against Liverpool was played on February 11 and United wouldn't be back in league action until February 26 when they

244

would face Norwich but before that they faced both legs in their Europa League round of 32 tie against Ajax with the first-leg taking place in Amsterdam. A 2-0 win in Amsterdam helped United book a tie with Athletic Bilbao in the round of 16. The 2-0 win helped United to a 3-2 aggregate win despite losing their fourth game of the season at Old Trafford. After winning through in the Europa League, United faced back-to-back away games in the Premier League against Norwich City and Tottenham. They secured two wins from these two away games with a 2-1 win over Norwich and a 3-1 win at White Hart Lane over Tottenham. The goals against Norwich came from the two old men of the team in Scholes and Giggs. The following week United travelled to Tottenham and second-half goals from Rooney and Ashley Young (2) gave United the points. City maintained a two point advantage at the top of the table as they mirrored United's wins. After the back-to-back away wins in the league, United welcomed Athletic Bilbao to Old Trafford in the first-leg of the round of 16 tie in the Europa League. The two sides have only met once before, in the European Cup in 1956/57 season but the Spanish were playing at Old Trafford for the first time as United's home game on that occasion was played at Maine Road because the floodlights at Old Trafford were not equipped at the time. Wayne Rooney gave United the lead on 22 minutes before an impressive Bilbao side scored three goals without reply and United needed a 90th minute strike from Rooney to salvage any hope of progressing in the competition. Following the loss to Bilbao, United welcomed West Brom to Old Trafford and another Rooney double gave United a 2-0 win and the three points. That win took United top of the league by one point with City in action the following day and United stayed there as City suffered a 1-0 defeat to Swansea. On the back of this United travelled to Bilbao looking to overturn their first-leg defeat and progress to the last eight of the Europa League, they needed to win by two goals to do so but were outclassed by Bilbao and lost the game 2-1 to go out 5-3 on aggregate. Wayne Rooney scored his third goal of the tie with a strike from 25 yards but this was a mere consolation as Ferguson's side were knocked out of a second European competition in one season and were left with just the Premier League title to aim for.

With ten games remaining in the league campaign, United sat one point ahead of their City rivals but City held an advantage on goal difference which could be crucial come the end of the season. The first of those ten games saw United on the road. Travelling to the Midlands to face Wolves. In a fixture United lost the previous season, they wouldn't want that to be repeated and it wasn't as they secured a 5-0 victory, with Jonny Evans notching his first senior goal after 21 minutes and by half-time, United were 3-0 up with further goals from Valencia and Welbeck. Hernandez notched a second-half double to complete the scoring The win saw United opening a four point gap with City not in league action for another three days and they beat Chelsea 2-1 to reduce the gap to one point again but the five goals for United had helped close the gap on goal difference. The following round of fixtures saw United hosting Fulham and City playing away to Stoke with City playing first but they could only manage a draw and despite dropping down to second, United knew a win against Fulham would take them three points clear. United got their win by one to nil with the only goal coming after 42 minutes when Ashley Young found Jonny Evans on the edge of the area who in turn found Rooney and he slotted in the only goal of the game. The next round of fixtures saw United playing after City once again, giving City the opportunity to draw level and place pressure on Ferguson's men but they could only draw 3-3 with Sunderland, giving United the opportunity to pull five points clear with a win over Blackburn at Ewood Park. Blackburn caused a shock by defeating United at Old Trafford earlier in the season and United gained revenge for that defeat with a 2-0 win. Blackburn held out in the first-half and almost took the lead but United had De Gea to thank for keeping the score at 0-0.

United continued to press in the second-half but had to wait until the 81st minute when a cross-shot from Valencia found the far corner of the net. Young added a second four minutes later to give United the three points that took them five points clear with seven games to play. The next matchday saw both United and City playing on Sunday April 8 2012, with United kicking off a half past one against QPR at Old Trafford and won the game 2-0 on a comfortable afternoon for Ferguson and his side, the opening goal came as Shaun Derry brought down Ashley Young in the box and Derry was sent off with Rooney converting the penalty. The game was won in the second-half when Scholes made it 2-0 as he fired a low drive into the bottom left-hand corner of the net from 25 yards. The win gave United an eight point lead and it remained that way as City suffered a 1-0 to Arsenal later that day.

With an eight point lead, United travelled to Wigan for a midweek fixture while on the same night City played host to West Brom. Since Wigan had been promoted to the Premier League in 2005, United had won all 13 thirteen of encounters between the two sides but this time Wigan would come out on top with a 1-0 win that came from a corner controversially given to the home side and was the first goal United had conceded in six games. Coupled this result with City's 4-0 win over West Brom, United's lead at the top of the table was cut five points with five games left to play and United and City were due to meet in the 36th game of the Premier League season. Before that United had home fixtures against Aston Villa and Everton. While City faced away games against Norwich and Wolves. City played before United in the first round of remaining fixtures and notched a 6-1 win against Norwich and reduced the point's gap to two points before United welcomed Villa to Old Trafford the following day. United restored their five point advantage with a 4-0 win over Villa, with goals from Rooney (2), Welbeck and Nani. Both teams registered big wins but it was still City who held an advantage on goal difference by six goals.

United's remaining four fixtures saw them facing Everton (H), City (A), Swansea (H) and Sunderland (A). With a five point advantage, a win against Everton and avoid a defeat to City would all but seal their 20th league title. Despite leading 3-1 and 4-2 against Everton they were held to a 4-4 draw. A result that meant a defeat to City in their next game would see City move above United on goal difference with just two fixtures remaining. Everton took the lead before goals from Rooney, Welbeck and Nani put United into a 3-1 lead with an hour played. Then two goals in two minutes saw Everton pulling one back before Rooney appeared to have put United in control in again but two late Everton strikes held United to the draw. A 2-0 win for City over Wolves reduced United's advantage to three points with three games remaining for both sides.

With three points between the two neighbours, United travelled to the Etihad Stadium knowing that if they avoided defeat they would maintain their advantage with two games remaining. While defeat to City would see their neighbours return to the top of the table on goal difference and knowing they would only need to match United's results to snatch the title away from them. City scored the only goal of the game in first-half stoppage time to take control of the title race. City had dominated the first-half and scored when Vincent Kompany rose to meet a corner, United struggled to create any real opportunities as Ferguson opted to start with Rooney as a lone front-man and played Park Ji-Sung to try and negate the potential influence of Yaya Toure on the game. Welbeck replaced Park Ji-Sung just before the hour mark but United still struggled to threaten the City goal and would have been lucky to get anything from the game. City took the three points and moved above United and United would now need to win their two remaining games and hope for a slip-up from their neighbours having at one point held a eight point advantage. The penultimate weekend of the season saw both United and City winning their games 2-0. United beat Swansea, having seen City beat Newcastle. The final fixtures saw United travelling to Sunderland while City played host to QPR. Wayne Rooney's first-half strike gave United a 1-0 win and as the full-time whistle blew at the Stadium of Light, United were top of the league as City entered stoppage-time losing 2-1 to QPR. United players and staff including Sir Alex Ferguson remained on the pitch at full-time awaiting any news of a result from the Etihad Stadium. Sunderland fans began to cheer and United fans, players and staff got the news that City had scored two stoppage-time goals to finish top of the league on goal difference. Despite the disappointment of missing out on the league title they could take solace in the fact that the 89 points achieved were the highest for any team in the Premier League without winning the title. The only trophy United could show for their season was the Community Shield won against City at the beginning of the season. That isn't classed as a major trophy though and therefore the 2011/12 season will go down as a rare trophyless season for Manchester United under Sir Alex Ferguson.

Chapter Eighteen: The Final Challenge

After losing out on the title to neighbours City and finishing the season without a major trophy for the first time since the 2004/05 season. United were looking to bounce back and make sure they won the Premier League title back. Losing the title is difficult for everyone connected with Manchester United but to lose out to Manchester City and with virtually the last kick of the season after holding an eight point advantage over their neighbours, really hurt. Ferguson went into the 2012/13, intent on making sure it didn't happen again. As well as losing out to City for the league title, United had a poor season in Europe having appeared in three of the previous four Champions League finals. United welcomed two new players to the squad on July 1 2012 with the arrivals of Shinji Kagawa from Borussia Dortmund and Nick Powell from Crewe. Kagawa joined United after helping Dortmund to the Bundesliga title and cost a reported initial £12million and the deal could rise to £17million based on appearances and achievements for United and Kagawa. Powell joined from Crewe for an initial £3million and the fee could rise to £6million. 18 year-old Powell signed for United after scoring 16 goals in 45 matches. Powell would be around the first-team squad but was clearly a signing for the future. The transfer saga of the summer revolved around United, City and Arsenal striker Robin Van Persie. Van Persie joined Arsenal for the 2004/05 season and after struggling with injury for much of his time in North London enjoyed an injury free season in 2011/12. Scoring 37 goals in 48 matches and 30 goals in 38 Premier League games to finish as the league's top scorer. Van Persie only had a year remaining on his Arsenal contract and on July 4 2012 announced that he wouldn't be signing a new deal for Arsene Wenger's side. Which prompted both United and City to express an interest in the Dutch striker. While Italian side Juventus were also said to be interested. So United and City were going head-to-head again but this time for the signature of a player rather than a trophy. You had to feel whoever won the race for Van Persie's signature would be favourites for the Premier League title. After months of speculate as to where Van Persie would go if Arsenal decided to sell and get a transfer fee for the forward. United reached an agreement with Arsenal on August 15 and looked to complete the transfer before the Premier League season kicked off on August 18. They would have to complete the transfer before midday on Friday August 17 if Van Persie was to be available for United's opening game on Monday August 20. United would pay Arsenal an initial £22.3million with an additional £1.5million if United won the Premier League or Champions League in the next four seasons. Van Persie signed a four-year deal with United. On joining United, Van Persie chose to wear squad number 20 because he was aiming to help United win a 20 league title in his first season at Old Trafford. Several players left Old Trafford with the majority of those to leave because they had struggled to break into the first-team squad. One notable name from those was Paul Pogba, who decided to leave United at the end of his contract and sign for Italian side Juventus. Despite being out of contract with United, they received a fee that was decided by tribunal. Tomasz Kuszczak and Micheal Owen both also left United at the end of their contracts while Park Ji-Sung and Dimitar Berbatov were also allowed to leave the club joining Queens Park Rangers and Fulham respectively. Further additions to the Old Trafford squad were made with the arrivals of Alexander Buttner and Angelo Henriquez. Buttner signed from Vitesse Arnhem to provide competition for Patrice Evra in the left-back position while

Henriquez like Powell was a signing for the future and would be loaned out to Wigan Athletic in the second half of the 2012/13 season.

With Robin Van Persie now a member of Sir Alex Ferguson's Manchester United squad, they travelled to Goodison Park for the opening game of the season. United played on Monday night in the final game of the opening weekend and despite Van Persie making his debut as a second-half substitute they went down to a 1-0 defeat with Marouane Fellaini scoring the only goal for Everton. The defeat was United's first opening day loss since the 2004/05 season. After the defeat to Everton, United welcomed Fulham to Old Trafford in a game that saw both Van Persie and Kagawa making their first starts for United at Old Trafford. Damien Duff gave Fulham the lead after just three minutes but Van Persie struck his first goal with his first shot with a spectacular volley on ten minutes after a cross from Patrice Evra. Then on 35 minutes, Kagawa followed Van Persie in striking his first United goal to give Ferguson's men the lead. Right-back Rafael made it 3-1 five minutes before half-time. On 64 minutes, Vidic and De Gea collided with the later back-heeling into to his own net but United held out for the three points and their first win of the season. Next United faced an away game against Southampton and another 3-2 victory thanks to a Van Persie hat-trick. Southampton led twice as Van Persie's first goal of the game was sandwiched between strikes from Rickie Lambert and Morgan Schneiderlin. Van Persie missed a chance to equalise from the spot before scoring two late goals to secure a second successive 3-2 and three crucial points. Following the win at St Mary's, United welcomed Wigan to Old Trafford and recorded a 4-0 victory. It took United fifty minutes to break the deadlock but scored four in just over half-an-hour once the breakthrough came. Scholes opened the scoring and was joined on the scoresheet by Hernandez and new signings Buttner and Powell both scoring their first goals for the club. Both Buttner and Powell

253

were making their first appearances with Buttner starting the game and Powell replaced Ryan Giggs after 72 minutes and scored ten minutes later to wrap up the scoring. Despite losing their opening game, United were second in the league after four games. Sitting one point behind early leaders Chelsea.

In the Champions League United went straight into the group stages after finishing in the top three of the Premier League and were among the top seeds when the group stages were drawn. They were drawn with Braga of Portugal, Galatasaray and Romanian champions CFR Cluj. United had faced both Braga and Galatasaray in previous seasons while CFR Cluj were a new opponent for both Ferguson and the club. United started their campaign with a home encounter against Galatasaray and a seventh minute goal from Michael Carrick gave United the 1-0 win. On the back of four successive wins, United travelled to Anfield to face Liverpool. While United had three wins from their opening four games, Liverpool were yet to record a victory and despite having midfielder Jonjo Shelvey sent-off for a challenge on Jonny Evans on 39 minutes. Liverpool took the lead when Steven Gerrard scored on 46 minutes before goals from Rafael and Van Persie gave United the three points and left Liverpool still searching for their first win. After wins against Galatasaray in the Champions League and Liverpool in the league, United welcomed Newcastle to Old Trafford in the third round of the League Cup. Ferguson once again opted to use the early rounds of the competition to blood some of the younger players on the fringes of the first-team and first-team squad members who hadn't had much football so far in the season. Goals from Anderson and Tom Cleverly gave United a 2-1 win and United's reward was a fourth round visit to Stamford Bridge. Next United welcomed Tottenham to Old Trafford in the Premier League and made a disastrous start, falling 2-0 behind with just over 30 minutes played. Nani pulled one back for United on 51 minutes but just a minute later, the Tottenham two-goal lead was restored only for Kagawa to pull another back just a minute after that. There wasn't to be another great comeback for United against Tottenham as the visitors held on to win at Old Trafford for the first time 23 years. The defeat saw United drop to third in the table, now four points behind leaders Chelsea and a point behind second placed Everton. Looking to bounce back from the defeat to Tottenham, United travelled to CFR Cluj in their second group game in the Champions League and a Van Persie double gave United a 2-1 win that took them top of the group after two wins out of two. On the road again but this time in the Premier League, United visited St James Park and came away with a 3-0 as two goals in the opening 15 minutes put United in control. Defenders Jonny Evans and Patrice Evra both scored headed goals from corners and the win was sealed when Cleverley curled in from 25 yards on 71 minutes. After beating Newcastle, United welcomed Stoke City to Old Trafford in a game that Wayne Rooney scored at both ends as United won 4-2. Rooney opened the scoring for Stoke before he equalised and goals from Van Persie and Welbeck either side of half-time made it 3-1. Stoke pulled one back before Rooney made it 4-2 to United. United then made it three wins out of three in the Champions League with a 3-2 win over Braga at Old Trafford.

After eight league games, United had 18 points and were level with neighbours and defending champions City but both Manchester clubs were four points behind early pacesetters Chelsea and Chelsea were United's next opponents in the league. United travelled to Stamford Bridge, having not won a league encounter at the ground for ten years but made the perfect start when a David Luiz own goal and Van Persie strike gave them a 2-0 lead after just twelve minutes. Juan Mata pulled one back on the stroke of half-time for Chelsea before Ramires levelled on 53 minutes and the game hung in the balance. Then Chelsea were reduced to nine men when Branislav Ivanovic received a straight red card before Torres received a second yellow card on 68 minutes. Javier Hernandez replaced Tom Cleverley on 65 minutes and the Mexican striker scored the winning goal on 75 minutes to move United to within one point of Chelsea and inflict Chelsea's first league defeat of the season. Four days later, Ferguson took his team back to Stamford Bridge, this time for a League Cup fourth round tie. It was another high scoring encounter but United were knocked out of the competition as they lost 5-4 after extra-time after it finished 3-3 after normal time. Next up United faced another rival from London as they welcomed Arsenal to Old Trafford, in a game which saw Van Persie facing his former side for the first time. Van Persie struck after just three minutes to give United an early lead. Rooney missed a chance to double United's lead before half-time but United were 2-0 up when Evra headed in Rooney's cross on 67 minutes. Two minutes later Arsenal were down to ten men when Jack Wilshire received a second yellow card. Santi Cazorla scored a consolation for Arsenal on 90 minutes but it was another three points for United and three points that took them top of the table as both Chelsea and City dropped points. After failing to make it through the group stages the previous season, United ensured their qualification for the knockout stages of the Champions League after just four games as they made it four wins out of four with a 3-1 over Braga in Portugal thanks to three late goals after Braga took the lead. After confirming their place in the knockout stages of the Champions League, United travelled to Villa Park and despite falling two nil behind they picked up the three points against Aston Villa. Andreas Weimann's double gave Villa the lead before Ferguson called on Hernandez and the Mexican striker struck a double to give United the win. Following the comeback win against Villa, United travelled to East-Anglia and Carrow Road. United fell to a 1-0 defeat, their third league defeat of the season with the winning goal scored by former United youth player Anthony Pilkington. The defeat to Norwich, left United second in the table, one point behind defending champions City. The way the table was shaping up it was looking like the two Manchester clubs would be fighting it out for the title once again.

With Champions League qualification confirmed, Ferguson opted to rest several of his first-team regulars for their final two group games and United suffered two 1-0 defeats to Galatasaray and CFR Cluj, despite the defeats United still finished top of the group. After defeat to Norwich in the league and Galatasaray in the Champions League, United welcomed Queens Park Rangers to Old Trafford. Rangers took the lead on 52 minutes through a Jamie Mackie strike before Jonny Evans and Darren Fletcher both scored from Wayne Rooney corners on 64 and 68 minutes. Hernandez scored a third for United to confirm the three points for Ferguson's men. Next up were West Ham in the league and a Van Persie strike after 31 seconds that deflected over West Ham keeper Jussi Jaaskerlainen gave United the 1-0 win and left them one point in front of City after 14 league games. After defeating West Ham, they travelled to Reading and secured a 4-3 win with all seven goals coming in the first 34 minutes. Hal Robson-Kanu struck for the home side on eight minutes before Anderson equalised five minutes later and three minutes after that United were in front when Rooney stroked home a penalty. Reading hit back though and were 3-2 up after 23 minutes as Adam Le Fondre and Sean Morrison both headed home from corners. Seven minutes later United were level when Rooney got his second of the game before he turned provider for Van Persie as he put United 4-3 up after 34 minutes and despite the flurry of goals in the opening 35 minutes, that's the way the score stayed and with the three points United moved three points ahead of City following their 1-1 draw with Everton. United's next league would see them travelling to the Etihad Stadium with a chance to open up a six point advantage over their neighbours and title rivals but before that though they had to finish off their Champions League group stage campaign with a home game against CFR Cluj. Once again Ferguson opted rest several of his first-team regulars and once again United fell to a 1-0 defeat just as they did against Galatasaray but that didn't stop them going through as group winners after winning their opening four games in the group.

Ferguson took his team across the city to face neighbours and defending champions City, looking to open up a six point lead over their opponents at the top of the Premier League table. Despite having lost three of their opening fifteen games, United came into the game three points ahead of a City team that were yet to taste league defeat in the 2012/13 league season. This was down to the fact that United were yet to draw a game and had won their other 12 league games so far, while City had only won nine out of their 15 games. Despite having less of the possession it was United who led at the break thanks to two goals from Wayne Rooney. Rooney's two goals gave him a record ten goals in Manchester Derbies. With the score at 1-0, City suffered a blow with the loss of captain Vincent Kompany to injury. In the second-half City continued to dominate and pulled one back through Yaya Toure on 60 minutes only seconds after United had a third ruled out for offside. City were level on 86 minutes through Pablo Zabaleta. With the scores level City looked the more like winners but Van Persie would have the final say. Both Ferguson and City manager Roberto Mancini knew that signing Van Persie would be crucial in their bids to win the league title but Van Persie chose United and a big factor in that decision was the opportunity to work with Sir Alex Ferguson. United were awarded a free-kick when Carlos Tevez fouled Rafael in the dying stages and Van Persie took the free-kick which took a deflection off the City wall before beating Joe Hart in the City goal to give United the three points and see them move six points clear of City at the top of the table. As well as being six clear of City, they were also ten clear of early leaders Chelsea as the title race was fast becoming a two-horse race between the two Manchester clubs. The win over City was followed up with a 3-1 win over Sunderland at

Old Trafford, with goals from Van Persie, Cleverley and Rooney. Following this United played Swansea City at the Liberty Stadium and despite being given the lead by Evra, United were pegged back by Swansea through Spanish forward Michu and they had to settle for their first draw of league campaign. The point meant that United were four points clear of City on Christmas Day. After their away draw with Swansea, United finished 2012 with two home games and two wins against Newcastle and West Brom. Boxing Day saw United playing host to Newcastle and the game would turn out to be a classic as United edged a seven goal thriller. James Perch put Newcastle ahead after four minutes before Jonny Evans scored at both ends in the space of three minutes. First he equalised for United on 25 minute before putting through his own net on 28 minutes to give Newcastle a 2-1 half-time lead. That goal was originally ruled out for offside against Papiss Cisse, who was lurking behind Evans but referee Mike Dean allowed the goal to stand, judging that Cisse wasn't interfering with play. Evra scored against Newcastle for the second time in the season on 58 minutes, levelling the scores with a 25-yard strike. Ten minutes later Newcastle were back in front thanks to a sublime finish from Cisse on 68 minutes. United weren't behind for long though as Van Persie struck back three minutes later, then United repeated a trick of Sir Alex Ferguson's long reign with a late winner as Hernandez scored with just seconds of the 90 minutes left on the clock to give United a 4-3 win and with City losing away to Sunderland, United extended their lead at the top of the table to seven points. The calendar year of 2012 finished with a 2-0 win against West Brom with Van Persie sealing the win in the 90th minute after a 9th minute own goal from Gareth McAuley. The win over West Brom meant United went into 2013 with a seven point advantage over defending champions City in the league as they looked to win a 20th league title. While they were still in the Champions League and had the start of their FA Cup campaign to look forward to.

2013 started with a league fixture against Wigan at the DW Stadium. This fixture had been pivotal in United's failed title bid the previous and they got revenge for that 1-0 defeat with a 4-0 win thanks to doubles from Hernandez and Van Persie. Both players scored a goal in each half. The first weekend of 2013 saw the Premier League teams entering the FA Cup at the third-round stage and United were drawn against fellow Premier League team West Ham with the game taking place at Upton Park. Tom Cleverley gave United the lead on 23 minutes before a James Collins double gave the Hammers the lead and they looked set to knock United out until Van Persie finished supremely to equalise in the 90th minute and setup a replay at Old Trafford. That replay meant that United would have two home games in the space of four days with the replay against West Ham following a Premier League fixture against rivals Liverpool. The game against Liverpool, was won 2-1 with goals from Van Persie and Vidic. After Van Persie had opened the scoring on 19 minutes, and the game reached half-time with the score 1-0 to United. Vidic made it 2-0 on 54 minutes when he diverted a Patrice Evra header into the back of the Liverpool net and three minutes later Daniel Sturridge made it 2-1 but United would keep their lead and secure another crucial three points in their pursuit of a 20th league crown. A Wayne Rooney strike after 9 minutes secured a win for United in the replay with West Ham and secured them a home tie against Fulham in the fourth round. Four days after securing their passage in the FA Cup, United travelled to White Hart Lane in the league and came away with a 1-1 draw as Clint Dempsey equaliser in the dying seconds of the game to deny United the three points. After the draw with Tottenham, United held a five point advantage at the top of the table with 15 games remaining. Following the draw with Tottenham, United played host to Fulham in the fourth round of the FA Cup. Ryan Giggs scored from the spot after three minutes to give United the lead but they would have to wait until the 50th minute to double their lead when Rooney scored before two Hernandez strikes in 14 minutes gave United a 4-0 advantage. Fulham got a late consolation through defender Aaron Hughes. The draw for the fifth round pitted United against Premier League opponents again and another home tie, this time against Reading. United returned to league action with a home game against Southampton and a Wayne Rooney double gave Ferguson's men a 2-1 win after Southampton had taken an early lead through Jay Rodriguez. The win over Southampton was followed by wins over Fulham and Everton. Keeping clean sheets in both games as they won 1-0 and 2-0 respectively. While United picked up nine points from their three wins over Southampton, Fulham and Everton. City lost further ground with two draws and a loss, meaning United had a twelve point advantage at the top of the table after 26 games.

As United won their Champion League group, they would be drawn against a group runner-up in the first knockout phase and were handed a tie against Spanish champions Real Madrid. The tie would be the fifth time the two teams had faced each other in the competition, with Real Madrid winning the last tie between the two in the 2003 quarter-finals. The game also meant that Cristiano Ronaldo would come up against United and Ferguson for the first time since his £80million transfer from United to the Spanish giants. The first-leg took place at the Santiago Bernabeu on February 13 2013 and finished in a 1-1 draw as Ronaldo levelled for Madrid after Danny Welbeck had given United a 20th minute lead. Former Atletico Madrid keeper David De Gea returned to his home city and pulled off a string of fine saves to stop Madrid taking a lead into the second-leg while United also had opportunities to win the game, most notable through Robin Van Persie who had two opportunities to give United a lead ahead of the second-leg. In between the first-leg and second-leg against Madrid, United booked their place in the quarter-finals of the FA Cup with a 2-1 win over Reading with all the goals in the game coming in the final 25 minutes. This was followed by a 2-0 win over QPR at Loftus

Road and a 4-0 win over Norwich at Old Trafford. The win over QPR saw Giggs scoring on his 999th career appearance. While Shinji Kagawa scored a hat-trick against Norwich, making him the first Asian player to do so in the Premier League. The wins over QPR and Norwich maintained United's twelve point advantage with ten games left to play. Manchester United's Champions League hopes were ended for another season in controversial circumstances after the referee adjudged that a high foot from Nani on Real Madrid defender Alvaro Arbeloa on 56 minutes was worthy of a red card. At the time United were leading 1-0 after a Sergio Ramos own goal on 48 minutes and Madrid were struggling to get a foothold in the game. The sending-off caused Ferguson to run down from his seat in the dug-out and remonstrate with the fourth official and the referee. Real took advantage of the extra man and equalised through Luca Modric after 66 minutes. The equaliser on the night made it 2-2 on aggregate and Real took the lead on the night and in the tie when Ronaldo struck three minutes later. Ronaldo's goal meant United had to score two goals without reply to win the tie. With the Champions League dream over for another season, United had to concentrate on winning their 20th league title and looking to progress in the FA Cup. Following the disappointment of their Champions League, United played host to Chelsea in the FA Cup quarter-finals, United looked set to qualify for a semi-final when they went two nil up after 11 minutes with goals from Hernandez and Rooney before two second-half goals in ten minutes for Chelsea saw them draw level and earn a replay at Stamford Bridge.

Before that replay against Chelsea, United had two league games against Reading and Sunderland. As United kicked off against Reading, they knew they had the opportunity to extend their lead to fifteen points following City's loss to Everton earlier that day. United got their win thanks to a deflected shot from Wayne Rooney on 21 minutes. After the game against Reading, the Premier League had a break because of Internationals and after the break United travelled to the Stadium of Light to face Sunderland and secured another 1-0 victory thanks to an own goal from Titus Bramble as he deflected a Robin Van Persie shot past Simon Mignolet in the Sunderland goal. The win against Sunderland meant that United had won 25 of their 30 league games and therefore setting a new Premier League record. United's next league game would see them face City at Old Trafford, holding a fifteen advantage over their neighbours and title rivals. Before that they faced Chelsea in the FA Cup quarter-final replay at Stamford Bridge. United's hopes for domestic double of Premier League and FA Cup were ended by a Demba Ba strike four minutes into the second-half. United went into the game without Rooney and Ferguson opted to start Van Persie on the bench and United failed to find any cutting edge in the game. Following recent Derby games that have been pivotal in both teams winning trophies, this Manchester Derby wouldn't have an effect on the outcome of the title race with United holding a fifteen point advantage over neighbours City at the top of the table. City reduced the gap to twelve points with a 2-1 win but barring a meltdown from United it was only a matter of time before United were confirmed as champions of England for the 20th time and their 13th Premier League success. The defeat was United's first in 18 league games. Next United travelled to Stoke and came away with a 2-0 victory thanks to a second minute strike from Micheal Carrick and a penalty converted by Robin Van Persie in 66th minute. Van Persie had been struggling for goals in recent weeks and celebrated this goal by running to the touchline and embracing Sir Alex Ferguson. After the win over Stoke, United travelled to Upton Park for a midweek fixture against West Ham and despite twice falling behind they came away from London with a draw. Antonio Valencia levelled for United after Ricardo Vaz Te had put the Hammers in front. Then Mohamad Diame put West Ham back in front before Van Persie made it 2-2 just like he had done in the FA Cup tie at Upton Park. The draw with West Ham left United 13 points ahead of City though they had played a game more than City.

The next round of Premier League fixtures would prove decisive in United's quest to win back the title from their neighbours. United would play Aston Villa at Old Trafford on Monday 22 April with City in action the day before against Tottenham. After City suffered a 3-1 defeat against Tottenham, Ferguson and his team knew that a win against Villa would confirm the clubs 20th league title and a 13th Premier League crown all under the management of Sir Alex Ferguson. The title was confirmed with a 3-0 win thanks to a Robin Van Persie hat-trick in the first 35 minutes of the game. The opening goal came after just two minutes when Van Persie scored after a lay-off from Ryan Giggs. Then on 13 minutes came one of the strikes of the season and maybe the strike of many seasons as Van Persie volleyed the ball into the top corner of Aston Villa's net after a delightful ball over the top from Rooney. Van Persie completed his hat-trick on 33 minutes with Giggs once again provided the assist for the Dutchman to score. The former Arsenal man had proved a crucial signing in United winning their 20th league title and the striker who had decided to wear number 20 on joining United, his shirt number was at the centre of the title celebrations once the full-time whistle blew. This title gave everyone involved as much satisfaction as their first if it wasn't their first. Following the way that they had thrown the title away the previous season in losing the title on goal difference to neighbours City, everyone involved took great satisfaction in the way this title as won. Already thirteen points clear before kick-off, the three points from the win over Villa took them sixteen points clear and now the aim would be to make sure they finished as many points clear of City as possible. United biggest title winning margin was 18 points in the 1999/2000 season. To beat that winning margin was surely the target for United now. Next for United was a trip to the Emirates Stadium to face fierce rivals and

Robin Van Persie's former side Arsenal. As traditional in a team's next game after being confirmed as champions they were given a guard of honour by their opponents. Despite the Arsenal players giving Van Persie and United a guard of honour. The former Arsenal striker didn't receive the greatest reception from the fans who used to adore him. Arsenal took the lead through Theo Walcott in the second minute despite calls for offside from United. On the stroke of half-time United were awarded a penalty when Bacary Sagna fouled Van Persie in the area and the Dutchman stepped up to score against his former side once again. Having also scored against Arsenal at Old Trafford earlier in the season. The score remained at 1-1 despite both teams having chances to score. After the draw with Arsenal, United welcomed Chelsea to Old Trafford in what was the fifth game between the two sides in the season, having been drawn against Chelsea in both the League Cup and FA Cup with Chelsea knocking Ferguson's team out of both domestic cup competitions. It was non-event of a game until Juan Mata's shot was deflected off Phil Jones before hitting the post and finding the back of the net in the 87th minute to give Chelsea a 1-0 win. The match also saw Rafael sent-off in the 89th minute following a clash with fellow Brazilian David Luiz.

In the week following the defeat to Chelsea, came the day that all Manchester United fans knew was getting closer but were dreading. On May 8th 2013 Sir Alex Ferguson announced that he intended to step down as Manchester United manager at the end of the current campaign and retire. The night before the announcement, newspaper reports had emerged that Sir Alex Ferguson was considering his future as United manager. There was speculation as to whether he would step away completely and retire or would he stay on for another season and work with his successor before they took complete control. By the time he would step down, Ferguson had been in charge of Manchester United for 26 and a half years. Making him the longest-serving manager of not just United but also of any English club. During his time as manager of Manchester United, Ferguson had seen his team win 38 trophies including, 13 Premier League titles, five FA Cups, four League Cup and two Champions League. He had also won ten Charity/Community Shields, UEFA Super Cup, Intercontinental Cup and a FIFA Club World Cup. He had also been honoured with many individual managerial awards including the League Managers Association (LMA) Manager of the Year on four separate occasions and he was named the LMA Manager of the Decade for the 1990s. He won Premier League Manager of the Season on eleven occasions including his last season. On 27 occasions Ferguson was awarded the Premier League Manager of the Month award. Sir Alex later revealed that he took the decision to retire in December 2012 and not many people knew about it because he wanted it that way after seeing the performances of his team dropping off the previous time he announced he would retire. Following the confirmation that Sir Alex would be retiring come the end of the season, attention turned to who would have enviable task of succeeding the Scot in the Old Trafford hot-seat. Everton manager David Moyes was in the final year of his contract at Goodison Park and had already announced he no intentions of signing a new deal with Merseysiders. Moyes was immediately installed as the favourite for the job with the bookmakers, closely followed by Real Madrid and former Chelsea manager Jose Mourinho. The board decided that Ferguson's recommendation of appointing Moyes was the right one for Manchester United and his appointment as Sir Alex Ferguson's successor was announced on a six-year contract. With the appointment of Moyes confirmed, Manchester United and Ferguson had two games remaining before the season was finished. Starting with his final home game against Swansea City, where after the game, United would be presented with the Premier League trophy for the 13th and final time under the leadership of Sir Alex Ferguson.

Following the announcement that Sir Alex Ferguson had decided to retire from his position as Manchester United manager he took charge of his 723rd and final game as United manager at Old Trafford. His final opponents at Old Trafford were Swansea City managed by Michael Laudrup. As Ferguson waited in the tunnel to make his entrance, there were 70,000 red flags being waved in unison inside the Theatre of Dreams and Manchester United matchday announcer introduced the Scot as "the man who made the impossible dream possible." As he walked on to the pitch, Sir Alex was given a guard of honour by both sets of players. Sir Alex was given a thunderous round of applause from all four corners of famous ground as he made his way to his seat in the dug-out. As Ferguson walked out the scoreboards showed the figures 26 and 38 for 26 years of management for Ferguson and 38 trophies won. Before the title celebrations could be begin and a final farewell to Ferguson at the ground he had called home for over 26 years there was a game to be played. The game itself was afterthought on a day that the Old Trafford also said goodbye to Paul Scholes as he retired for a second time and made his 717th appearance for the club. After a Javier Hernandez opener had been equalised by Swansea it was fitting that United won the game with a late goal and they did so when Rio Ferdinand scored a rare goal as he smashed home with three minutes to go from a Van Persie corner. Scholes was given a rapturous ovation as he was replaced on 66 minutes by Anderson. Ferguson stayed in his seat throughout the game and entered the pitch at full-time to address the Old Trafford as he would do at the end of any season. This time though it was to say goodbye and thank everyone who had involved in this great journey and to ask everyone involved with the club to give his successor the same support that he had received over his 26 years in charge of Manchester United. Ferguson left the arena for a short while and returned with his squad to receive the Premier League trophy for the 13th time in the Ferguson era.

Ferguson's final game as Manchester United came against West Bromwich Albion at the Hawthorns and it was fitting that match would see one final Premier League record for Ferguson. The game finished 5-5, making it the first Premier League game where both teams scored five goals. The game was Ferguson's 1500th in charge of United and he was denied one final win as Romelu Lukaku struck a second-half hat-trick for West Brom. United were 3-0 up within 30 minutes thanks to goals from Kagawa, Buttner and an own goal. West Brom pulled the score back to 3-2 as James Morrison and Lukaku both struck. Van Persie made it 4-2 before Javier Hernandez struck the final Manchester United goal of the Sir Alex Ferguson era in the 63rd minute of this game. With the score at 5-2 and less than half-an-hour remaining on the clock. Ferguson looked like he was going to end with a win but West Brom had other ideas as Lukaku completed his hat-trick and a strike from Mulumbu ensured that the game would finish in a high-scoring draw. Ferguson was given another guard of honour by both sets of players as he made his out of the tunnel and was once again given a grand ovation by all four corners of the ground before the game. After the game, Ferguson acknowledge the United travelling fans before disappearing down the tunnel of a Premier League ground for the final time. The final results of the season saw United eventually finishing 11 points clear of Manchester City at the top of the Premier League table. After losing the title to City the previous season on goal difference, this was a fitting end to Sir Alex Ferguson's time in charge of Manchester United.